IMAGES
of America

CAMPBELLSVILLE

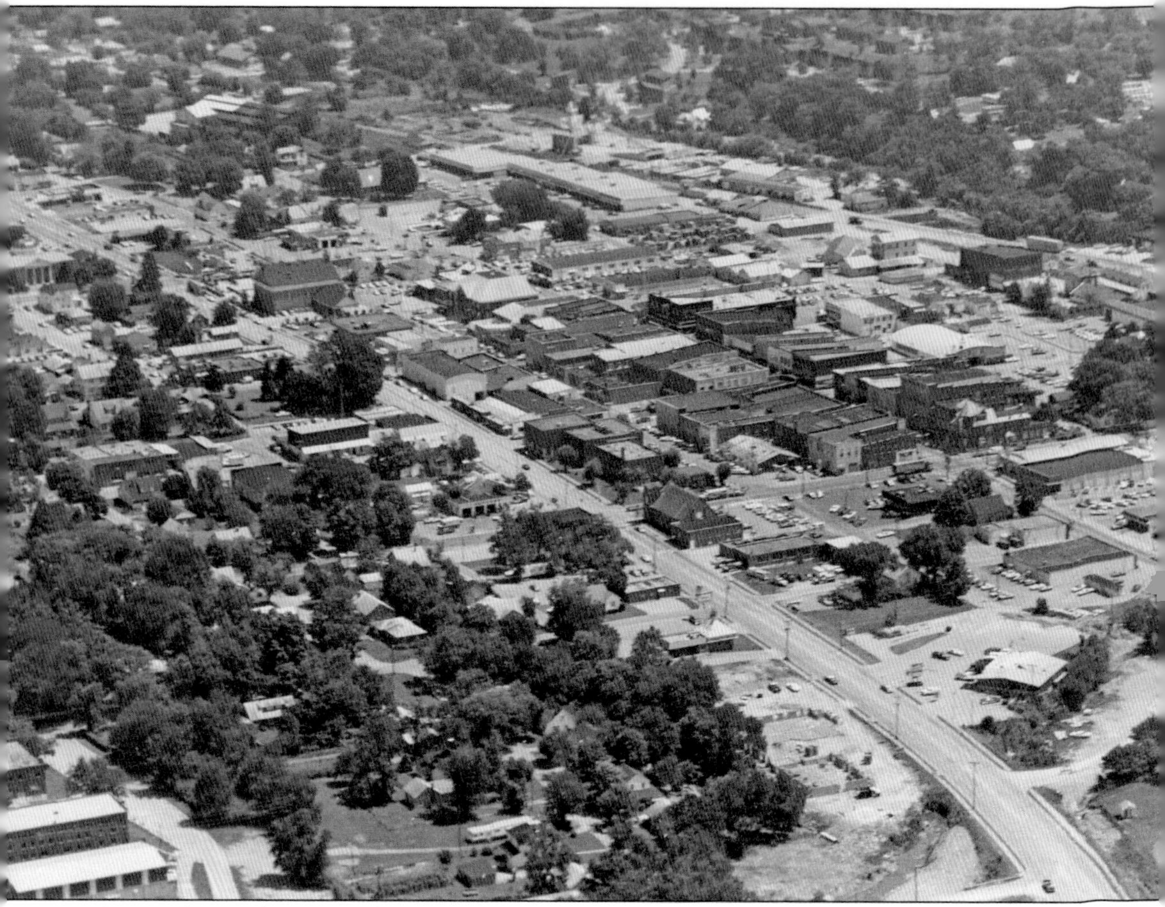

Located near the geographical center of Kentucky, Campbellsville is home to approximately 12,000 people. U.S. Highway 68 provides the main east-west artery and can be seen running on a left to right diagonal in this 1970s photograph. A portion of Campbellsville University is visible in the lower left corner, with the downtown area covering most of the photograph's center. Campbellsville shares an international Sister City connection with Buncrana, County Donegal, Ireland. (TCHS.)

On the Cover: In this c. 1957 photograph, Campbellsville celebrates the Fourth of July with a parade through downtown. Campbellsville holds the distinction of having one of the largest Independence Day celebrations in Kentucky, bringing thousands of people downtown each year. (TCHS.)

IMAGES
of America

CAMPBELLSVILLE

Joseph Y. DeSpain, John R. Burch Jr.,
and Timothy Q. Hooper

ARCADIA
PUBLISHING

ISBN 978-0-7385-8656-4

Published by Arcadia Publishing
Charleston, South Carolina

Printed in the United States of America

Library of Congress Control Number: 2010925919

For all general information, please contact Arcadia Publishing:
Telephone 843-853-2070
Fax 843-853-0044
E-mail sales@arcadiapublishing.com
For customer service and orders:
Toll-Free 1-888-313-2665

Visit us on the Internet at www.arcadiapublishing.com

Taylor County's success rests on the collective efforts of those born within her borders and those who arrived from other locales. These efforts produced agricultural, athletic, commercial, and educational achievements, from the farmer who tried new agricultural methods, to the individuals who risked personal lives, energy, and capital, to the teacher and worker whose skills helped develop the county's talents and products. To that community of individuals, we dedicate this book.

Contents

ACKNOWLEDGMENTS

Any work of this size stands on the shoulders of many past and present who have collected and preserved photographic history. We are particularly grateful to all who have granted us permission to scan from their collections. Individuals who have been generous with their photographs include Barkley Blevins (BB), Raymond Burress (RB), Tom Caldwell (TC), Paul Campbell Jr. (PC), Elizabeth Money Coakley (EMC), Virginia Crabb (VC), J. B. Crawley (JBC), Barbara Curtis (BC), Terry Dabney (TD), Emily Ann DeSpain (EAD), Larry DeWitt (LD), Donabeth Doyle (DD), James Flowers (JF), Ruth Graham (RG), Mary Jewell Graves (MJG), Julia Hartfield (JH), Faye Howell (FH), Paul Johnson Jr. (PJ), Lynwood Kessler (LK), Margaret Hodgen Liddell (MHL), Marshall Lowe (ML), Thomas McMahan (TM), Jane Felts Mauldin (JFM), Rodger Monson (RM), Russell Montgomery (RuM), Mark Newcomb (MN), Sam Newcomb (SN), Sheila Newcomb for Kentucky Utilities (KU), Ron Rafferty (RR), Ronald and Walter Ramsey (R&WR), Walter "Corky" Scott III (WS), Seymour "Buddy" Shaw (SS), Margaret Wood Smith (MWS), Charles Sparks (CS), Margaret Stewart (MS), Gwynette Sullivan (GS), Bonnie Webster (BW), Laura Wilds (LW), Jay Wilson (JW), and Murrell Young (MY). Bobbie Tremain (BT) offered use of the Ann Eliza, Texas, map cited by her father, Joe Chumbley. In addition, the large photographic collections of Carolyn Beard Gupton (CBG), Frank and Chris Kidwell (F&CK), Ricky Malone (RiM), and the Fred H. Buchanan Collection of Jane B. Routin (FHB) offered additional help. Institutions and personnel who made contributions include the A. B. Colvin Baptist Collection and Archives, Montgomery Library, Campbellsville University (ABC-CU); Melinda Robertson for Pikeville College Special Collections (PCSC); Stan McKinney Central Kentucky News-Journal Digital Image Collection, Montgomery Library, Campbellsville University (SM-CKNJ); Elaine Munday and the staff of the Taylor County Library (TCL); and Jason Flahardy of the University of Kentucky Special Collections (UK). Finally, through the generous gifts of many individuals, the Taylor County Historical Society Collection (TCHS) has developed a photographic collection that helps preserve the county's history. We are eternally grateful to all of these people and institutions for their help and for their commitment to preservation and, specifically, to the preservation of our photographic history.

In addition to help with the photographs, we want to give special recognition to the following people who have provided support: Gwynette Sullivan (president of the Taylor County Historical Society), Dr. Robert L. Doty for his script editing, Betty Jane Gorin-Smith, Alexandra Burch, Betsy Burch, Christopher Burch, Idalia Burch, John Burch Sr., Kayleigh Burch, Morgan Burch, Samantha Burch, Robin Cox, Ann DeSpain, Clay Hooper, Glen Hooper, Neil Hooper, Venita Hooper, Patty McDowell, Fred Miller, Ted Schultz, Mary Street, Glen Taul, and Regina Thompson.

In conclusion, this work hopes to awaken all readers to the breadth and depth of Campbellsville and Taylor County life and to the contributions and accomplishments made by some of those who have lived here.

Introduction

Euroamerican settlers first began arriving in the land that would eventually become Taylor County during the mid-18th century, although permanent settlements would not begin to be constructed until the 1770s. The land was attractive for families who planned to subsist on the agricultural goods they grew because of the availability of waterways, such as Pitman Creek, Robinson Creek, and the Green River. Settlement was quickly followed by the establishment of churches, beginning with Campbellsville Baptist Church in 1791. Good Hope Baptist and Bethel Presbyterian Church also had established congregations by 1800.

Taylor County became the 100th county in the Commonwealth of Kentucky when it was created on March 1, 1848. The county was named after Zachary Taylor, who gained fame as a general in the Mexican War and eventually became president of the United States. The town of Campbellsville, which was created in 1817, was selected to serve as the newly formed county's seat of government. At the time of its founding, Taylor County was sparsely populated and supported an economy primarily based on agriculture.

The outbreak of the Civil War impacted Campbellsville and Taylor County, as it did other communities throughout the United States. Men from the region enlisted in both the Union and Confederate armies. Confederate forces under the command of General John Hunt Morgan passed through Taylor County on three occasions, including a raid in 1864 that resulted in the razing of Taylor County's courthouse in Campbellsville.

The post–Civil War era saw Campbellsville prosper as the community became a transportation center for the region. The availability of railroads in the vicinity spurred significant economic growth, including the construction of a flourmill and sawmill. By the late 1800s, the community had grown enough to support a bank and several hotels. Unfortunately, many of the buildings constructed during the latter portion of the 19th century were lost to fires that ravaged Campbellsville in 1911 and 1914.

The dawn of the 20th century found many Baptists in Taylor County wanting to improve educational opportunities in their community. To that end, they founded Russell Creek Academy in 1906. The academy included a Normal School, which educated people to be teachers. Russell Creek Academy evolved into Campbellsville Junior College in 1924. In 1959, Campbellsville Junior College began offering a four-year curriculum and became known as Campbellsville College. University status was achieved in 2007. Today Campbellsville University has a student body of approximately 3,000.

The first five decades of the 20th century were marked by substantial growth in Campbellsville's population. One of Campbellsville's major employers, the Union Underwear Company, came to the community in 1948. The plant came to manufacture products for Fruit of the Loom. At its peak, the plant was one of the largest textile structures of its type in the entire country and employed more than 4,000 people. Unfortunately, the plant closed at the end of the 1990s, which was economically devastating for the community, considering it did not have a broad employment base.

Tragedy spurred change, which resulted in Campbellsville and Taylor County addressing their economic issues by retraining large numbers of workers and recruiting new employers, such as Amazon, to the community. Today the county features a diversified economic base that serves a population of 24,069. Campbellsville remains the county seat and is inhabited by 11,010 people.

Throughout its history, the growth of both Campbellsville and Taylor County has been marked by both boom periods and severe trials and tribulations. Despite the difficulties faced by the residents of Taylor County, its citizens have always shown admirable grit and determination in improving the circumstances of their families and community.

One

Main Street

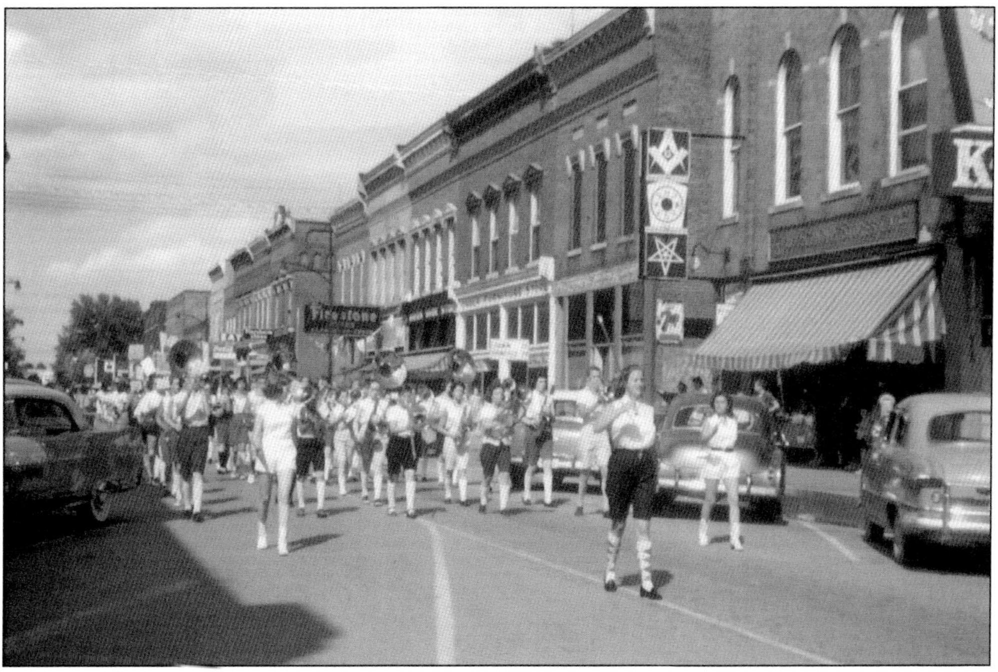

Gayle Creel leads the Campbellsville High School Band in a Fourth of July parade around 1957. While the buildings remain much the same on Campbellsville's Main Street, signs and business names are long since gone. But the photograph demonstrates a vibrant, progressive Main Street whose life is reflected in the following photographs. (TCHS.)

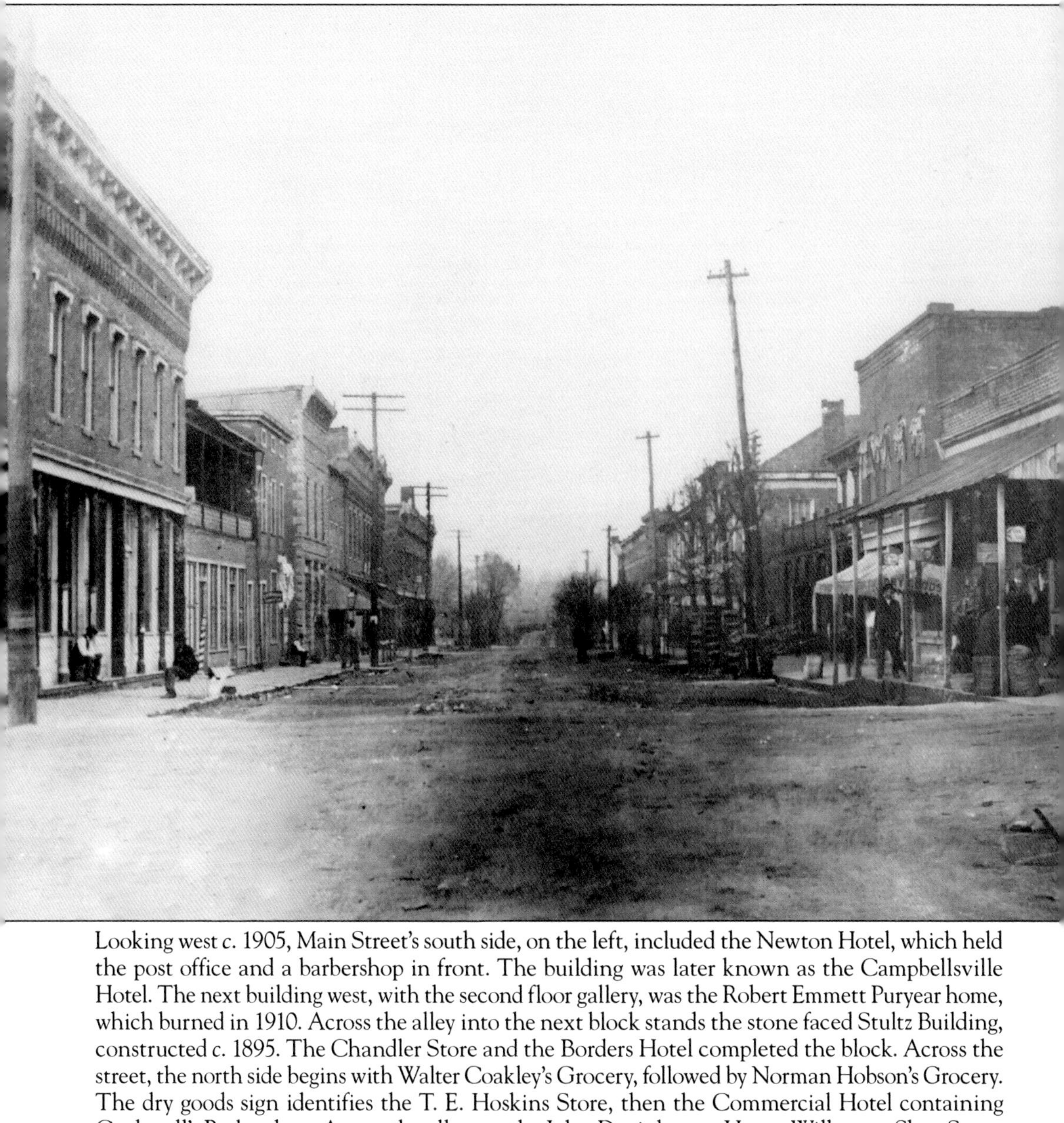

Looking west *c.* 1905, Main Street's south side, on the left, included the Newton Hotel, which held the post office and a barbershop in front. The building was later known as the Campbellsville Hotel. The next building west, with the second floor gallery, was the Robert Emmett Puryear home, which burned in 1910. Across the alley into the next block stands the stone faced Stultz Building, constructed *c.* 1895. The Chandler Store and the Borders Hotel completed the block. Across the street, the north side begins with Walter Coakley's Grocery, followed by Norman Hobson's Grocery. The dry goods sign identifies the T. E. Hoskins Store, then the Commercial Hotel containing Cockerell's Barbershop. Across the alley are the John Davis house, Henry Wilkerson Shoe Store, Bob Chandler Drugstore, Moberly Grocery, and Chandler and Davis Hardware. The latter three would later become Taylor National Bank, now the location of Citizen's Bank. (TCHS.)

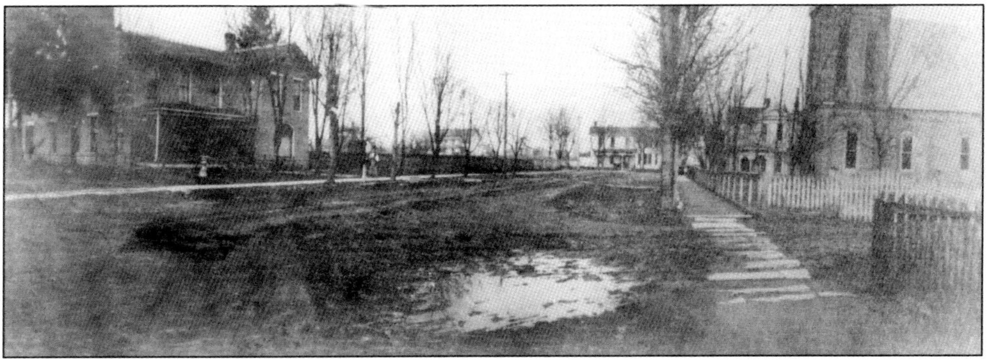

Here is an early photograph of Main Street looking east. Paved streets did not arrive in Campbellsville until the 1930s. Only after Kentucky created a State Highway Commission in about 1920, under Gov. Edwin P. Morrow, did paved streets and roads become a reality. In addition, funding through the Works Progress Administration brought further improvement in roads and bridges. (TCHS.)

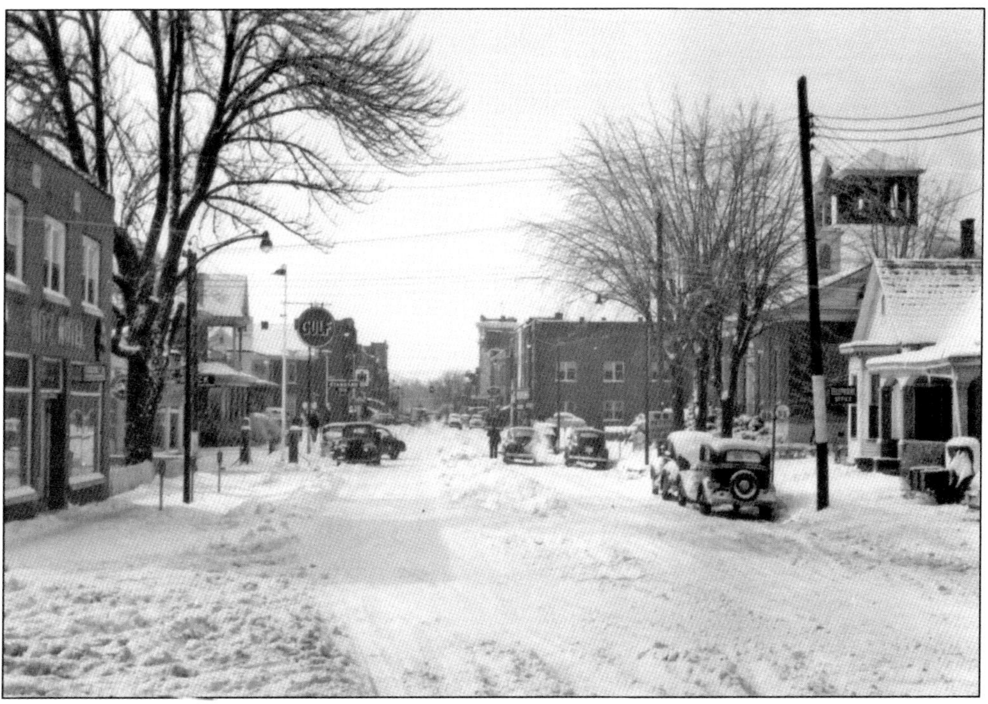

A major snowstorm blankets Main Street c. 1960. This picture looks west down Main Street and shows the dramatic changes during the first half of the 20th century. Paved streets, cars and trucks, promotional signs with national brand names, and telephone and electric lines, all signal a changed economy and pace on Campbellsville's Main Street. (TCHS.)

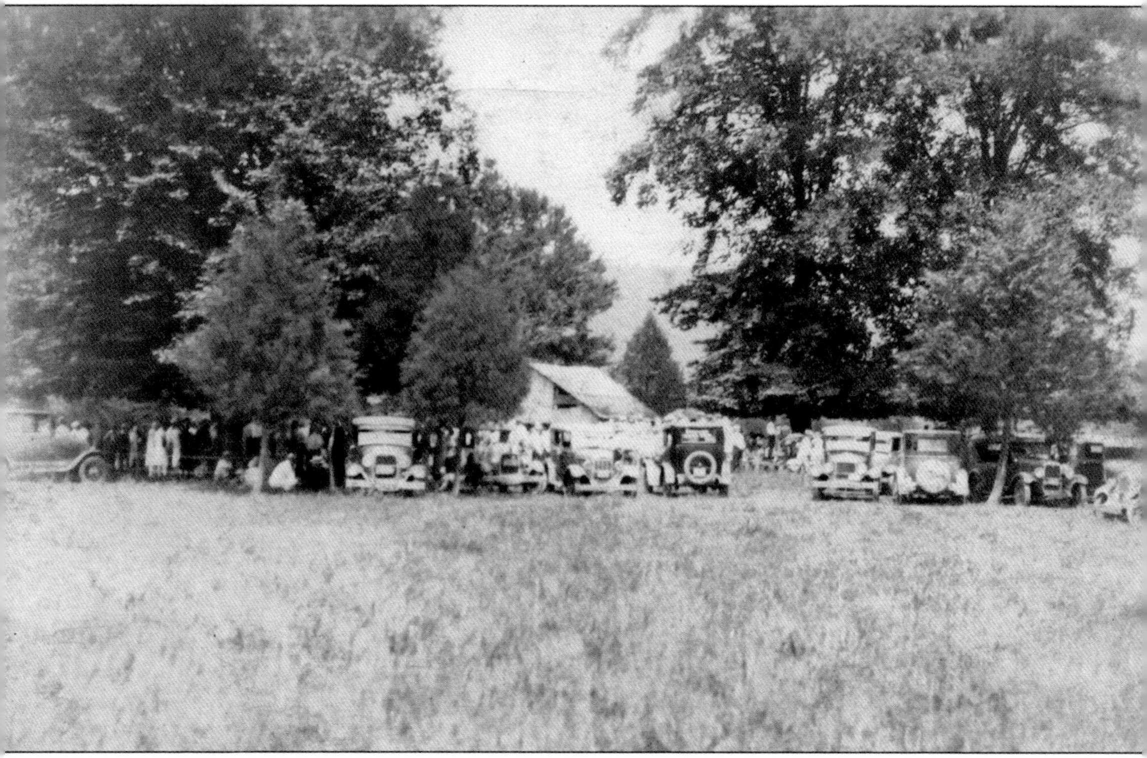

When the federal government proposed a highway from Chicago to Miami, named the "Lakes to the Gulf" route, the Campbellsville Lions Club and other public leaders joined with community leaders from Nelson, Washington, Marion, and Adair Counties to promote the Sergeant York Trail Bee Line Highway. The group expected to connect the Kentucky route with the York Highway already established in neighboring Tennessee. An estimated 5,000 to 6,000 people gathered on the Campbellsville College campus in July 1925 and formed an association to promote the Sergeant York Trail. Local individuals looked to capitalize on the efforts. Burr H. Gilpin opened the York Trail Restaurant in Campbellsville, a business R. Walker Wilson bought in 1926 and renamed the Wilson Confectionary and Coffee Shoppe. At Burdick, Sallie Sublett advertised a "first-class lunch room at her place on the York Trail." Her riverside camp was also "open to campers and tourists." (FHB.)

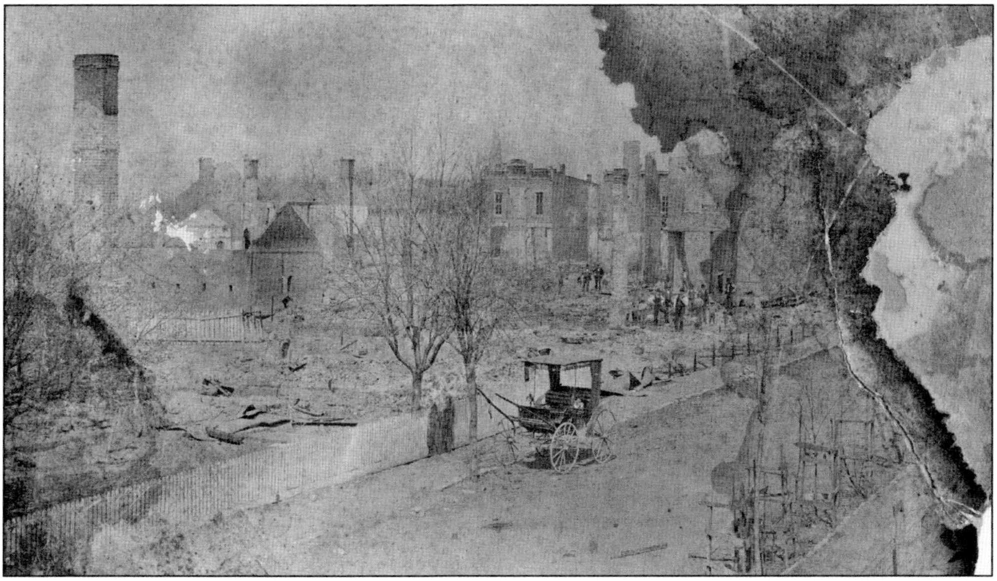

Over the years, fires have plagued downtown Campbellsville. The picture above captures the results of a fire that took place around 1895 and destroyed most of the buildings on the south side of Main Street and Central Avenue. Below, Campbellsville suffered another major fire on Saturday, March 18, 1911, that destroyed two city blocks. Beginning in the kitchen of Brack Sanders' general store, the fire ruined the north side of Main Street from present-day Citizens Bank east to Central Avenue. Little or no insurance covered the estimated $50,000 loss. The makeshift building in center may be the printing office of *The News-Journal.* Major losses included the Taylor National Bank and the Commercial Hotel. Buildings on the south side of Main Street suffered, with many windows broken and stock damaged. The Campbellsville Hotel lost windows, but the adjoining R. E. Puryear Building burned completely. (TCHS, above and below.)

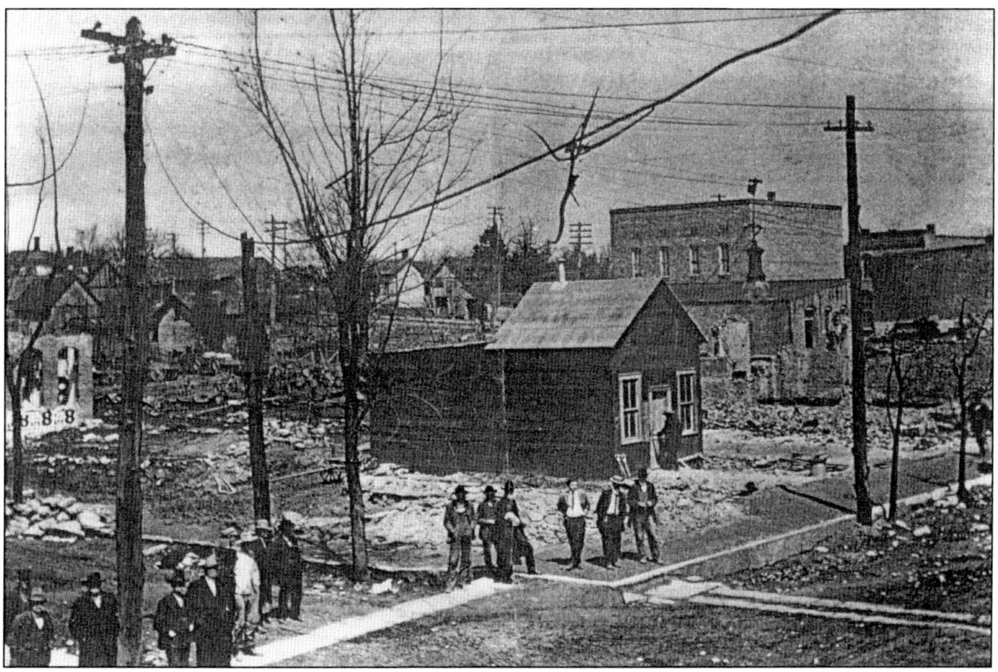

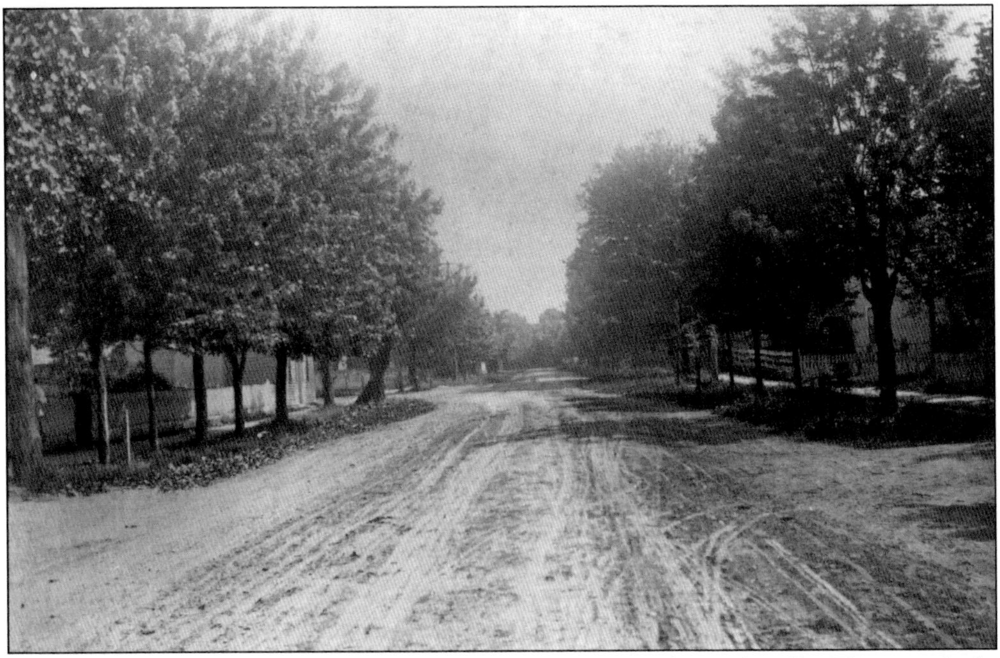

This early picture captures life on Main Street prior to any mechanical traffic. This view looks east. The first building on the left is the Redmon Tavern, which was later the location for the Bank of Campbellsville. Other identifiable businesses are the Bass and Bryant Drugstore and a hardware store that sells Tennessee wagons. (TCHS.)

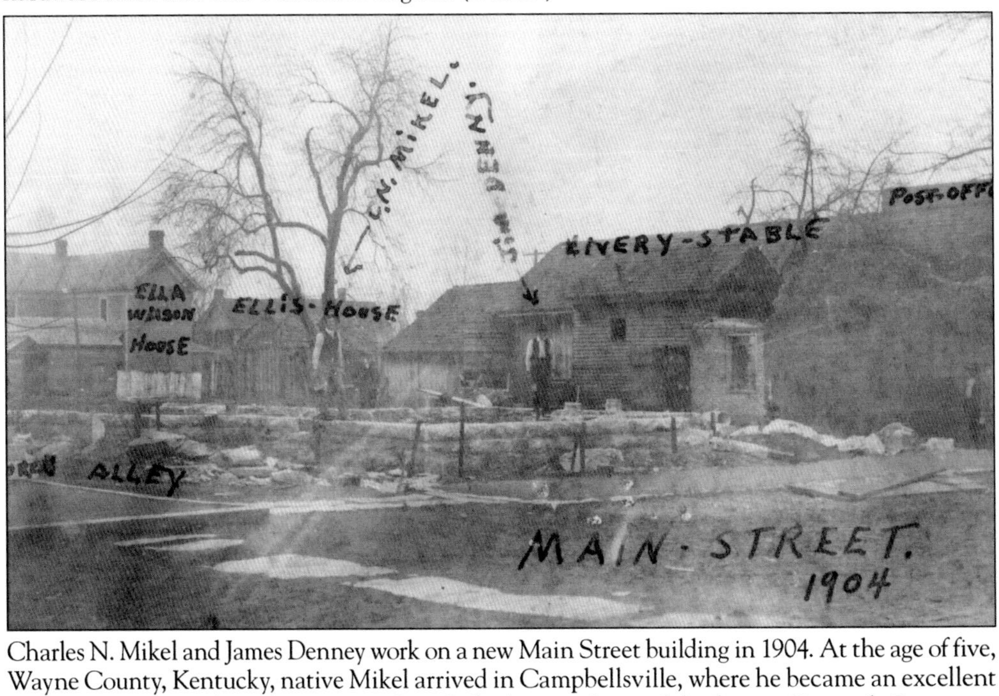

Charles N. Mikel and James Denney work on a new Main Street building in 1904. At the age of five, Wayne County, Kentucky, native Mikel arrived in Campbellsville, where he became an excellent stonemason. Examples of his stonework include the storefront of the former Coppock Garage on Court Street, completed with the help of African American stonemason Wallace Bottoms, and the foundation and stone columns on the present United Methodist Church. (TCHS.)

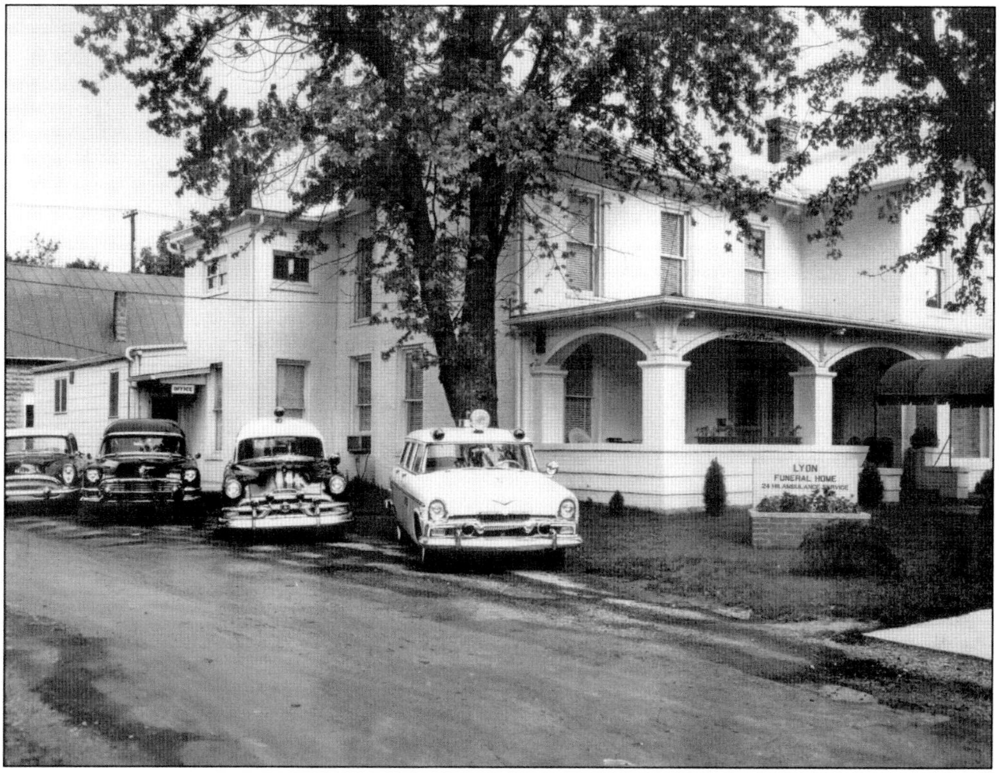

In September 1934, the Eads-Walker-Cloyd Funeral Home became the Lyon Funeral Home when Lucy Lyon and her son, Marshall, bought out other partners. At the time, the company conducted business on the second floor of the Willock Building. Later the company moved east to a house adjacent to the Central Sales Building before moving to this house on East Main Street across from Bethel First Presbyterian Church. (LD.)

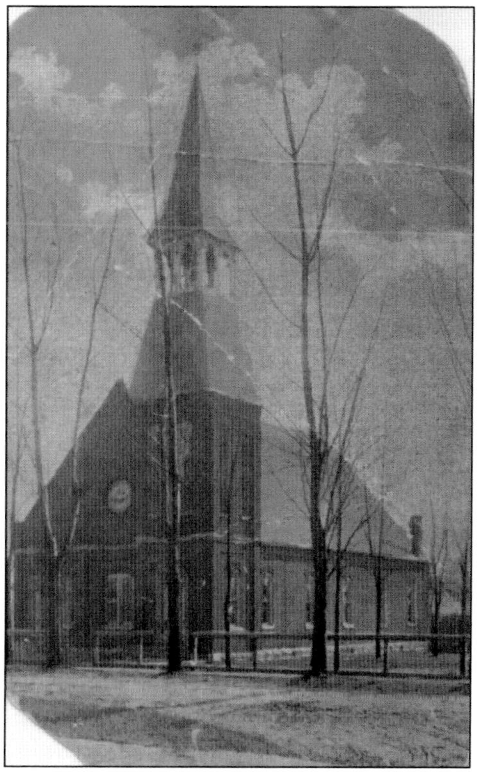

The present Bethel First Presbyterian Church resulted from a 1966 merger between Campbellsville's First Presbyterian and Bethel Presbyterian, the latter located on the Columbia Highway. Prior to building their first church in 1884, Presbyterians in Campbellsville held services in the Methodist church for almost 30 years. First Presbyterian lost its first church building in an 1892 fire. Using many of the bricks from that building, First Presbyterian Church constructed the present church. (SS.)

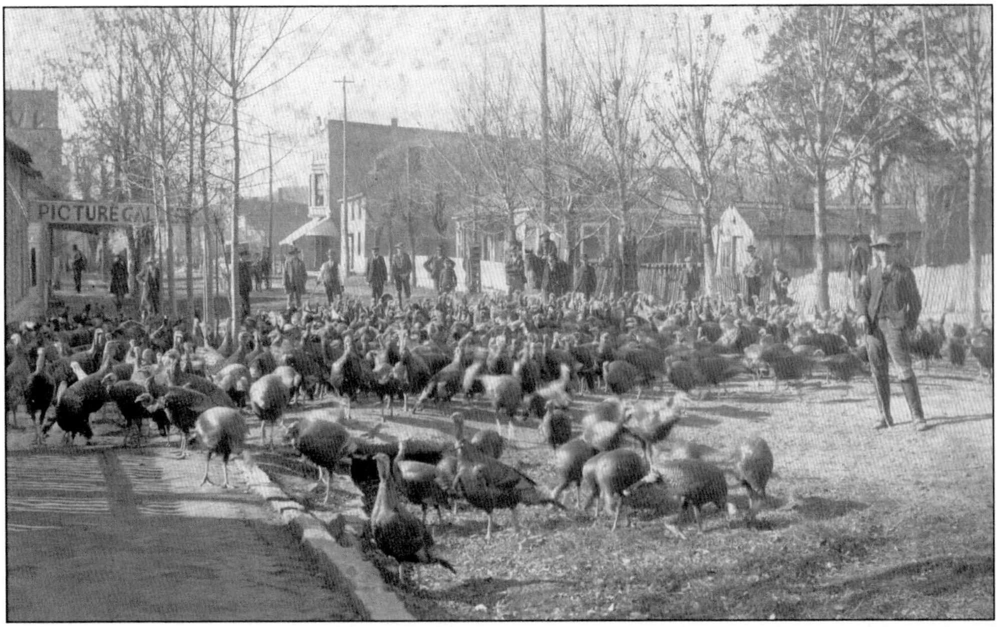

S. H. Grinstead Produce Company's Campbellsville office shipped turkeys by way of the railroad to Louisville and eastern markets, demonstrating one aspect of the railroad's significance to Campbellsville in the early 20th century. As they had done prior to the railroad's arrival, some producers still drove turkeys to the shipping point. Identifiable persons in the c. 1902 picture above include Robert B. Wilson of Cane Valley, with a cane at left center, and his son William Lester Wilson, second to Robert B. Wilson's right. Below, J. T. Morris demonstrates the continued value that poultry had for local producers. This photograph also illustrates the dramatic changes that were made in 30 years in the methods of bringing livestock from the farm to the market. In 1947, Taylor County native William "Wickie" Durham, president of the Southeastern Poultry and Egg Association, presented Pres. Harry S. Truman two pedigree turkeys for the White House Christmas dinner. (TCHS, top, FHB, below.)

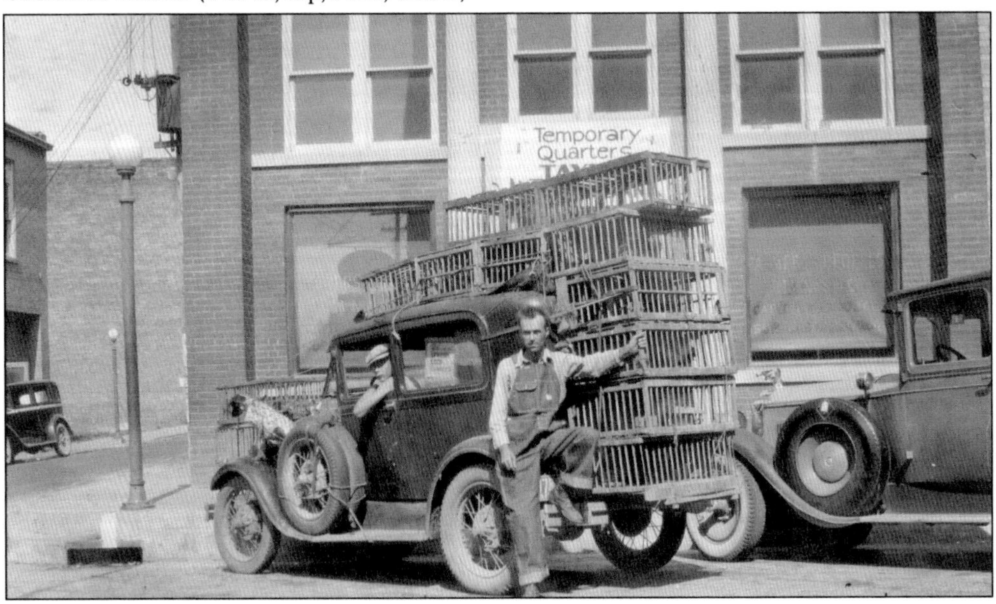

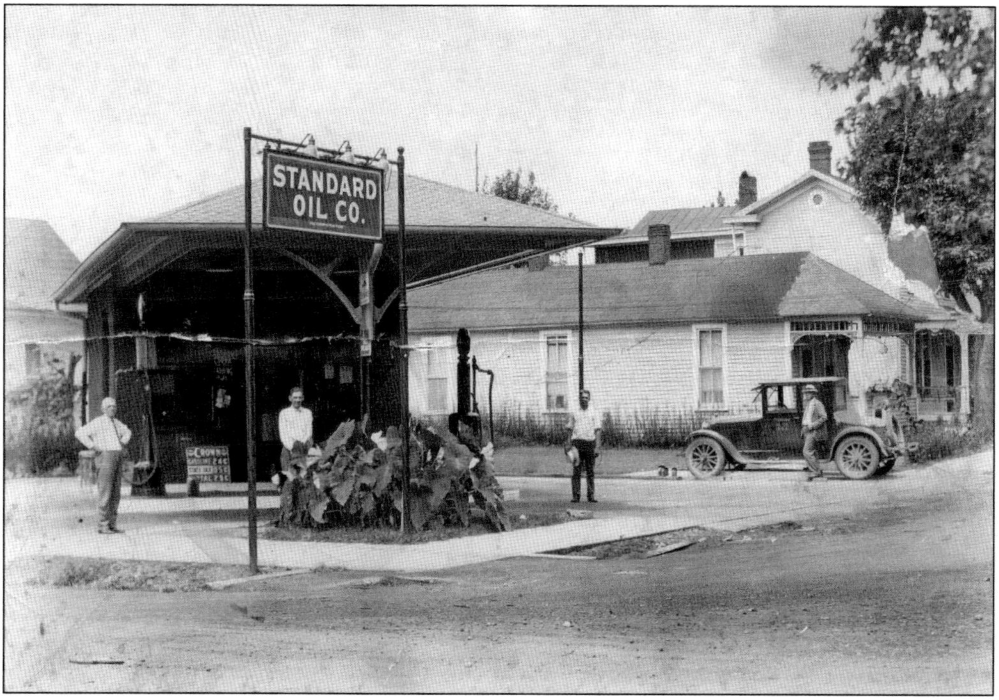

Henry Edrington opened the first gas station in Campbellsville, a Standard Oil dealership, on the corner of Main Street and Lebanon Avenue. Individuals in the picture are, from left to right, Standard Oil representative Steve Noe, distributor Henry Edrington, Paul Coakley, and Mr. Hannah of Kentucky Utilities. Beginning in December 1928, Maggie Collins and Betty Lawson operated a boarding house called the Wayside Inn in the two-story frame house on the right. (EMC)

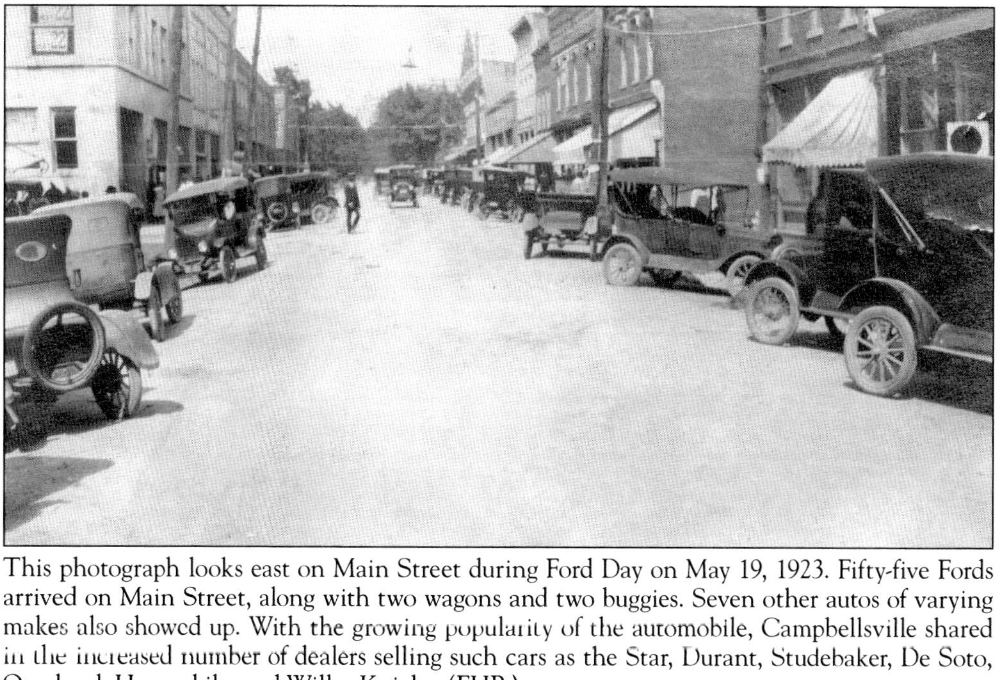

This photograph looks east on Main Street during Ford Day on May 19, 1923. Fifty-five Fords arrived on Main Street, along with two wagons and two buggies. Seven other autos of varying makes also showed up. With the growing popularity of the automobile, Campbellsville shared in the increased number of dealers selling such cars as the Star, Durant, Studebaker, De Soto, Overland, Hupmobile, and Willys-Knight. (FHB.)

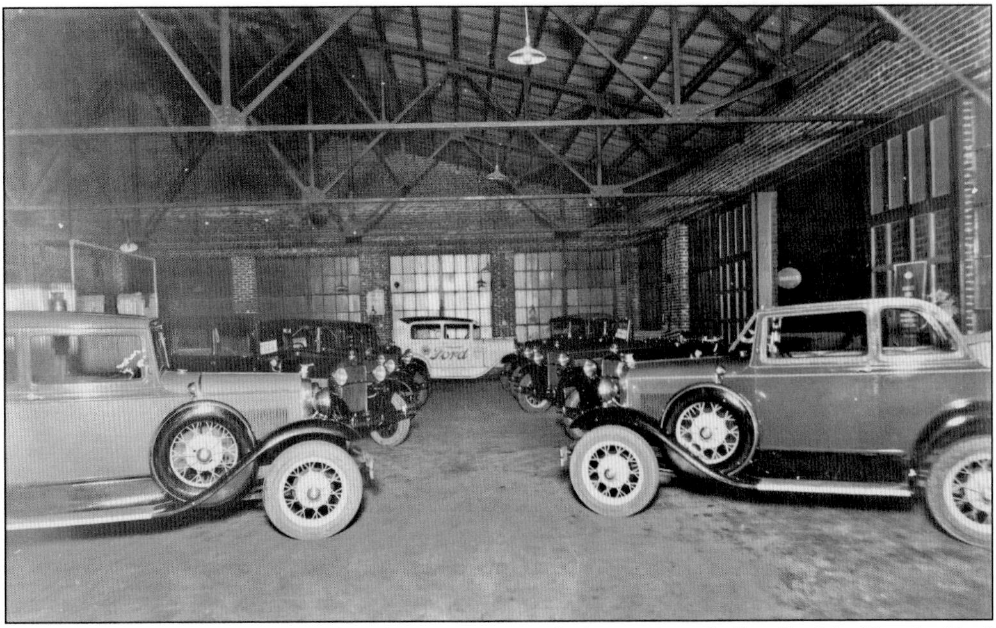

On August 11–12, 1931, the Ford Deluxe Caravan rolled into Campbellsville. Used by the Ford Motor Company as a way of introducing its new line of cars and trucks, this caravan consisted of a radio car, convertible sedan, convertible cabriolet, deluxe tudor, and deluxe coupe, which were all displayed at Central Sales. (FHB.)

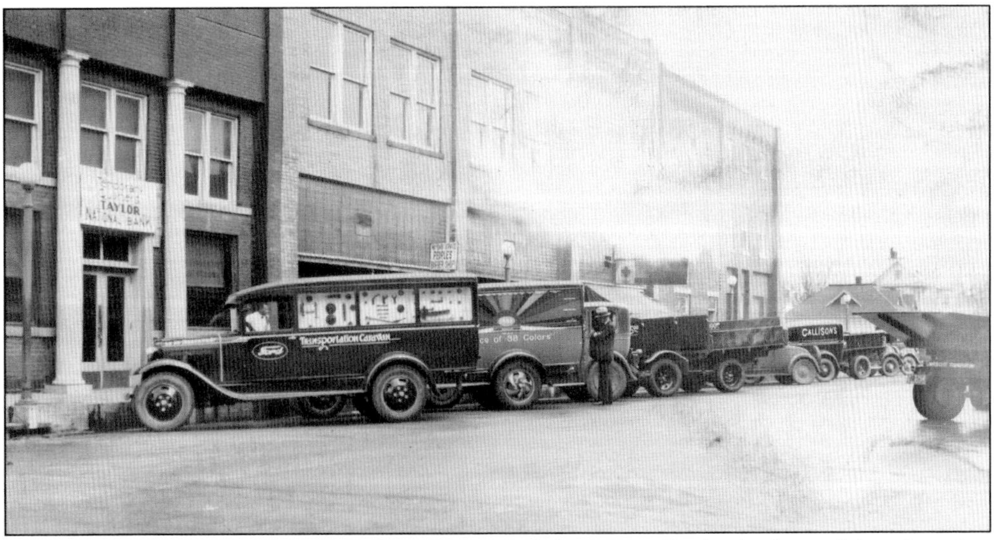

The Ford Transportation Caravan of 1932 promoted the newest Ford vehicles and their benefits, including color choice and price, as noted by the truck bumper to the right touting "lowest cost transportation." The Taylor National Bank, Peoples Barbershop, and Callison's Grocery, pictured from left to right, operated in the buildings on the left. The Peoples Barbershop owner, W. Thomas Hodgen, may be visible through the windows of the first car on the left. (FHB.)

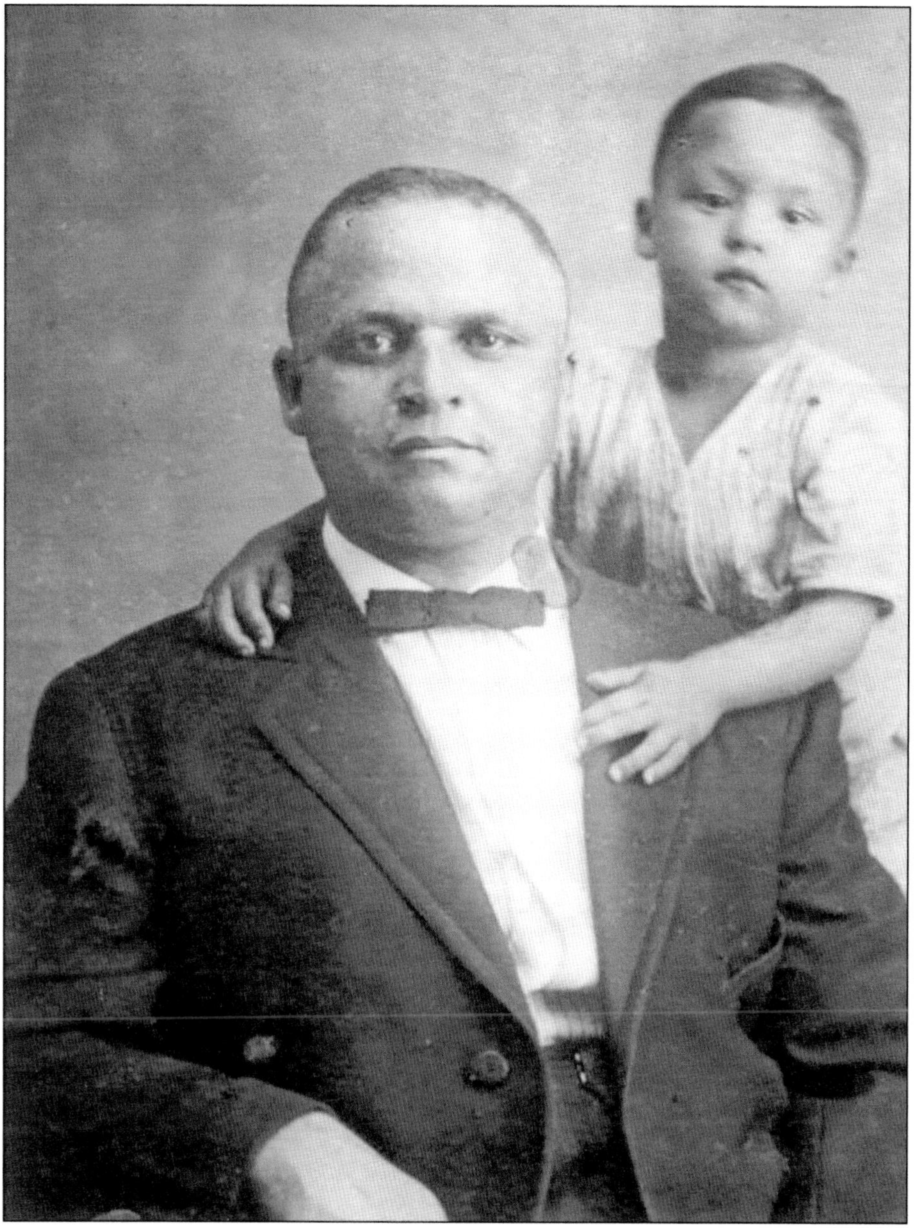

William Thomas Hodgen barbered successfully in Campbellsville for over 50 years in the Peoples' Barbershop. He advertised a sanitary barbershop containing three chairs and an electric vibrator, and his advertisements showed an important understanding of how to use the media. He offered coupons, drawings for free gas, promoted ice water from a drinking fountain as a concern for public health, and showed broad interest in supporting community efforts such as the Campbellsville College girls' teams. In addition, he was an entrepreneur, opening a movie theater for blacks in 1920 and starting a metal cane factory. Hodgen also developed a wide reputation as a wholesale and retail dealer in wild animals. On one occasion, he advertised for 1,500 rabbits for which he would pay 15¢ a rabbit. As Pres. Woodrow Wilson planned for his White House marriage in 1915, Hodgen offered opossums, groundhogs, and "one pair nice tame baby black bears" for a series of White House dinners. Hodgen is shown here with his grandson Woodie. (MHL.)

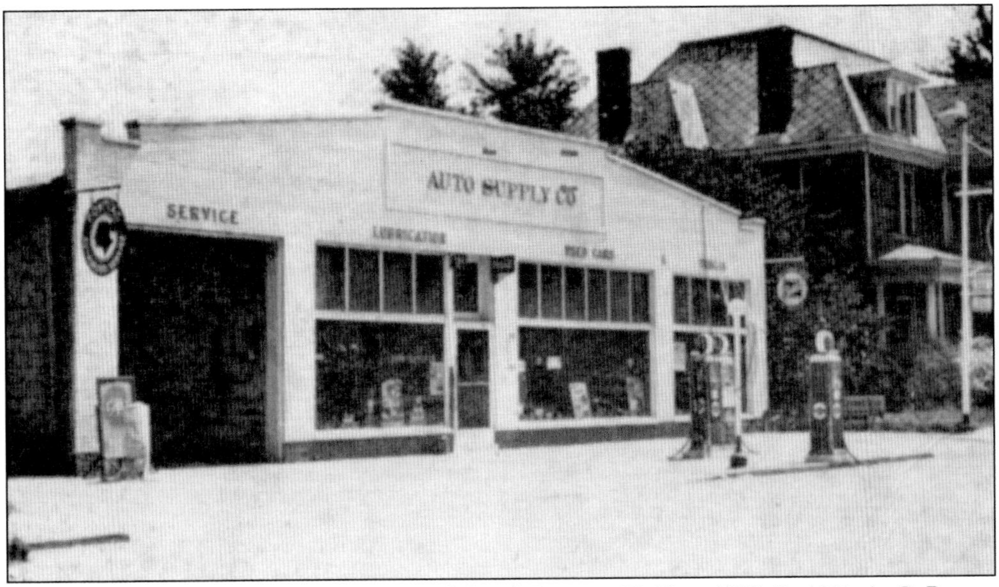

Auto Supply changed its name to Newcomb Buick-Pontiac-GMC in 1978. By 1911, A. C. Burrey handled the Buick dealership in Campbellsville. Wood Coppock took over the Buick franchise around 1918 and ran Auto Supply for about 44 years before retiring. The building stood on Main Street's south side east of the Colonial House, a boarding house operated by Fannie Wilson. (TCHS.)

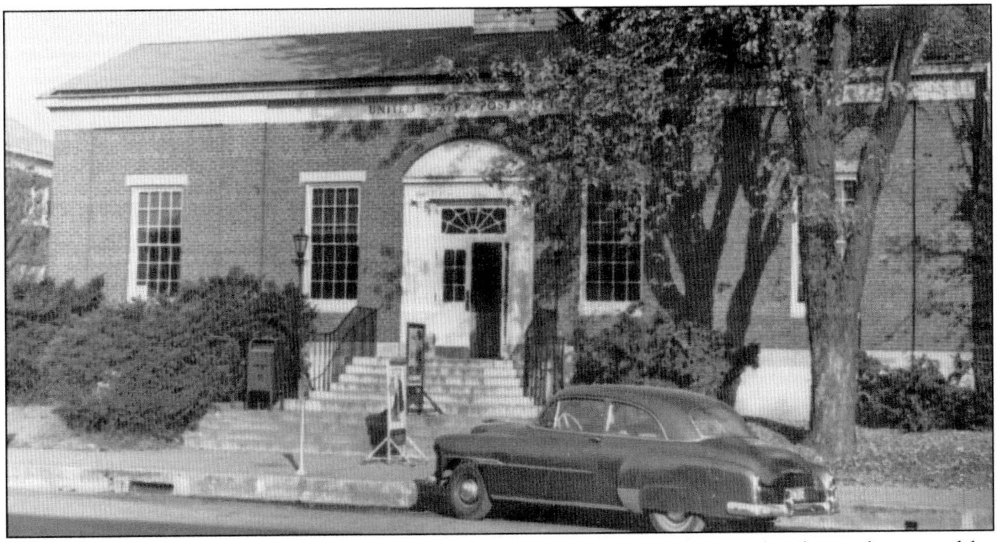

Completed in 1936, the former Campbellsville Post Office stands on a lot formerly owned by Drs. William Burr Atkinson, Frank I. Buckner, Edwin L. Gowdy, and Mr. John A. McRoberts. The lot had also previously been known as the stagecoach lot. To complete the brick building, contractors removed the McRoberts house. The building now houses the Bertram, Cox, and Miller Law Offices. (TCL.)

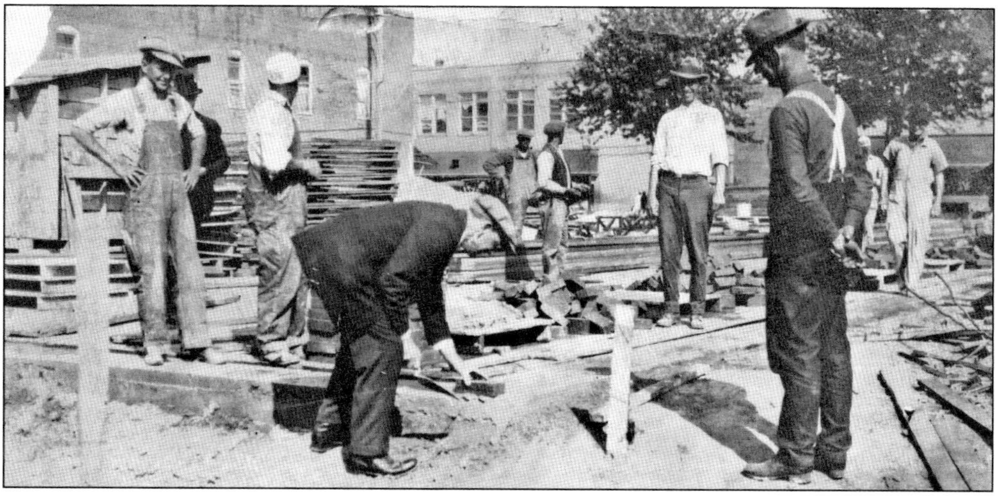

Started in 1922, the Central Sales Building represented an expansion of the Buchanan-Lyon Company. J. T. Phillips and R. G. Goodwin contracted to complete the two-story building that included a showroom, a customer waiting room, and garage. Originally, Buchanan-Lyon intended to put all of its business in the building. However, by 1924, the board of directors decided to separate the Ford agency, splitting the hardware and implement business from the wholesale grocery business and locating the new division, Central Sales Company, in the new building with managers Thomas W. Buchanan and Robert J. Lyon. Robert's brother, William J. Lyon, became the buyer for the wholesale grocery company. Building construction finished in 1923. The above photograph shows the first brick being laid on May 7, 1923. Below, the construction continues with the photograph showing a view looking south on Central Avenue. (FHB, above and below.)

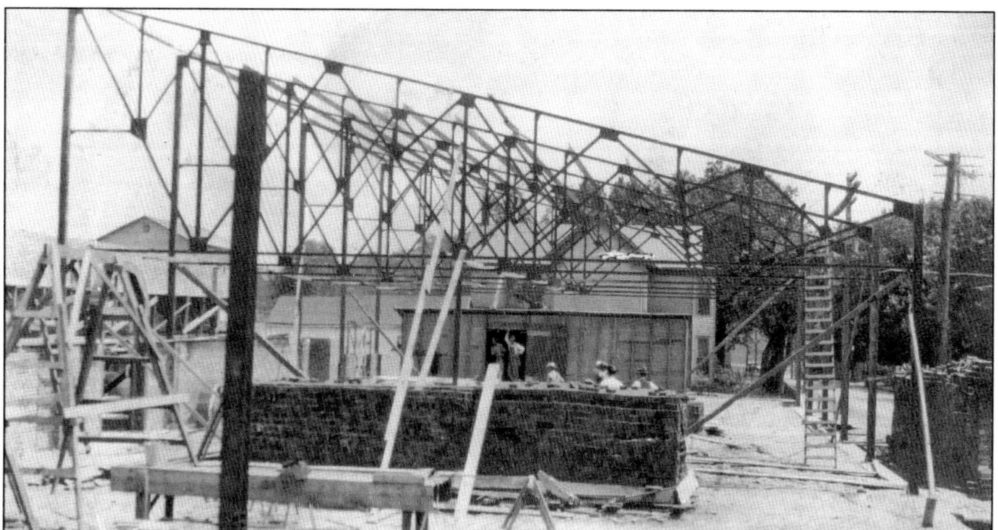

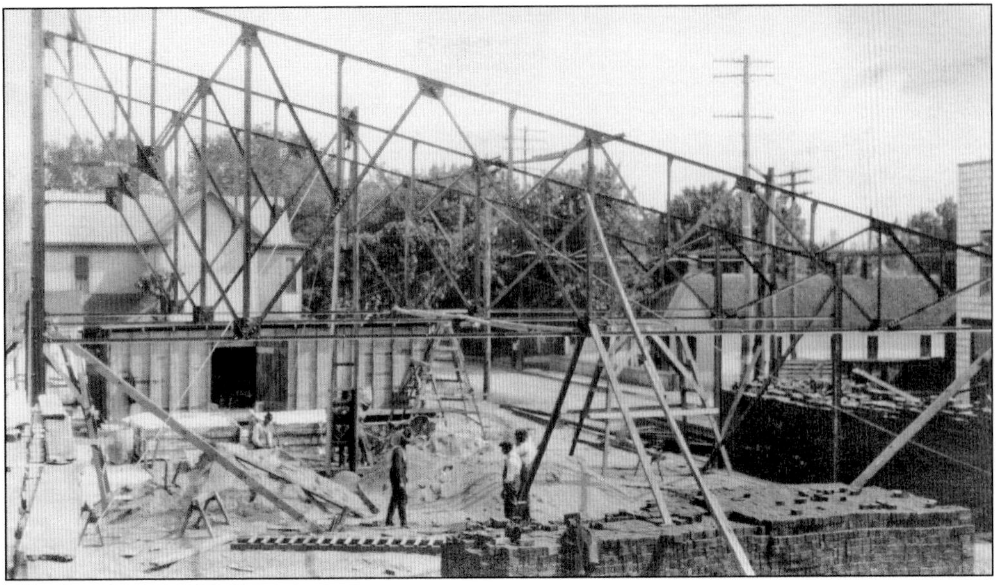

Fred Buchanan, Thomas W. Buchanan's son, took several pictures of the Central Sales Building's construction. This particular photograph, taken from the building's second floor, captures a view looking south on present-day Central Avenue. The houses seen here no longer exist. The two-story house left of center is George H. Willson Jr.'s birthplace. George and his wife Mildred later ran the Blue Bunny. The photograph below catches workers who have paused from their work on the building's eastern wall. To the right, the top of Campbellsville Milling is visible. The brick house seen just above the wall later became the Lyon Funeral Home, which was replaced in 1960 by the Howell Drugstore. (FHB, above and below.)

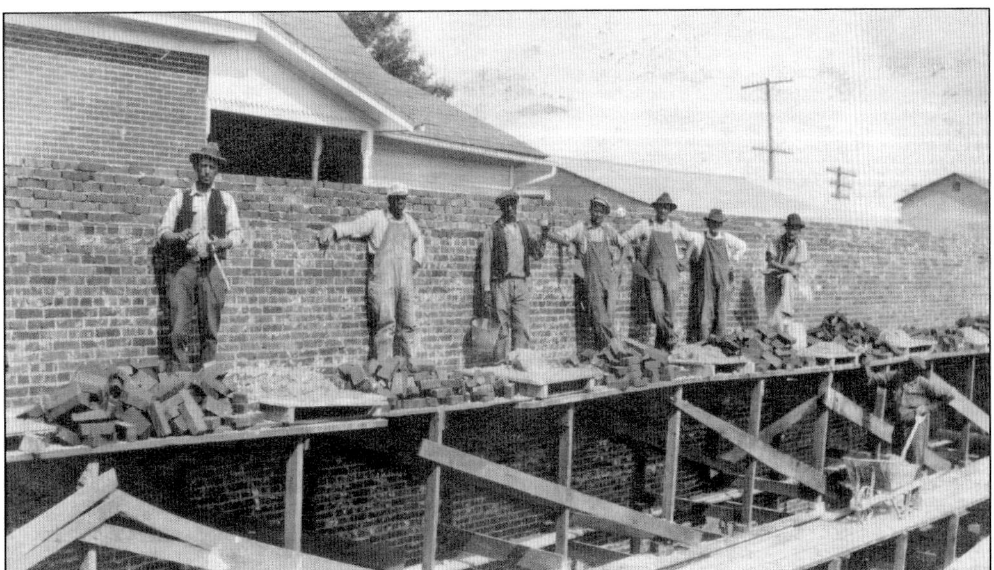

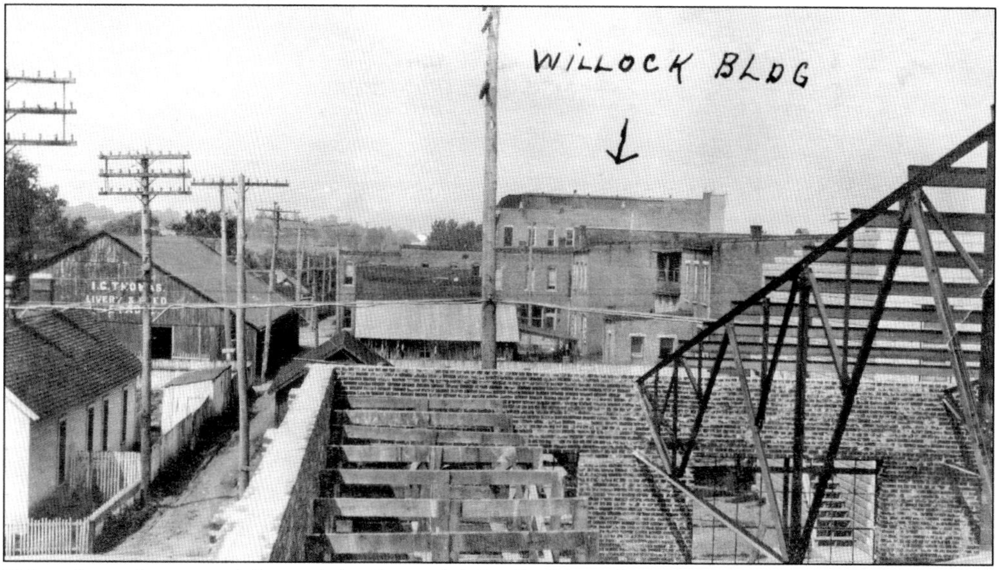

Taken from the second floor of the Central Sales Building during construction, this photograph looks west. Fred Buchanan probably identified the Willock Opera House on the picture because it was the location for the Buchanan-Lyon Wholesale Grocery Company. To the left of the Willock Building is the I. G. Thomas Livery and Feed Stable. This photograph provides an interesting contrast, considering the photographer is standing on a newer livery. (FHB.)

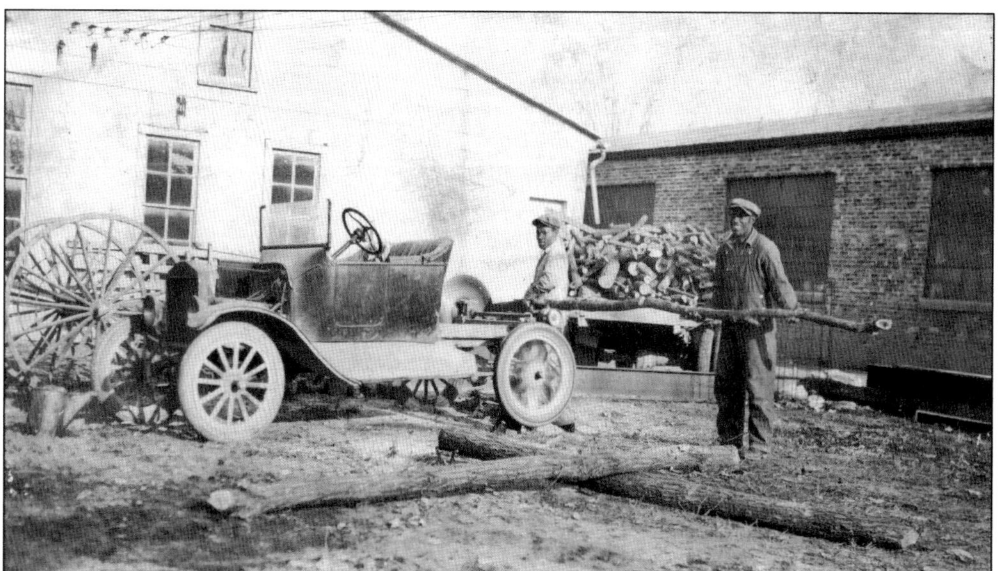

Displaying great ingenuity, two unknown workers have connected a Ford automobile to a saw. They have attached a saw to the car frame with the saw at one end and a drive wheel at the other. By jacking up the Ford with blocks placed under the rear axle, the car's drive wheel connects with the saw drive wheel, turning the vehicle into a portable sawmill. (FHB.)

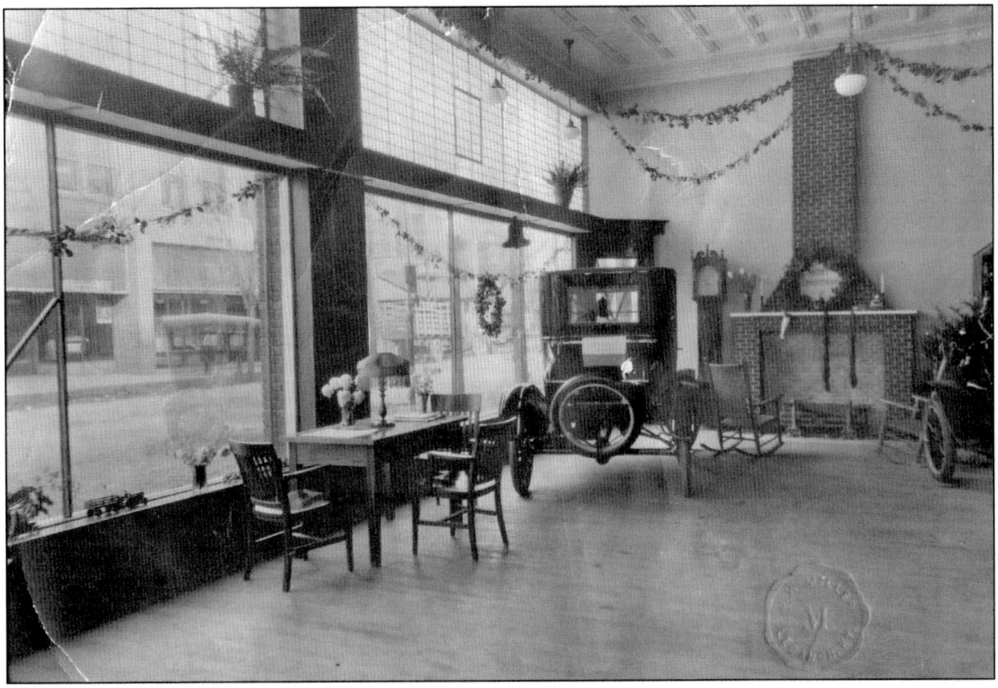

The Central Sales Showroom's large, plate-glass windows helped to better display its cars. Also, they provided an excellent view of Main Street life, something noted by *The News-Journal*, Campbellsville's newspaper, which called them a "Real Show Window." The sign on the building across the street identifies the Buckner and Vaughn Store, a plumbing business. A fake fireplace and hearth help convey the Merry Christmas message written above the mantle. (RiM.)

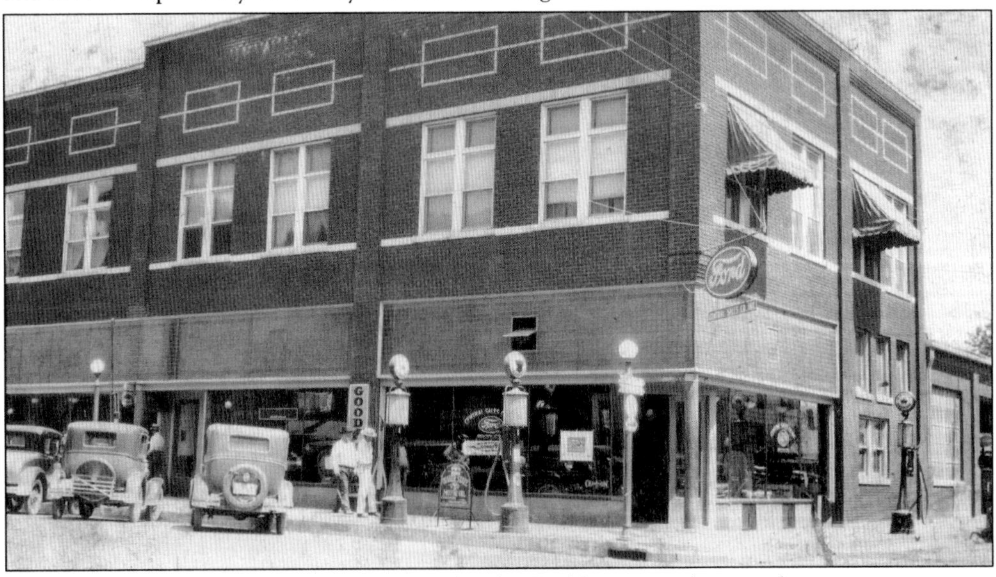

This photograph shows the finished Central Sales Building several years after construction was completed. Like most automobile dealerships of the time, the company added gasoline pumps on the street. Also, automobile growth brought national marketing and brand development. In addition to Ford automobiles, Central Sales sold Crown Gasoline, Goodyear tires, Quaker State motor oil, and Champion spark plugs. (FHB.)

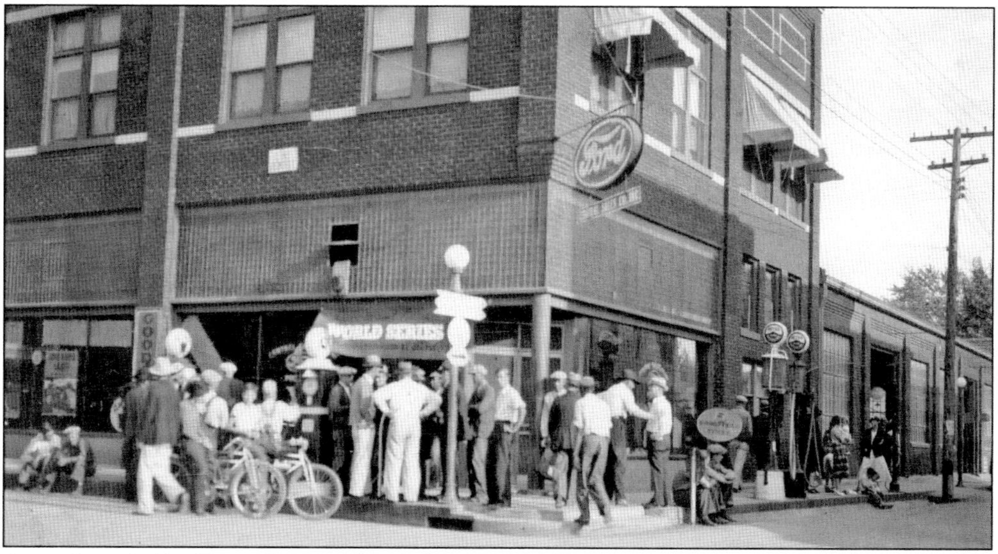

Some Campbellsville residents gather to listen to the 1934 World Series between Detroit and St. Louis. St. Louis won the series 4–3 based on the four wins by the Dean brothers. According to local reports, business was almost suspended during the World Series because of local interest. The Ford Motor Company purchased broadcast rights for it, and as a Ford dealer, Central Sales made the broadcast available for Main Street. (FHB.)

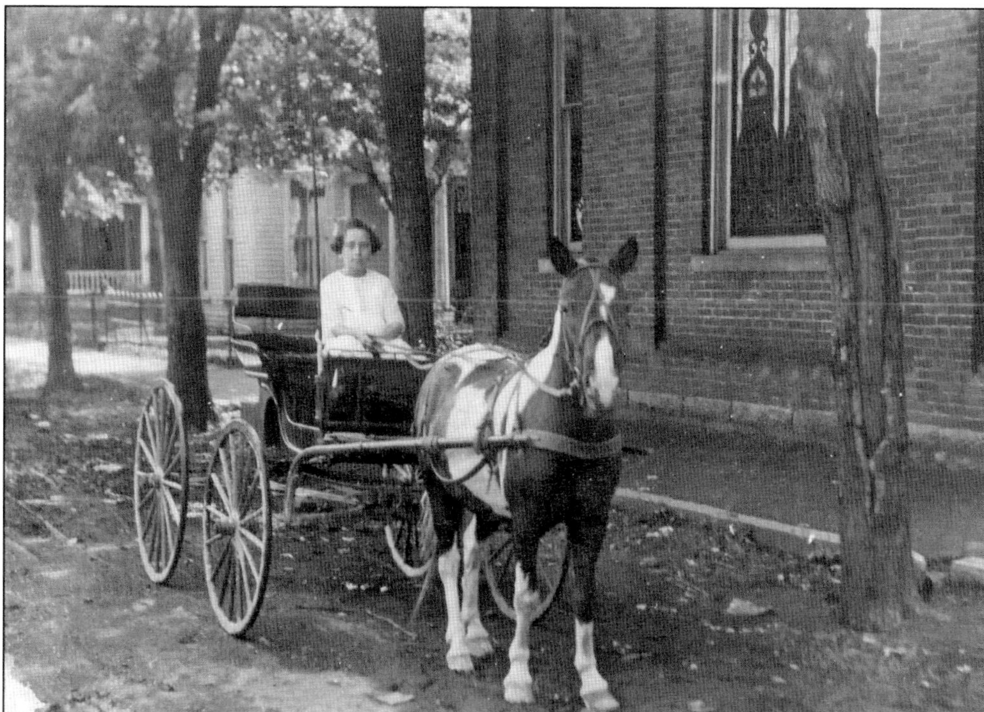
Margaret Miller Beard, daughter of Samuel Tilden Miller, takes her pony for a buggy ride on Main Street. She is parked in front of the third Methodist church that sat on the south side of Main Street. The Campbellsville Oil Company tore the church building down in 1927 for its new Texaco service station. The site now holds the Taylor County Judicial Center. (CBG.)

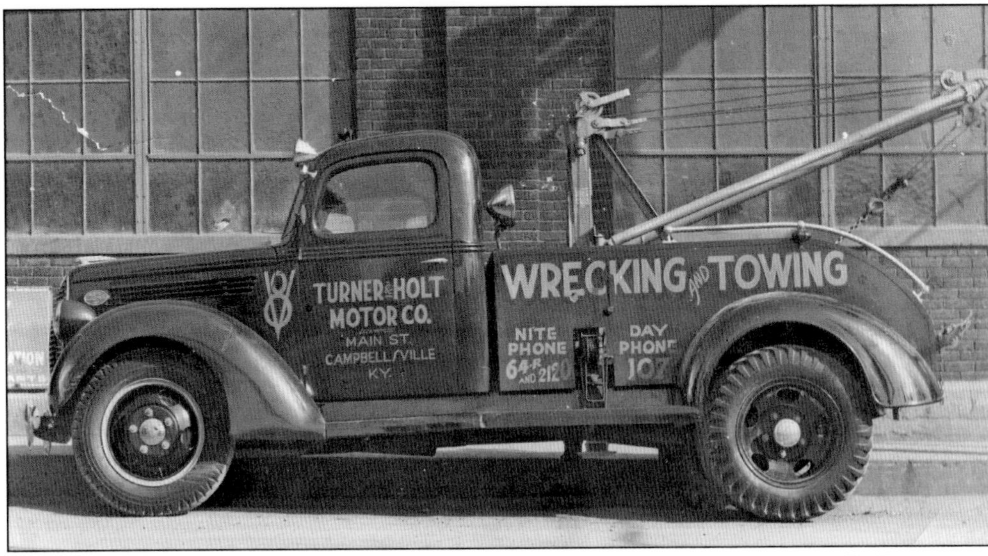

When Fred Buchanan sold Central Sales Company to George R. Turner, Henry R. Turner, and Paul Holt in October 1935, he ended the longstanding Buchanan association with the Ford dealership. The Turners had formerly held a Chrysler dealership in Campbellsville, while Holt was already employed with Central Sales as a salesman. With the change in ownership, the company became known as Turner and Holt Motor Company. Below, the Turner and Holt employees include, from left to right, Turner Gaddie, Dave Barnett, John Humphress, Bill Malone, Maxie Marcum, unidentified, Bill McGlockin, Howard Malone, Jake Cox, and George Rice (kneeling). Later Ford dealerships included Campbellsville Motor Company, managed by Ira Vaughn, and McCubbin Motors. (RiM, above and below.)

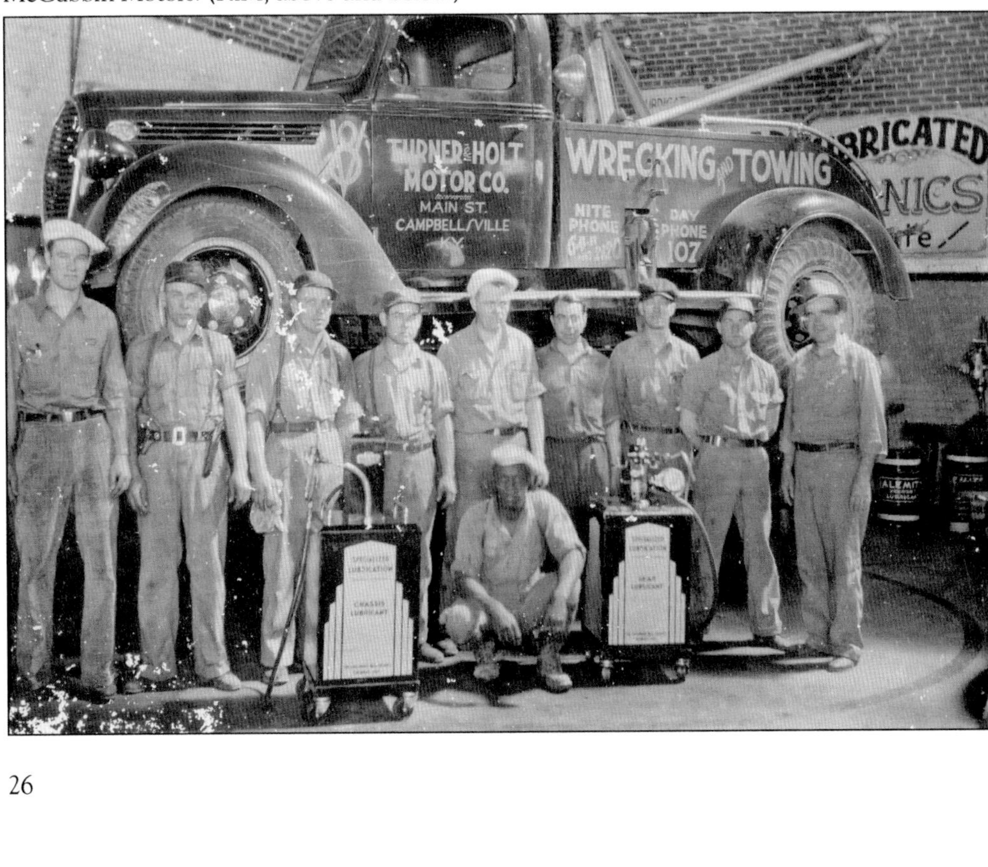

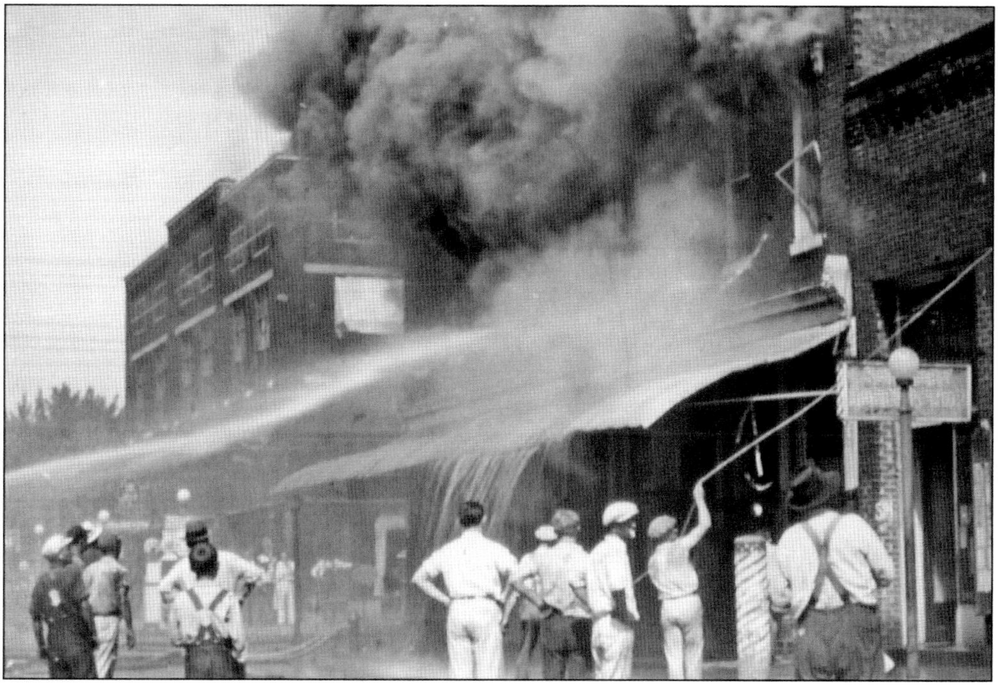

On July 13, 1934, fire broke out in the Campbellsville Hotel, completely destroying the hotel's interior, the post office inside the hotel, and Smith Lee's Barbershop. Fire also damaged an adjoining building to the rear that contained George Marple's restaurant, which opened the day prior to the fire, the Central Avenue Barbershop, and the apartment over them occupied by J. T. and Dorothy Coomes. The fire department brought the fire under control within two hours, but not before an estimated $25,000 worth of damage had been done. The post office moved into the former Farmers and Peoples Bank Building across the street. At the time of the fire, Mr. and Mrs. Raymond Hill were managing the hotel. (TCHS, above and below.)

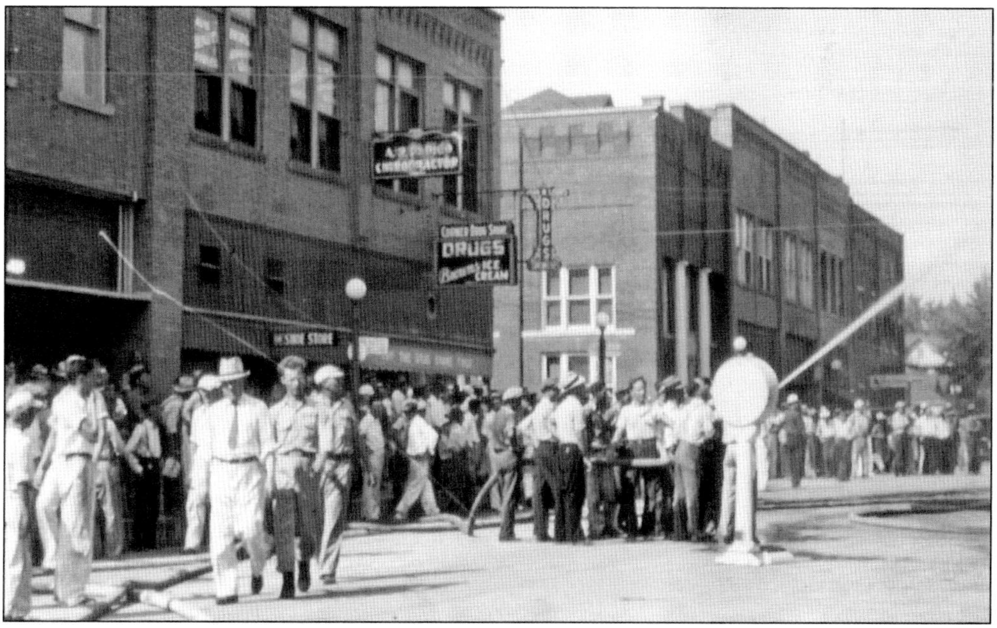

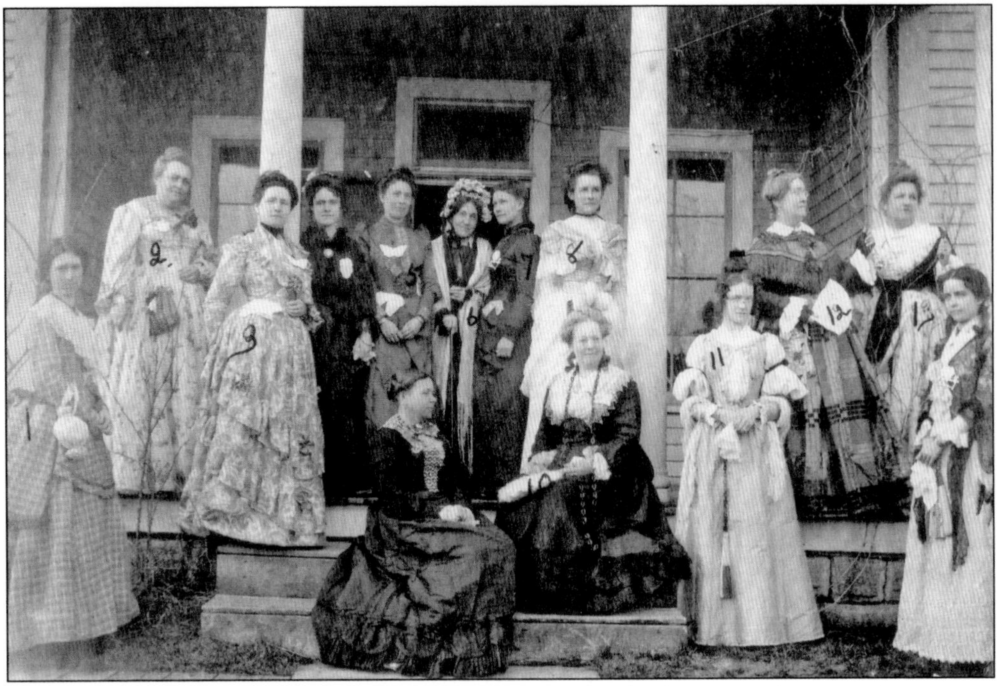

Around 1910, the Dr. Jefferson Lee Atkinson home was the location of a fancy dress party. Pictured on the porch are, from left to right, Minnie Walling, Mae Goode, Mrs. Lee Hobson, Mrs. Virgie ?, Katherine Thompson, Mattie Hill, Florence Bass, Lora Gowdy, and Melisa Davis. Those off the porch are, from left to right, Lizzie Jackson, Lizzie Durham, Ivy Lyon, unknown, and Mary Turner. (TCHS.)

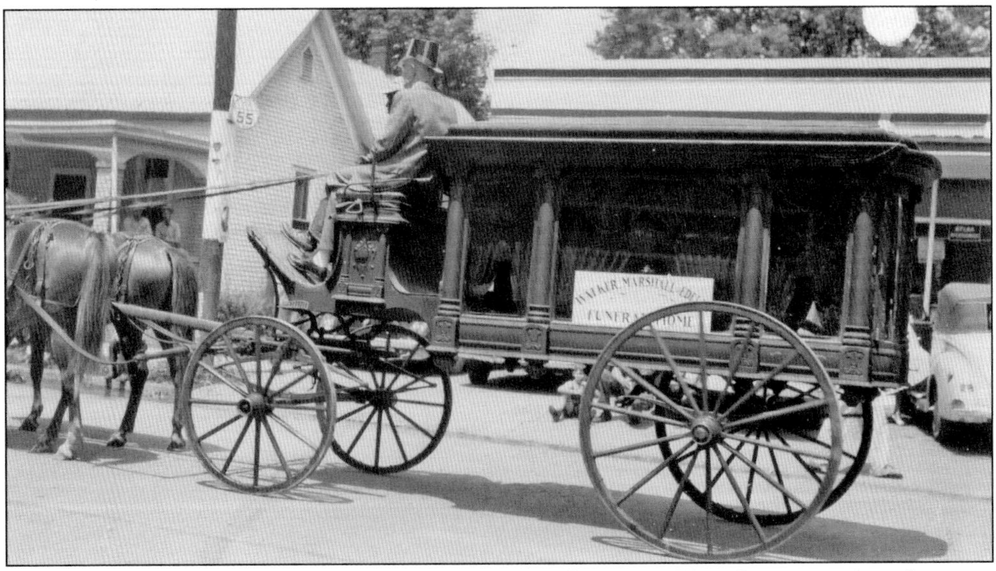

When C. Alex Edelen, formerly with the Taylor Funeral Home at Vine Grove, purchased a major interest in the Walker Marshall Funeral Home in November 1947, he became manager of the firm and changed the name to Walker, Marshall, and Edelen Funeral Home. The other partners were U. V. Walker and Richard Marshall. Buddy Newton remained as an assistant. An unidentified man drives this hearse in the 1948 centennial parade. (FHB.)

Martin Luther Spurling, local photographer, undertaker, and one time Overland and Willys-Knight automobile dealer, produced this postcard of the First United Methodist Church, built in 1899. When tearing the building down, workers found a penny that Fulton B. Netherland had placed in the mortar during construction when he was employed as water boy for C. R. Hoskins. The old Methodist church sat on the south side of Main Street. The location is now covered by the Taylor County Justice Center. The bell from this church was given to Campbellsville College Dining Hall. Methodists replaced the old church with a new structure built across the street from the 1899 structure. Campbellsville Oil Company purchased the building and lot in 1927 and replaced the building with a new Texaco service station. (F&CK, right and below.)

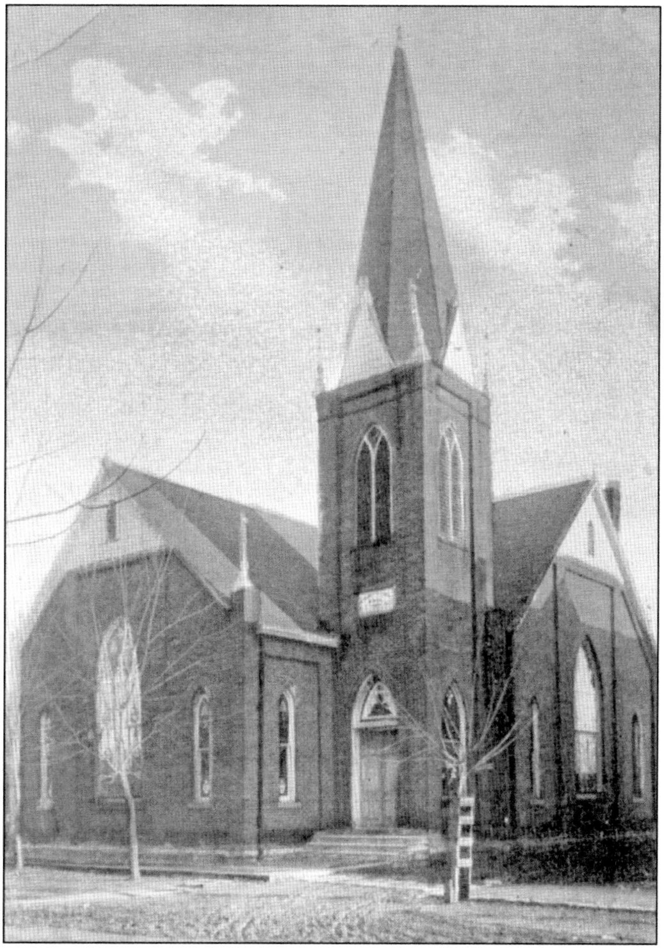

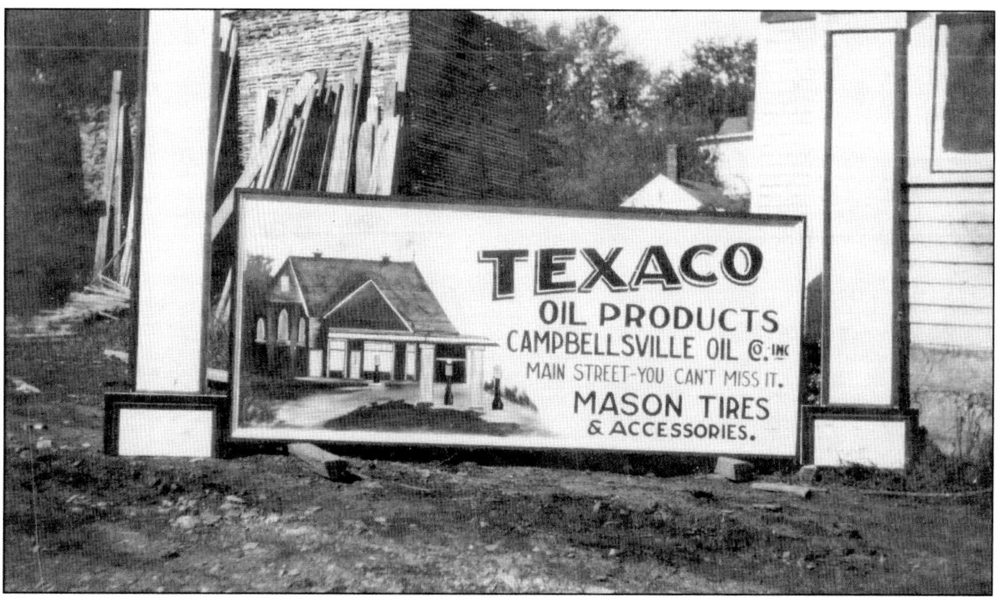

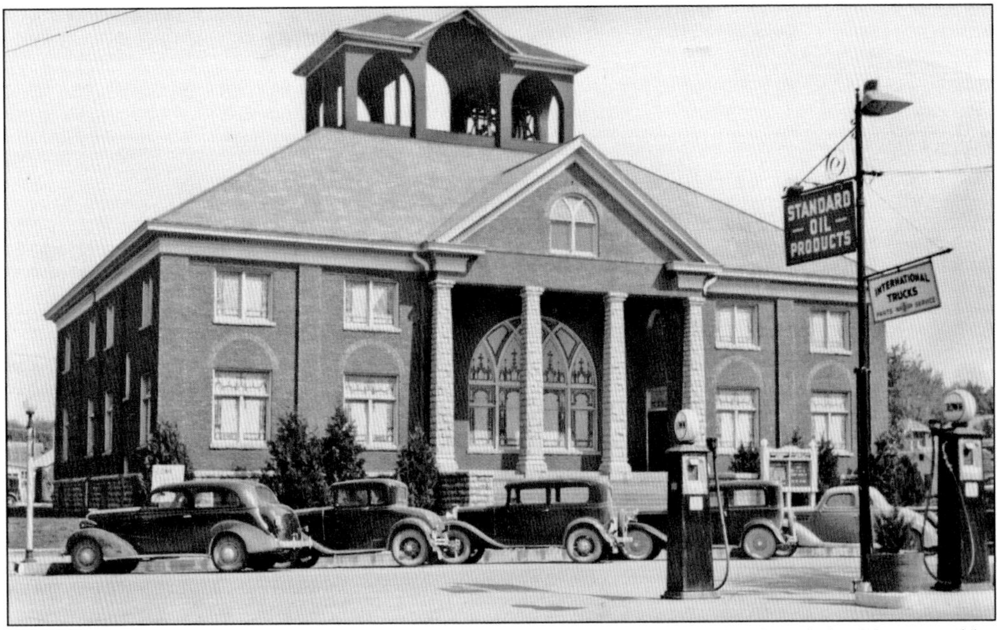

Built between 1920 and 1921, the First United Methodist Church is the fourth building used by the Campbellsville Methodist Church. The congregation built its first church around 1844, across the street from the present building. Campbellsville Oil Company tore the previous church down to build its new service station. The station's pumps can be seen in the right foreground. The congregation laid the cornerstone for this building on July 17, 1921. (MJG.)

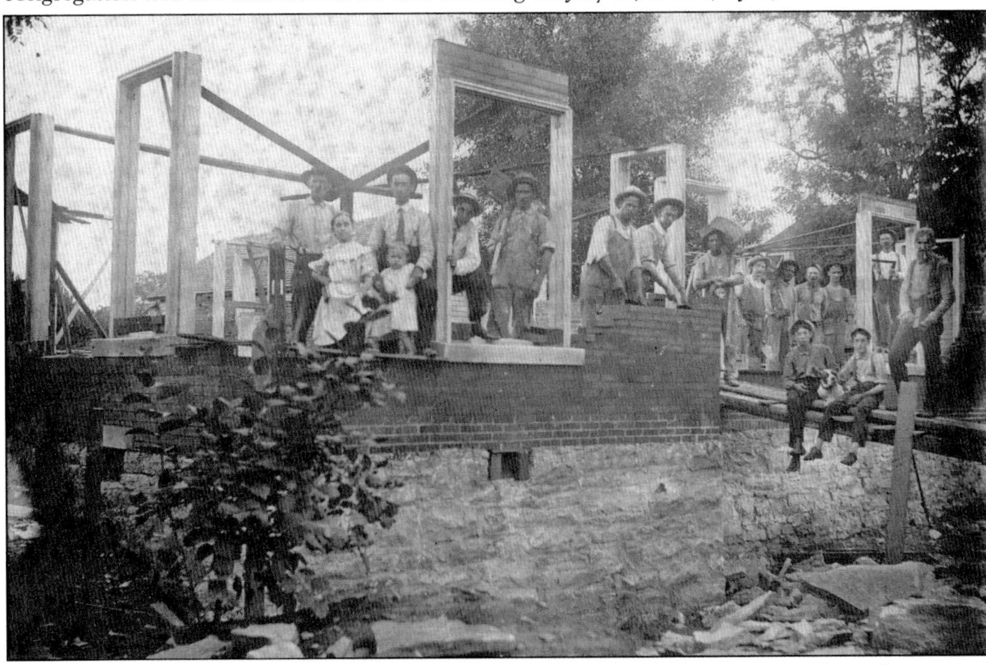

Completed in 1907, the William I. Meader home sat on Main Street across from the present Bertram, Cox, Miller Law Offices. Standing next to the center window frame, Meader is holding the small girl. Fred Buchanan is seated on the plank on the right. The house later became known as the Colonial Inn, which was torn down in 1960 to make room for a parking lot. (FHB.)

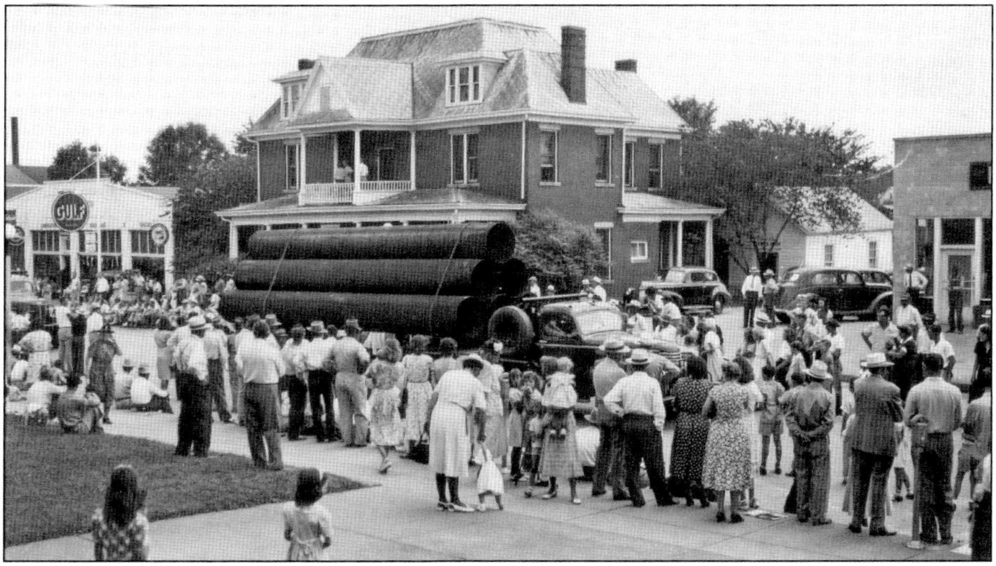

Taken during the 1948 Taylor County Centennial celebration, this photograph shows R. Walker Wilson's Colonial Inn and Colonial Flower Shop. The inn provided meals for the Community Clinic, a small clinic with an operating room located two doors east. The picture also includes the A&P Store, which was previously located in buildings west of this location. Both the Inn and the A&P Store are gone. (FHB.)

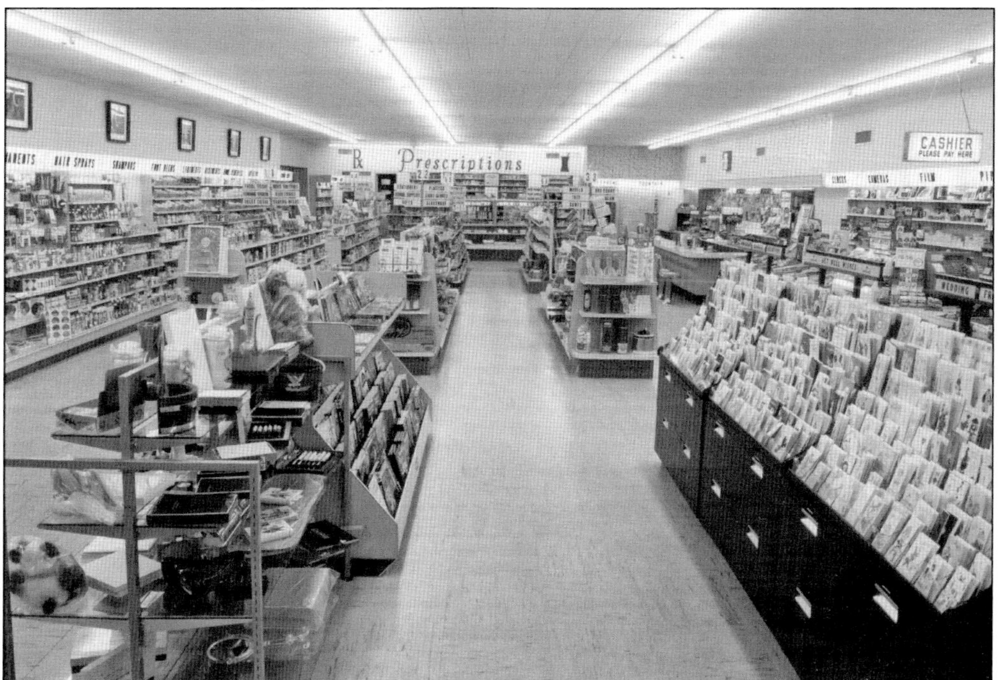

James Hugh Howell Sr. opened his new brick and concrete block building as Howell Drugstore in February 1960. Offering a completely modern drugstore with fountain and luncheonette service, hospital and sick room supplies, and veterinary medicines, the building replaced the former Lyon Funeral Home, which had moved farther east on Main Street. (TCL.)

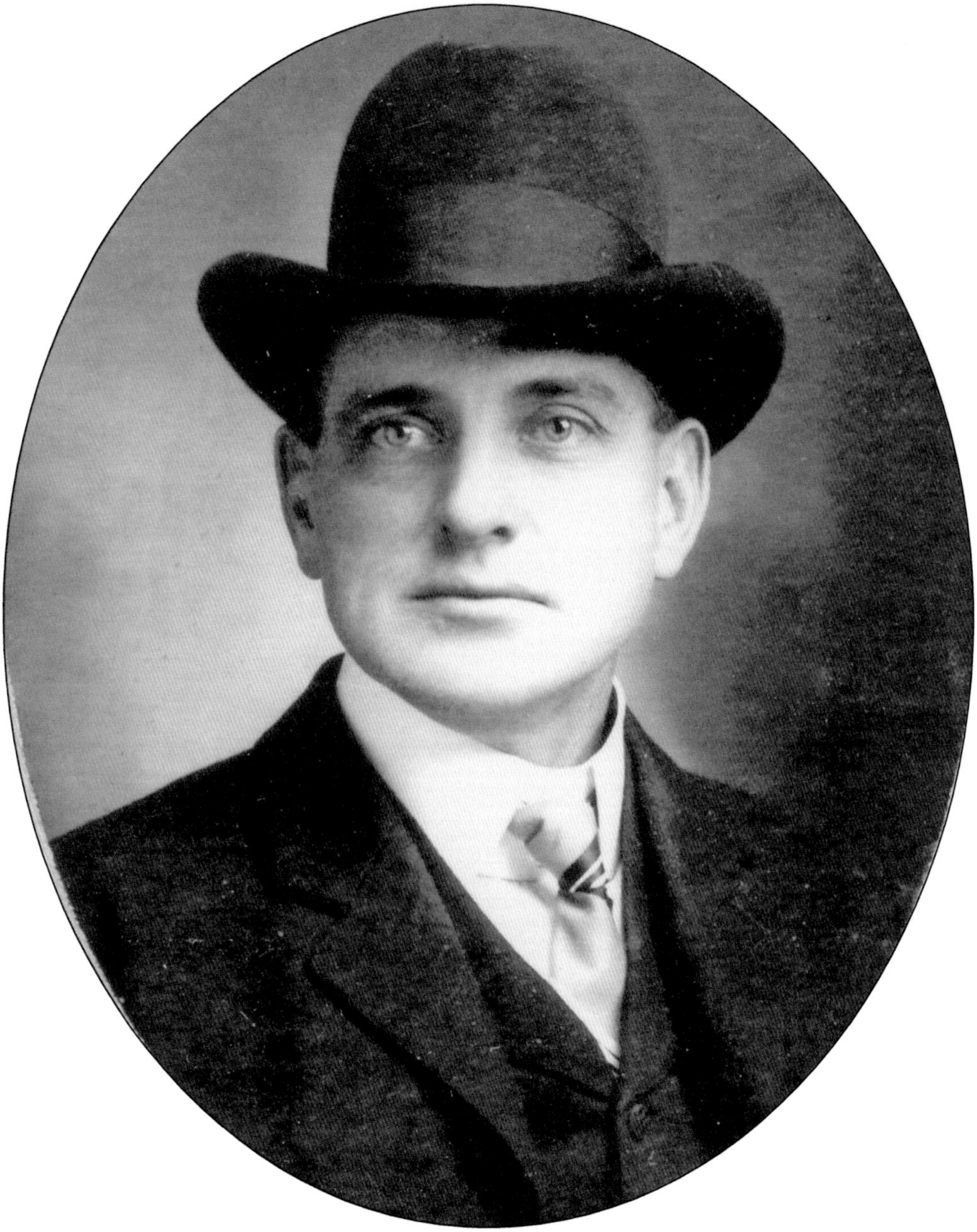

Born in Adair County, Kentucky, William Robert Lyon came to Campbellsville in 1893 to operate the Commercial Hotel. In 1896, he and Henry R. Turner purchased the Turner and Wright buggy company and renamed it the Turner and Lyon Company. He joined with Thomas W. Buchanan in 1909 to create one of the first wholesale grocery houses in the area, eventually buying the Campbellsville branch house of Louisville's wholesale grocer, H. Wedekind and Company, for whom he worked. Buchanan-Lyon expanded its grocery business through branches in Greensburg, Columbia, and Lebanon. Buchanan-Lyon also added automobile sales by becoming dealers for Maxwell and Ford. In 1923, the board of directors agreed to split the automobile and farm implement sales off as Central Sales. W. R. Lyon remained with the Buchanan-Lyon Wholesale Grocery Company as president until his death in 1926. (TCHS.)

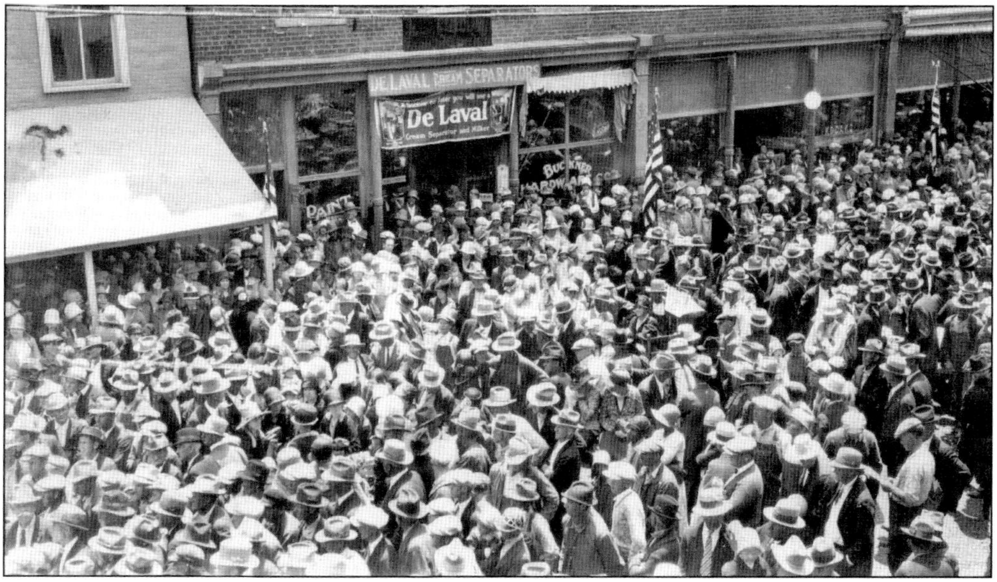

The Buchanan-Lyon Company demonstrated a business savvy and marketing awareness that was new to Campbellsville. It produced the first major Main Street promotion in April 1912 that included demonstrations and prizes. The first prize for coming the longest distance and hauling 82 people went to the Wolford Brothers of Casey County. An estimated 3,000 people attended the event. (FHB.)

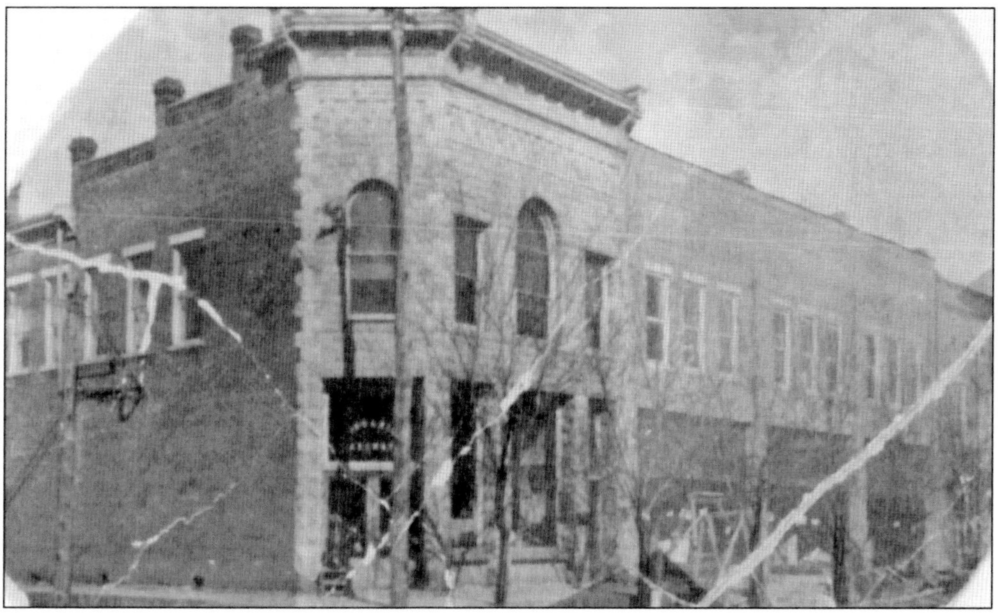
At present the offices of Wise, Buckner, Sprowls & Associates accounting firm, this building initially housed a hardware store. The second floor formerly held the telephone exchange, owned by G. V. Murray, with three daytime operators, Mabel Allen Russell, Minnie Ashbrook, and Nina Barbee, and one nighttime operator, Richard Hord. The building also housed several banks including the Farmers and Peoples Bank (seen here), the Taylor National Bank, and Taylor County Bank. (SS.)

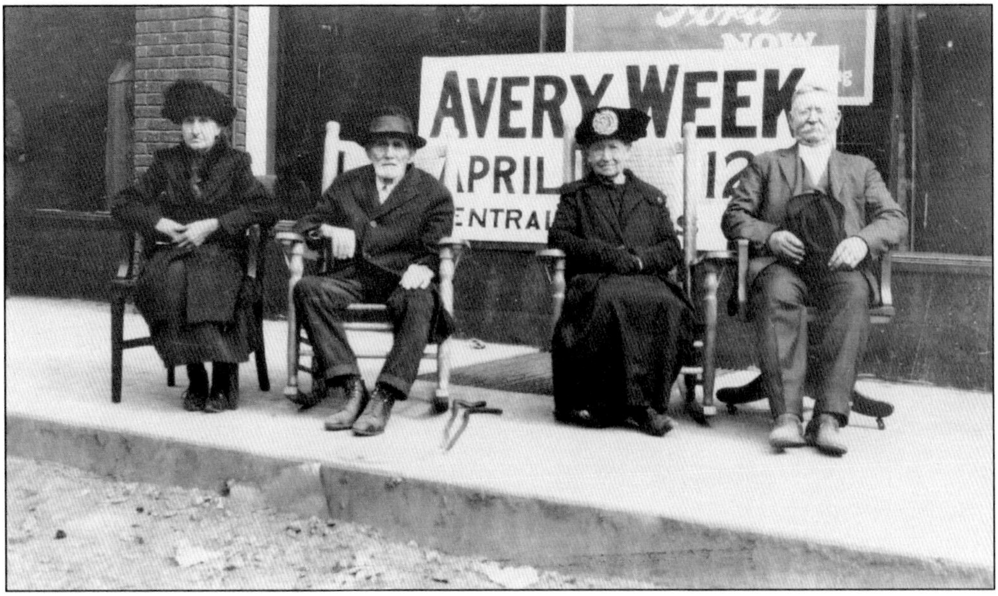

Central Sales and the B. F. Avery Company, Louisville, sponsored Avery Week in April 1924 to promote Avery equipment. The companies used various prizes to encourage attendance. One prize went to the farmer and his wife who had lived together on the same farm for the greatest number of years. In the picture above, first prize winners were, from left to right, Charles and Ellen Bragg, ages 89 and 82, having lived on the same farm for 61 years. Second prize went to B. F. and Elizabeth Caffee, ages 72 and 73, who claimed 52 years. Farmers were also invited to enter a contest for the best pair of mules. Eleven pairs of mules entered. Although the gentlemen in the picture below are unidentified, first prize winner S. L. Fisher from Adair County and second prize winner Fletcher Cox might be pictured. (TCHS, top, and FHB, below.)

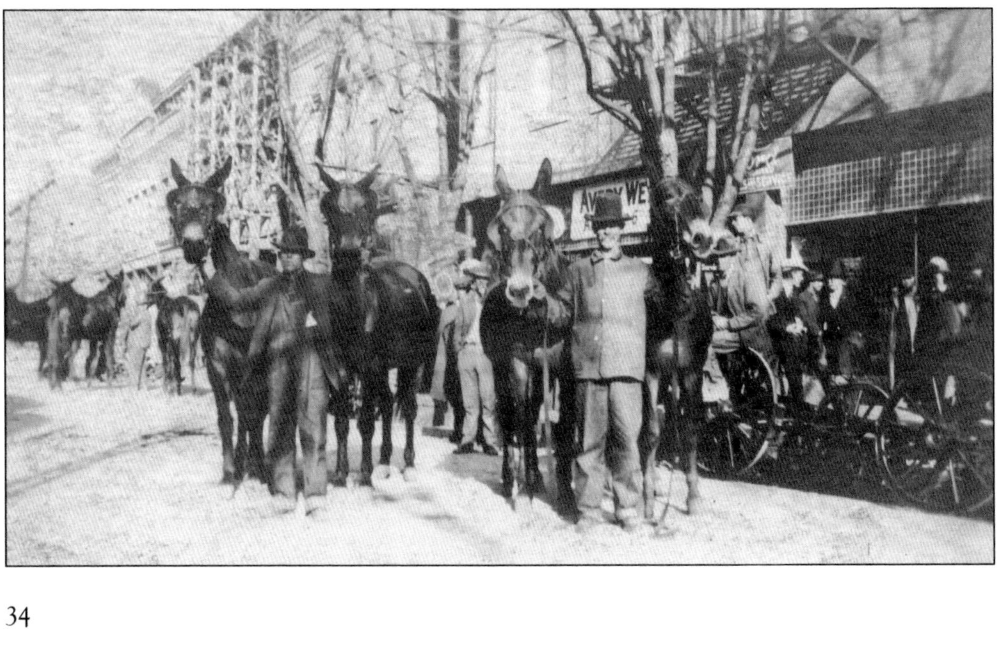

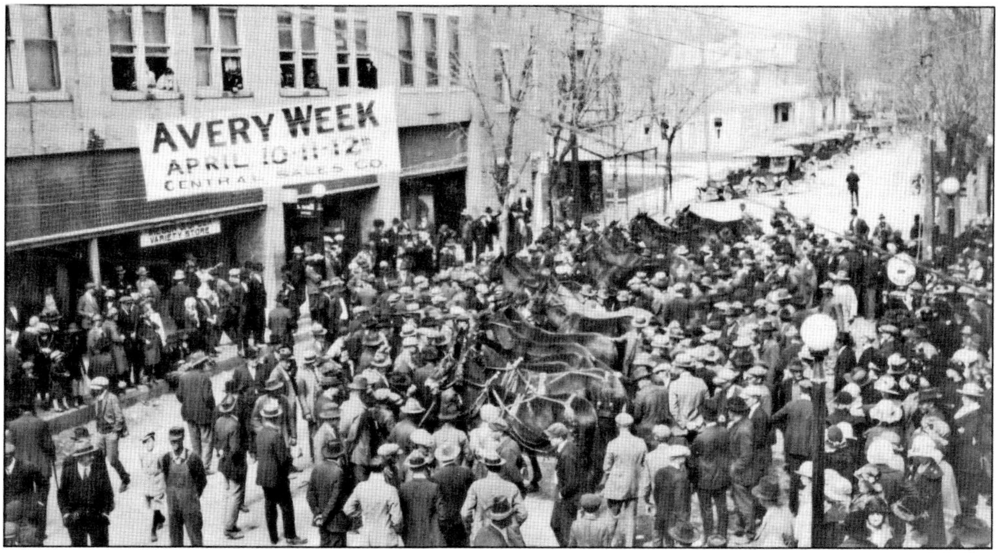

Avery Week reportedly brought one of the largest crowds ever to Campbellsville. In addition to the event's contests, the sponsors brought speakers such as C. S. Jones, from the University of Kentucky's Experiment Station, James Speed of the *Southern Agriculturist*, and Judge Huston Quinn, Mayor of Louisville. As John Deere would do in the future John Deere Days, Avery included movies at the Alhambra for farmers and children. (FHB.)

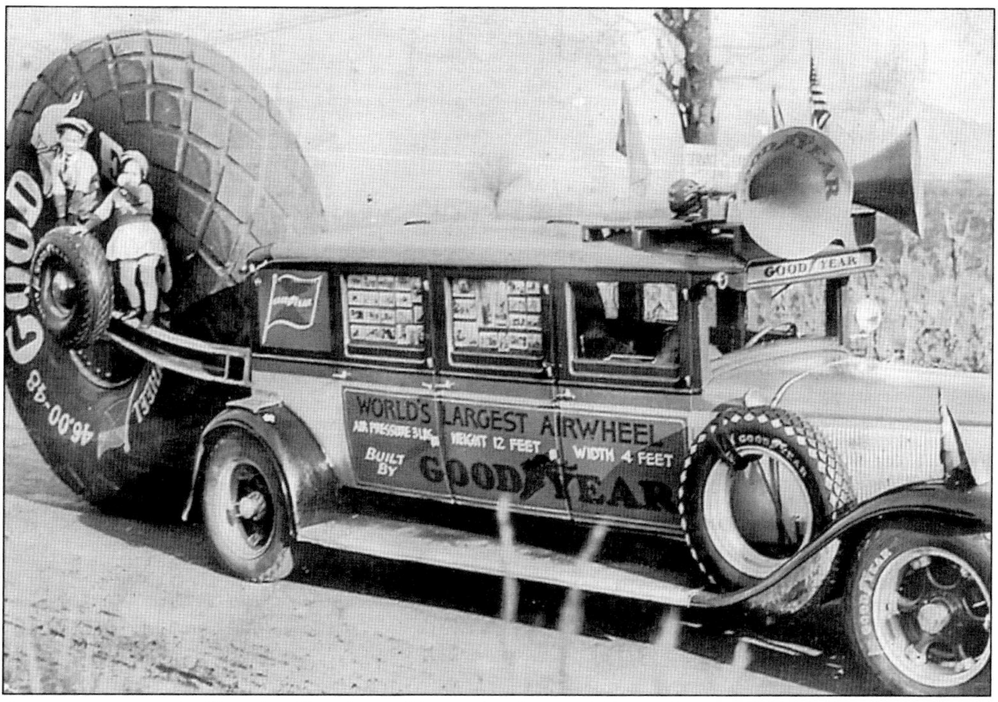

As a promotional effort for Goodyear Tires, the Central Sales Company brought the "World's Biggest Balloon Tire" to Campbellsville on November 21, 1932. Pulled by a small bus, the 12-foot-tall, 4-foot-wide Airwheel tire weighed over 1,000 pounds but was inflated to only 3 pounds of pressure. The inner tube weighed 125 pounds. Goodyear built three of the tires at its factory in Akron, Ohio. (FHB.)

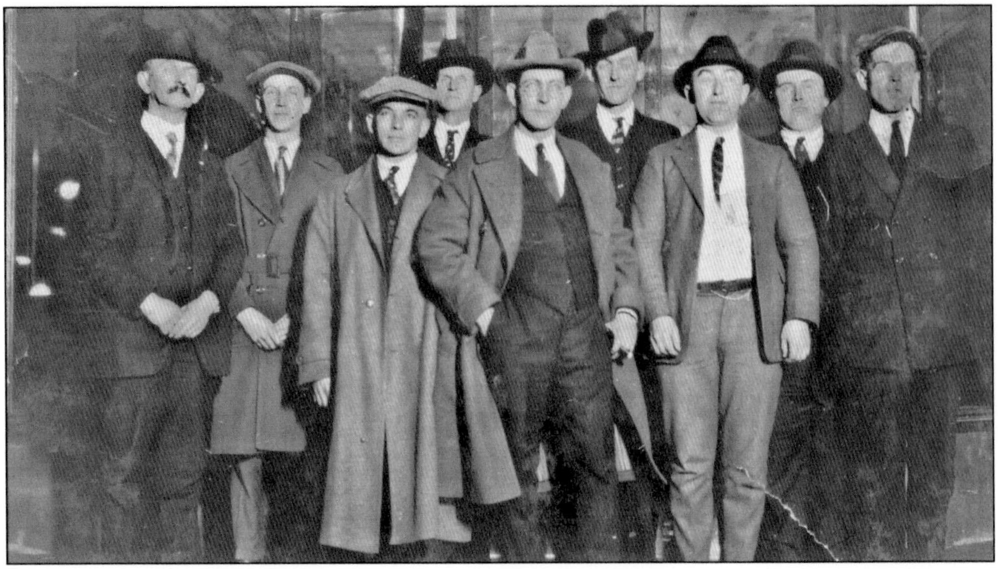

Local contractor Joseph Thomas Phillips, at center with glasses and cigar, is seen here with some employees at the completed Central Sales Building on the corner of Main Street and Central Avenue. He also built the present First United Methodist Church in 1921, and he remodeled the Kerr Building on Main Street for the new Monson's store in 1934. Upon his death, the newspaper called him the "dean of contractors and carpenters here." (FHB.)

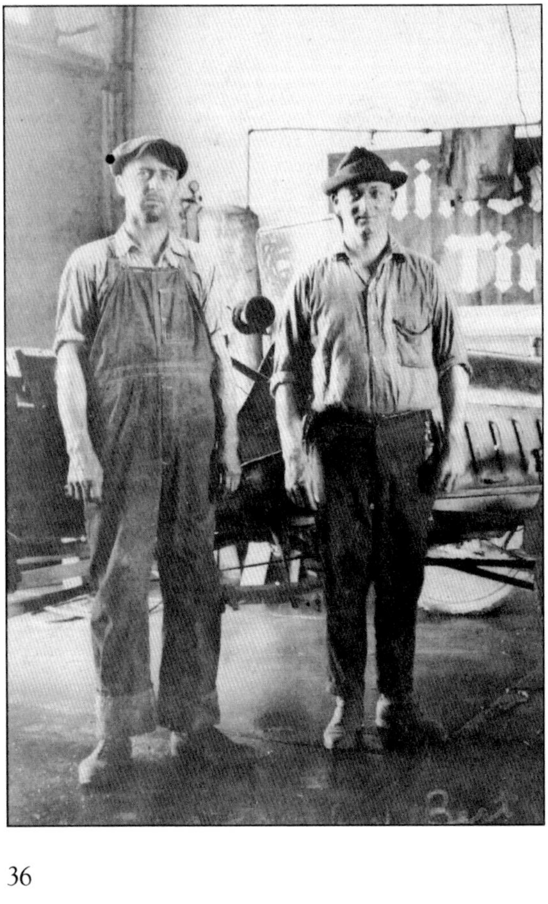

Wood Coppock (left) and Bert Cox (right) spent most of their lives in the automobile business. Coppock owned Auto Supply Company for 44 years in addition to being the Gulf Oil distributor for the area. He was also instrumental in starting the Campbellsville-Taylor County Industrial Foundation. One of Campbellsville's first auto mechanics, Bert Cox opened a garage with Abel Puryear in 1922 before going into business on his own. (CBG.)

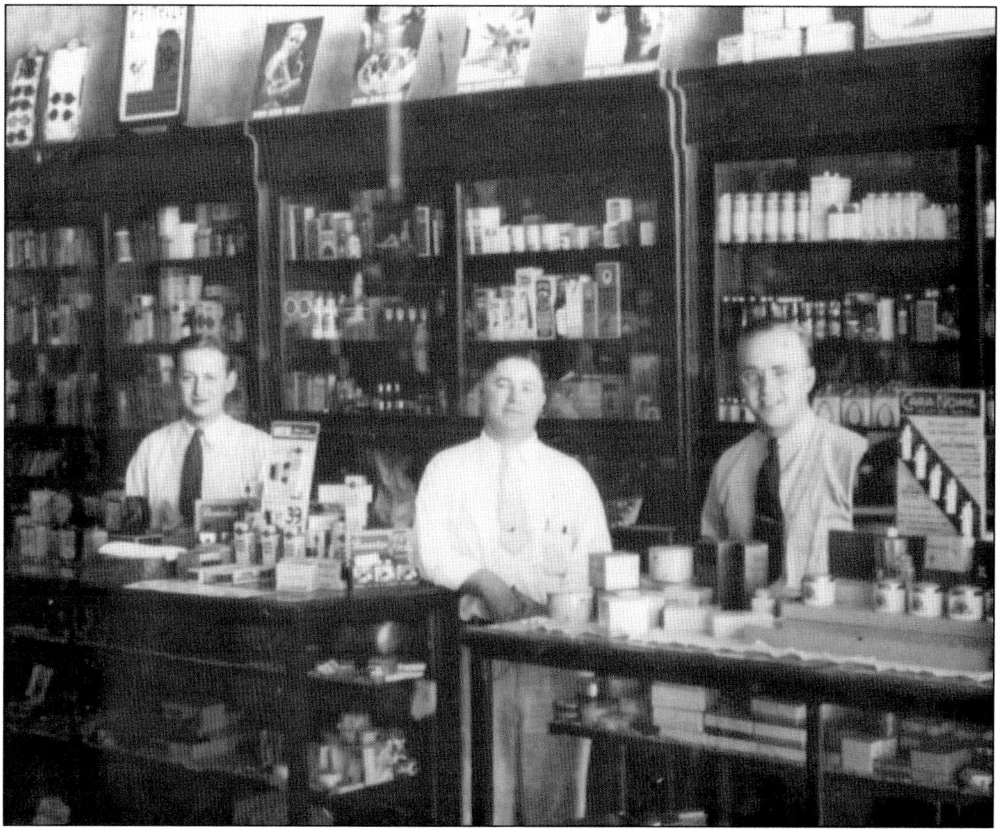

In 1927, Edward N. Leachman sold his interest in the Pruett-Leachman Drug Company to his partner J. G. Pruett. The new firm came to be known as the Pruett Drug Company, owners of the "Corner Drugstore." James W. Smith of Burkesville, Kentucky, who also owned a drugstore with his brother in Burkesville, bought the Corner Drugstore at a public auction in August 1929. Smith is pictured in the above photograph with Charlie Brake (left) and Clifford Hutchinson (right). The photograph on the right probably illustrates the March 1935 advertisement for the recently opened Luncheonette Department with a new electric grill, new dripolator coffee urn, and other equipment. Evan Watson stands beside the store's new ice cream machine. (TCHS, above, and MJG, right.)

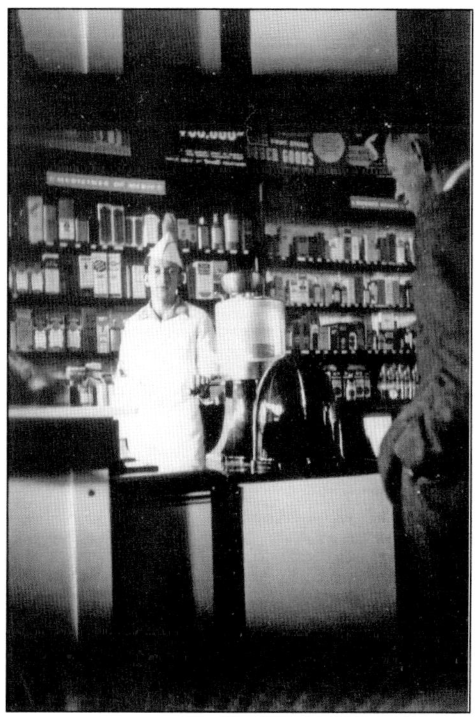

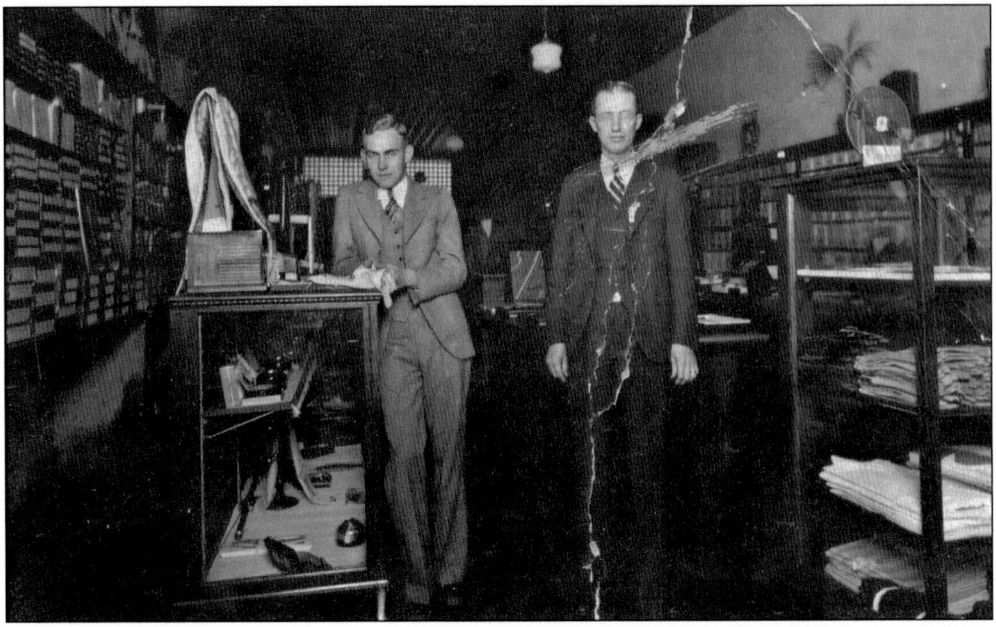

Lynn Mitchell (right) joined with his brother-in-law, Daniel Hatcher, to start Hatcher-Mitchell in 1911. Originally housed in the Willock Block, which is west of its present location, the company moved to its present site in the 1920s and has remained there since. Continuing to be operated by the Mitchell family, Hatcher-Mitchell is the second oldest business on Main Street. Eugene Bryant "Zimmie" Shively stands in the store with Lynn Mitchell. (LW.)

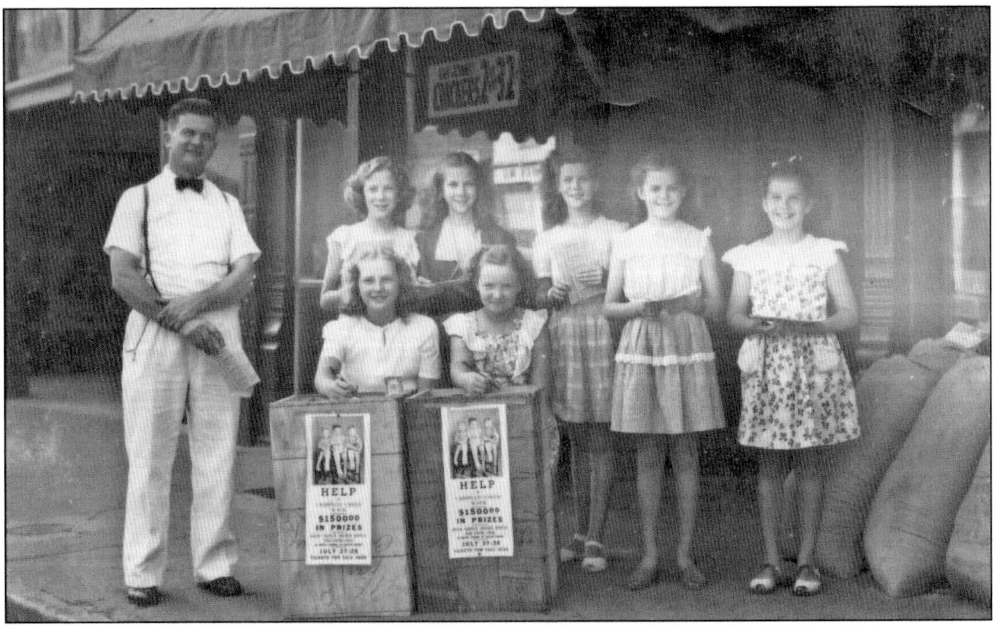

Irvin Ratcliffe, manager of the local A&P Store, joins young ladies in an effort to raise money for the Kosair Children's Hospital in Louisville. The girls' tables appear to be cabbage crates from the A&P Store. Seated are, from left to right, Montie Ray Waggoner Jones and Martha Coakley Carroll. Standing are, from left to right, Georgie Edwards Rodgers, Jocelyn Phillips Bartley, Donna Newcomb Stoess, JoAnn Durham Trinkle, and JoAnna Durham Tudor. (EAD.)

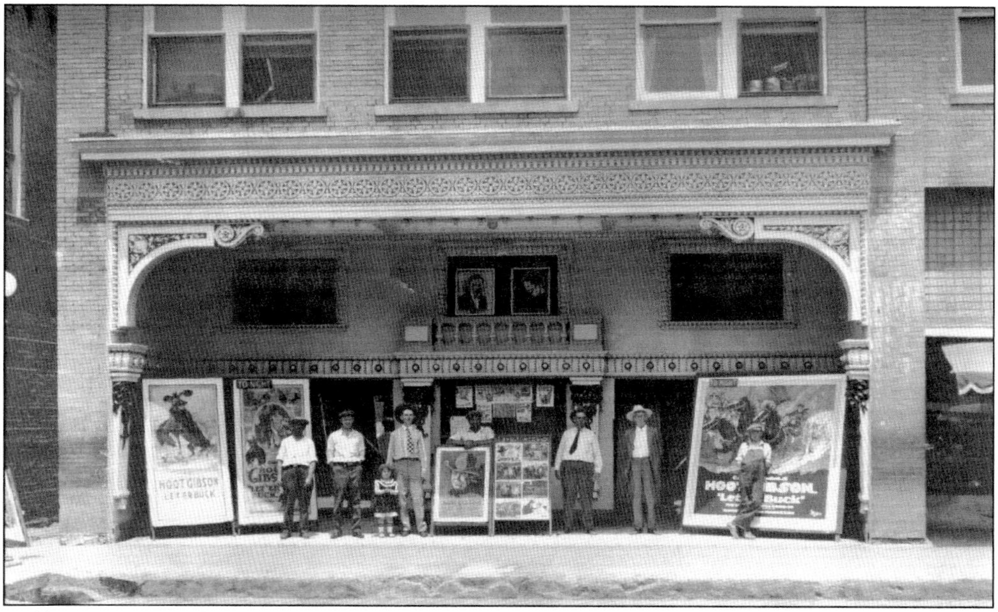

William I. Meader built the Alhambra Theater in 1916, and it reportedly had the backing of John E. Davis, who did not want his name publicized because of his Baptist Church affiliations. For power, Meader installed a 15-horsepower kerosene engine and dynamo. In keeping with the theater's name, he used elaborate Moorish decorations on the facade. Low attendance brought brief closings during and after World War I. However, Paul (at right) and Brack Sanders acquired the theater about 1922, bringing stable, creative management that introduced talking pictures on July 22, 1929. Through creative marketing strategies, such as showing pictures of local people and businesses on the screen as a "see yourself in the movies," Sanders turned the Alhambra into Campbellsville's longest running theater. (LK, above and right.)

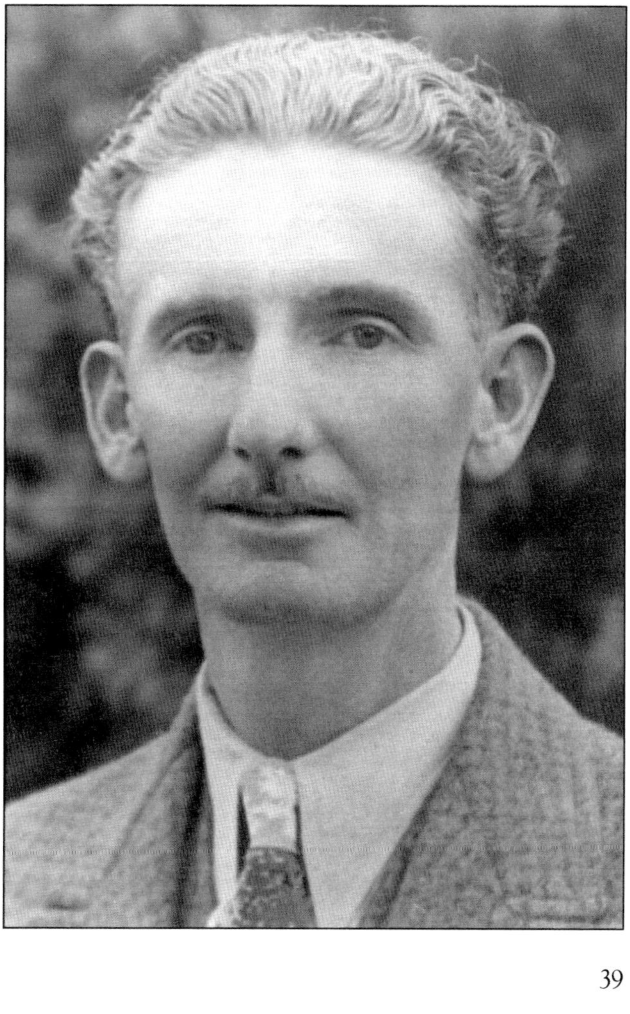

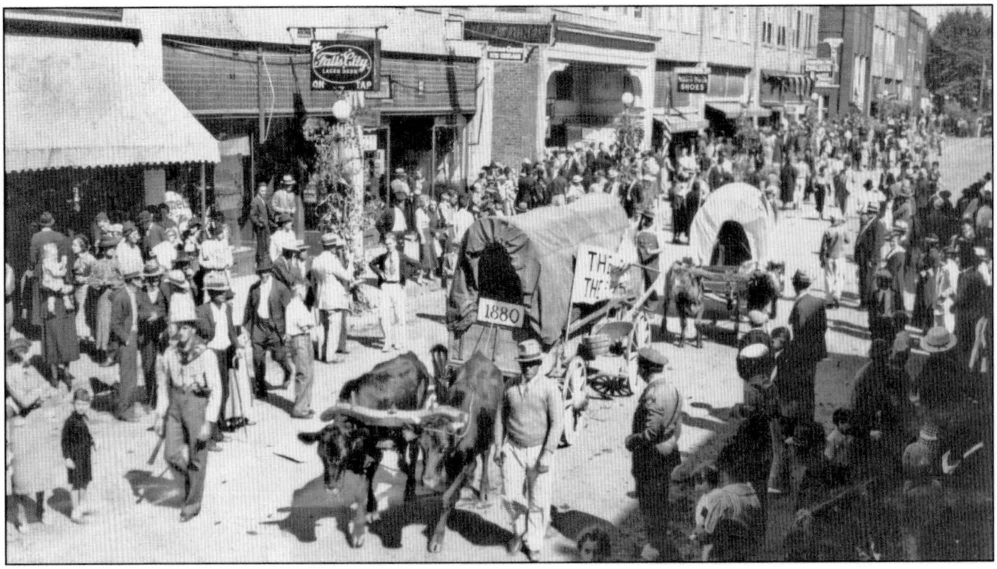

Taken during the 1934 Community Fair, this Main Street photograph shows most of the businesses lining Main Street between Court Street to the west and Central Avenue to the east. On the left is a billiard parlor advertising Falls City beer. Dr. M. M. Hall's office is on the second floor. Next is a confectionery and restaurant on the alley, known as the Green Cottage, with a sign advertising Cream Crest Ice Cream, followed by the Alhambra Theater, Hatcher-Mitchell advertising Nunn-Bush shoes, and the Corner Drugstore. In this photograph and one other, a Falls City sign is visible. Like most of the surrounding counties, Taylor County voted to go dry in the late 19th century. However, with the repeal of Prohibition, alcohol sales became legal in 1933, and some Campbellsville businesses applied for an alcohol license. Legal sales of alcohol lasted about three years until the county again voted for the local option to eliminate legal sales. However, even during Prohibition, local companies like Coca-Cola and Buchanan-Lyon distributed beer. Coca-Cola handled Falls City, and Buchanan carried Oertels. (FHB, above and below.)

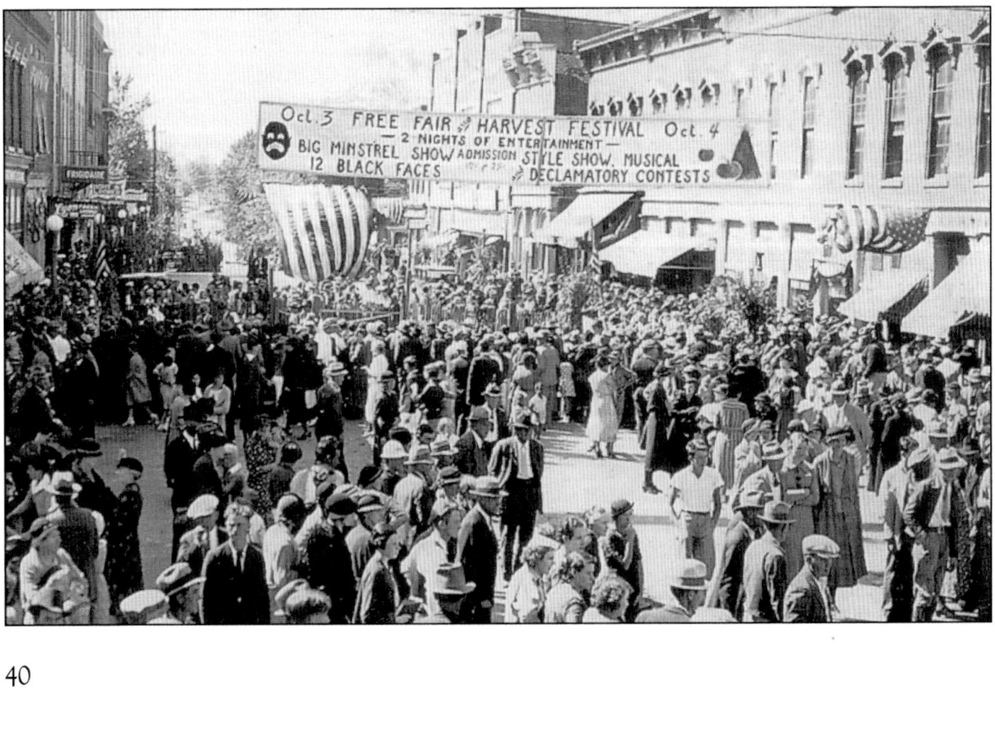

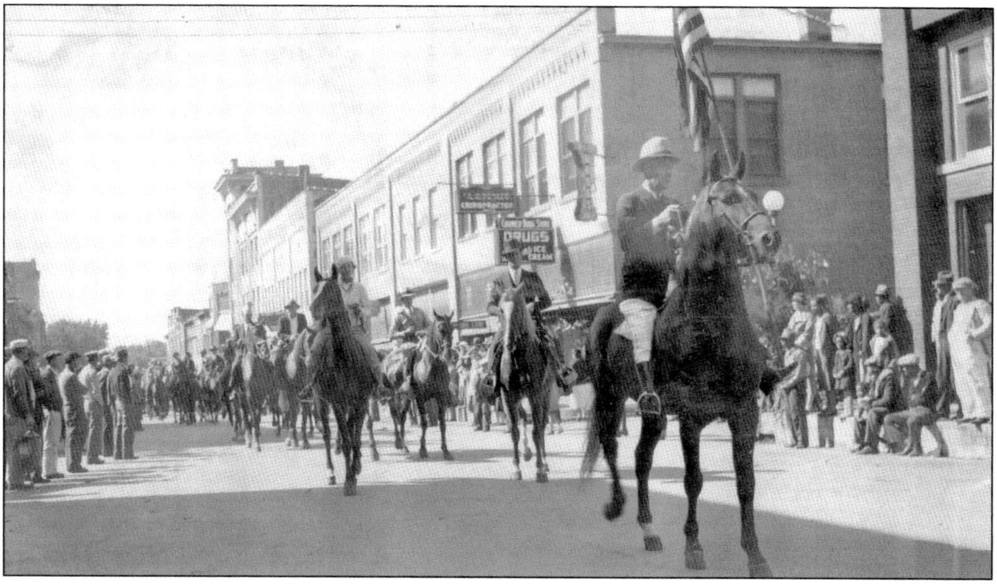

An estimated 3,000 to 4,000 people viewed the parade for the October 1934 Community Fair. The hour-long Main Street event began with a State Patrolman on a motorbike and ended with a parade of more than 50 horses and ponies. Signs identify the Shoe Store; A. R. Pedigo, Chiropractor; and the Corner Drugstore, which sold Brown's Ice Cream. (FHB.)

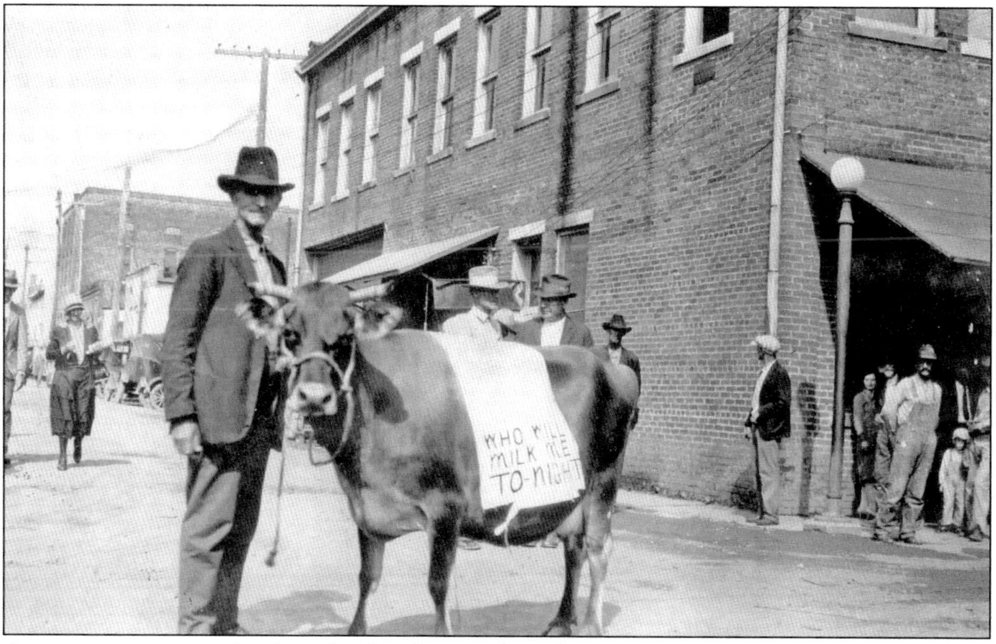

As a way to improve the dairy herd and strengthen downtown sales, the Campbellsville Dairy Promotion Association gave away a registered Jersey cow. Members of the Association provided free tickets to anyone who made a cash purchase in their stores. However, to be eligible to win the cow, the ticket holder had to be present at the time of drawing, thus the sign asking, "Who will milk me tonight?" (FHB.)

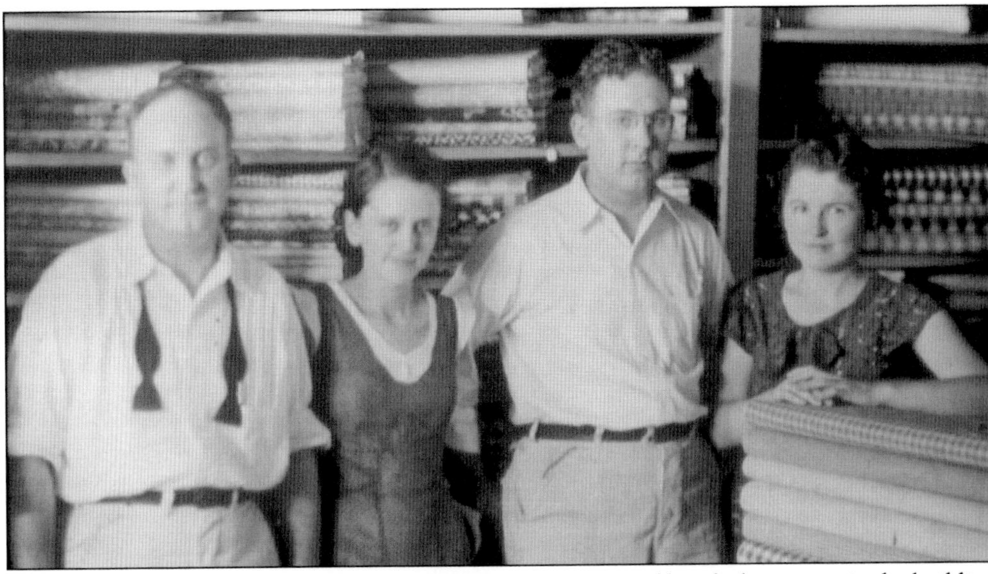

In September 1929, George Monson, a Cynthiana native, opened his clothing store in the building currently occupied by Sapp's Antiques. He moved across the street in 1934, finally settling in the Central Sales building on the corner of Main Street and Central Avenue in 1949, which was where the store operated until it was sold to Parks-Belk. Taken at the first store, this picture shows, from left to right, Willard Burress, unidentified, George Monson, and Jewell Monson. (TCHS.)

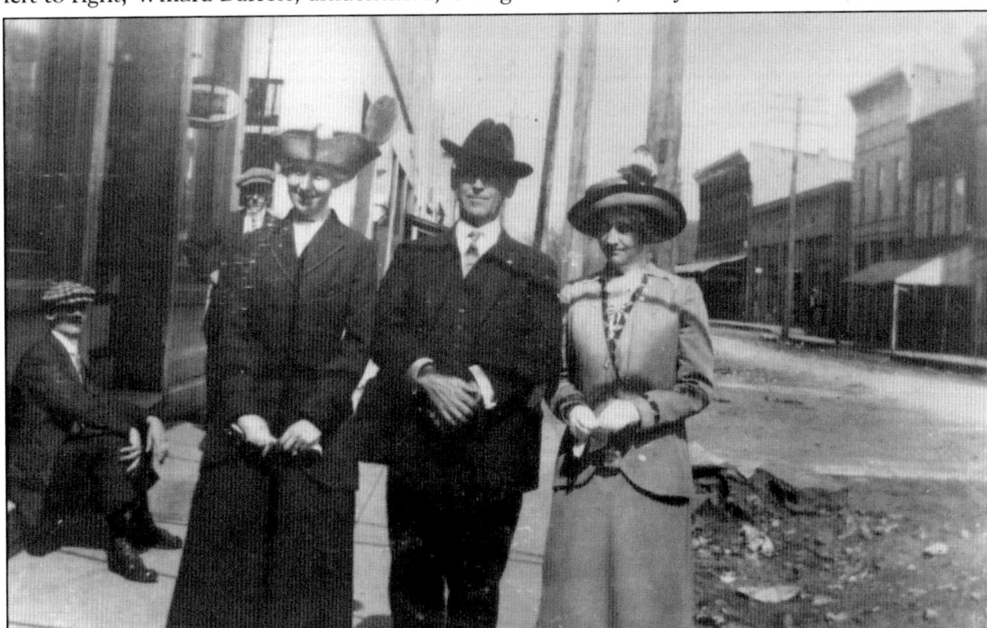

Pictured from left to right, William I. Meader Sr., Emma Black Wood, and Meader's daughter Aileen Meader Goodin, are standing in front of the Farmers Deposit Bank (now Tucker's Jewelers) in 1913. Meader began his business career in Columbia, where he operated a skating rink, before coming to Campbellsville. He started the Alhambra Theater, entered the insurance business, ran the New Commercial Hotel, and served as circuit clerk. (TCHS.)

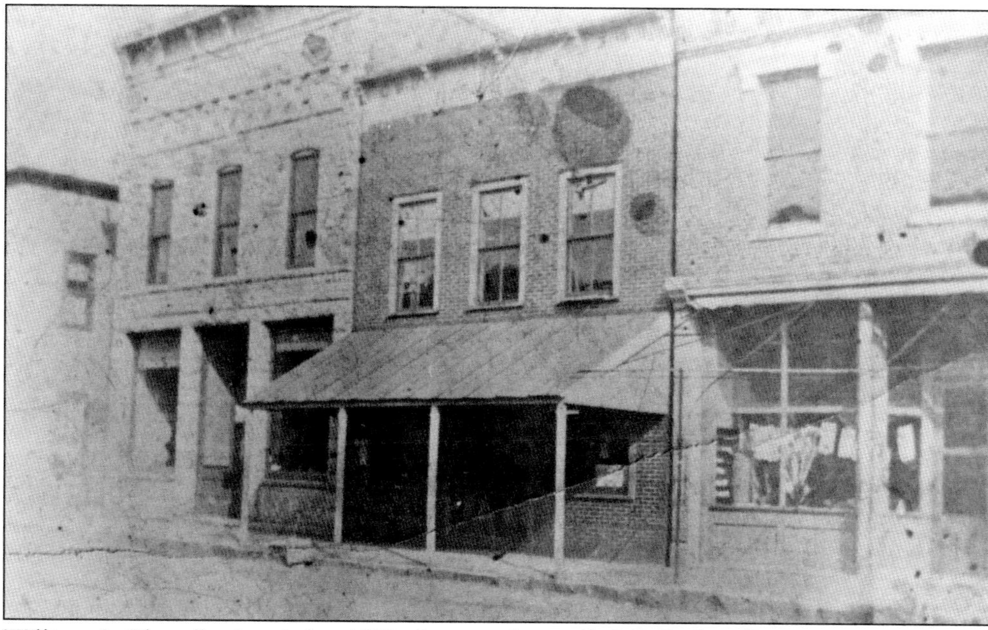

William A. Chandler founded in 1892 what was then called "Bill Chandler's store." The original store was a general store with a lunch counter. The company moved into the present location about 1894 and became known as Chandler Novelty Company. Today the building houses Chandler's Office Supply, and it continues the tradition of selling garden seed, stationery, and school supplies, along with its expansion into office furniture and equipment. (TCHS.)

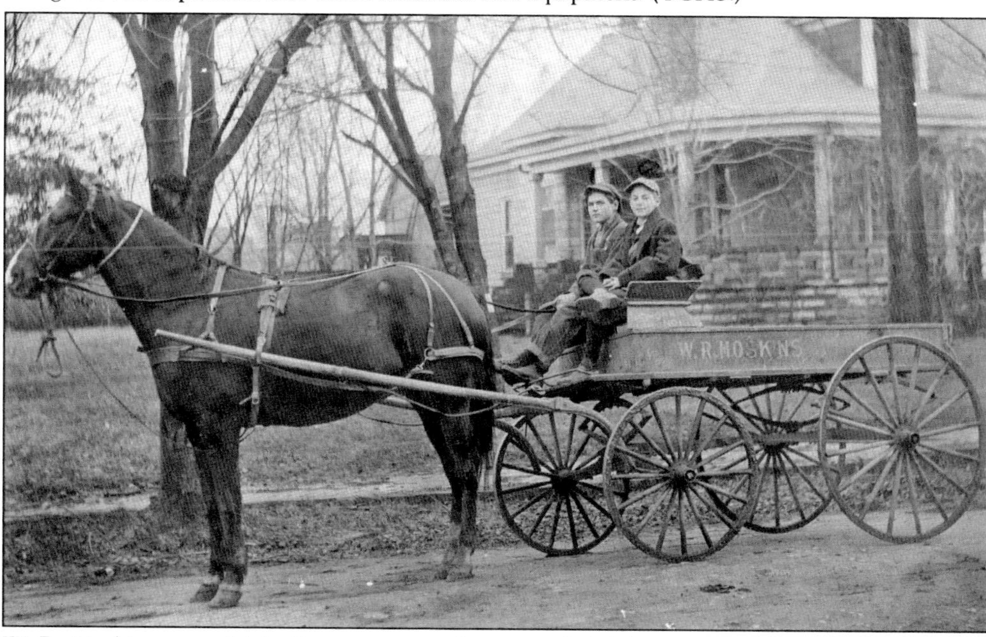

W. R. Hoskins ran a Main Street grocery that provided delivery. This photograph shows Ray Smith (left), regular delivery boy who later became an officer in Citizens Bank, and Keith Beck (right). W. R. Hoskins and Phone No. 1 are written on the seat. The picture was taken on Jackson Street in front of the Emmett Chandler home, which was later purchased and remodeled by James C. Miller Sr. (SN.)

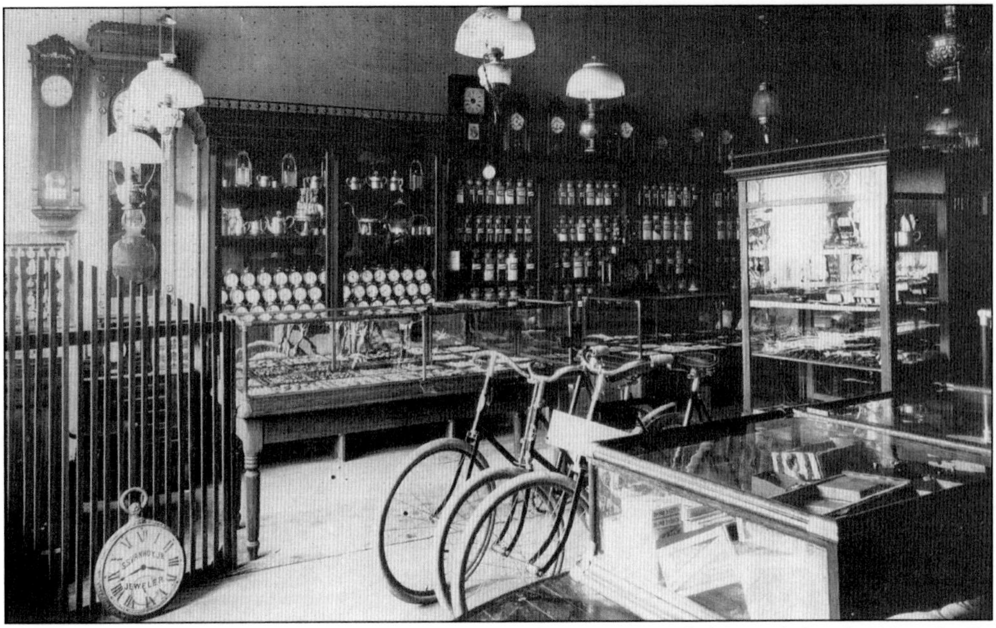

Robert Lee Hill began business in Campbellsville about 1893, probably with Jacob Odewalt. By 1899, he had joined with Shelby S. VanHoy to operate VanHoy and Hill Jewelers. After VanHoy moved to Shelbyville *c.* 1909, the store became known as The R. L. Hill Drugstore, and Hill ran it until 1928. In December 1930, William H. Stephens, a druggist from Lexington, purchased the store, renaming it Stephens Drugstore. Below, from left to right, are employees Lawrence Winfrey, Gladys Coe Coppock, and Robert Quehl, pharmacist from Newport, Kentucky. Charles H. Stephens, brother of the owner, ran the store, which included a fountain and a jewelry and silverware department. The building currently houses Altman's Pawn. (F&CK, top, TCHS, below.)

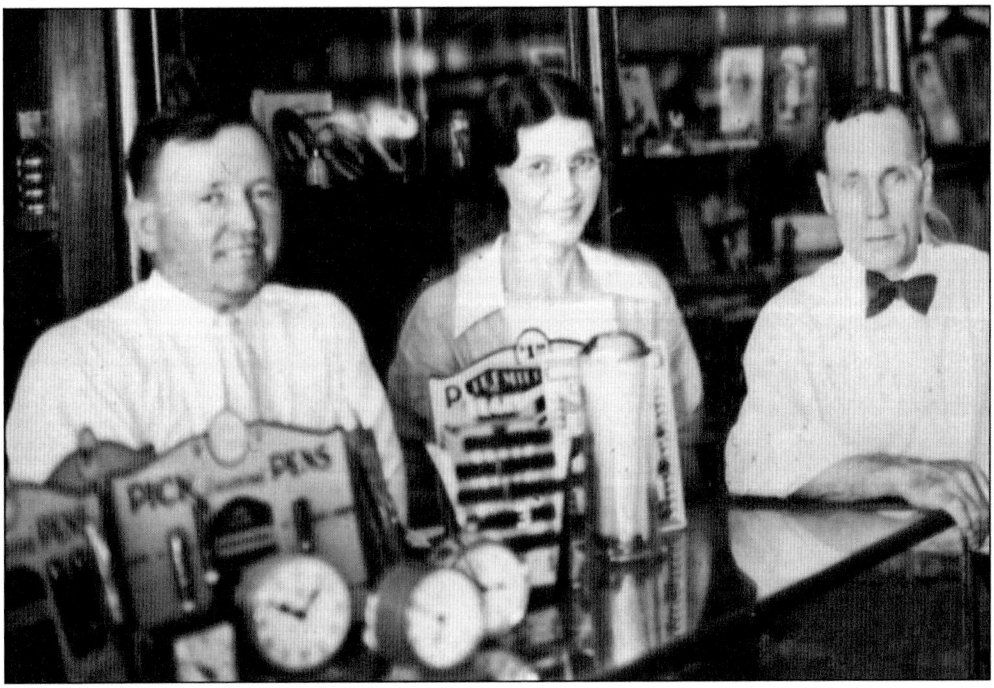

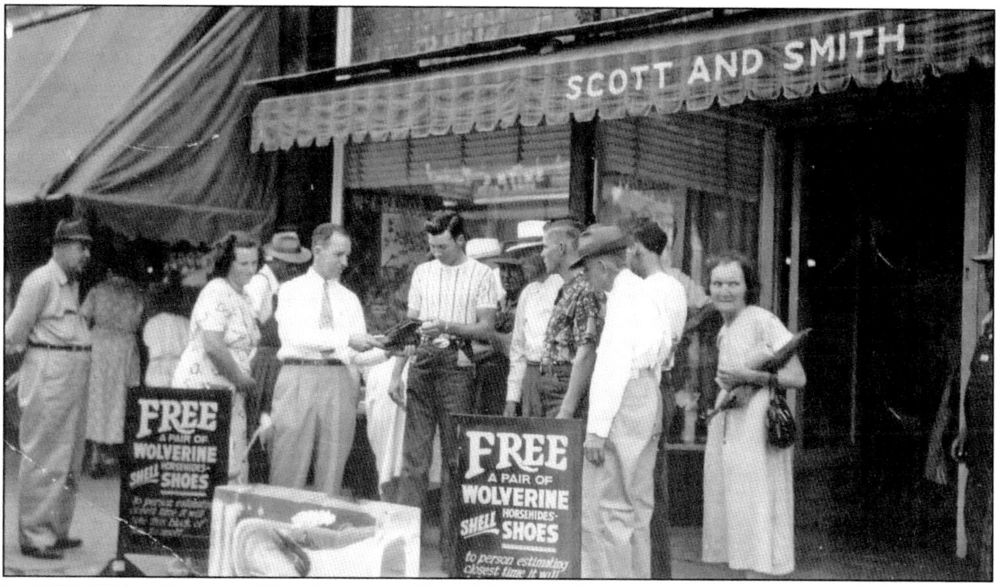

In 1926, Walter Scott and Ray Smith purchased the merchandise and fixtures of Ed and Armstrong Hill's store. One Scott and Smith promotion offered a free pair of Wolverine shoes to the customer who could estimate the approximate time the shoe would be freed from the melting block of ice. Walter Scott's grandson, Walter "Corky" Scott III, continues a Main Street business named, appropriately, Scott's. (WS.)

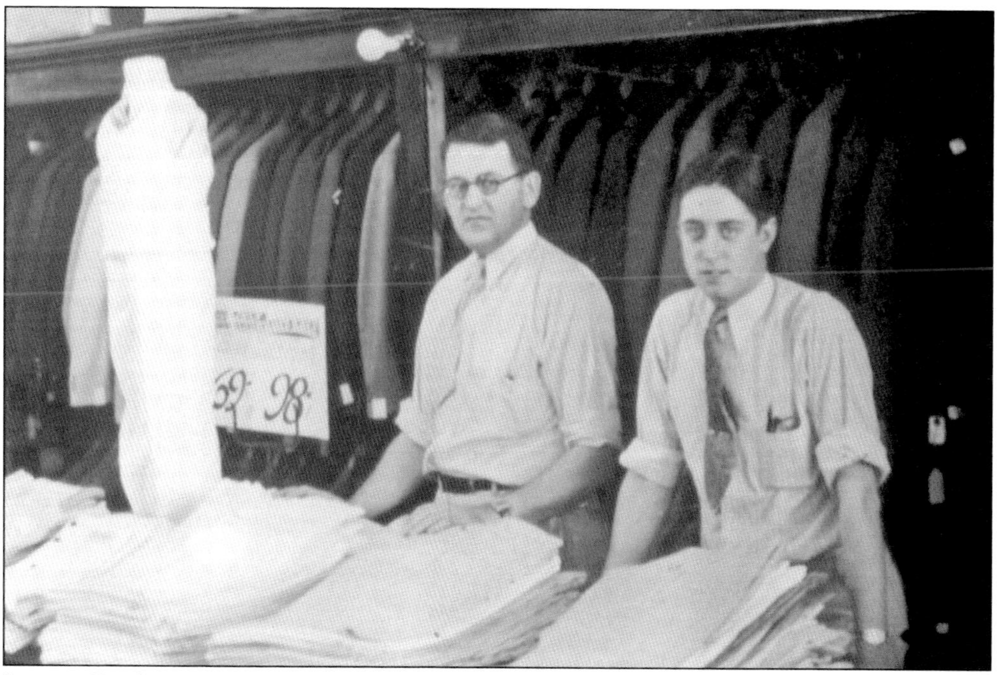

Lerman Brothers opened its Campbellsville women's and men's ready-to-wear store in October 1924. It was the chain's fourth store, with others being in Richmond, Cynthiana, and Lebanon. The company leased the store room formerly occupied by the Buchanan-Lyon Company wholesale grocery department. Burr Gilpin (at right) was a long-time employee of Lerman's. Chandler's Office Supply currently uses the building for display and storage. (TCHS.)

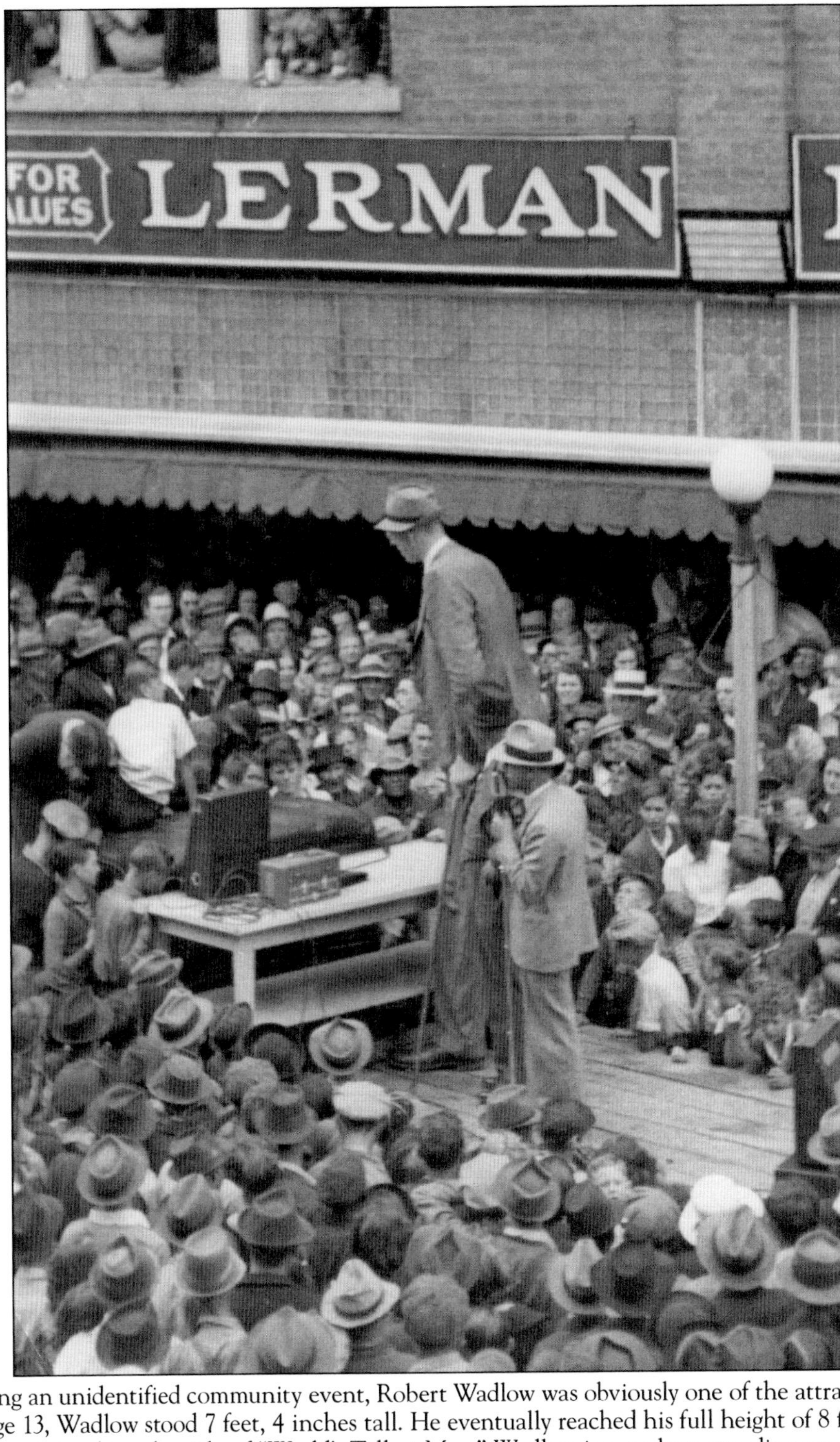

During an unidentified community event, Robert Wadlow was obviously one of the attractions. By age 13, Wadlow stood 7 feet, 4 inches tall. He eventually reached his full height of 8 feet, 11 inches, giving him the title of "World's Tallest Man." Wadlow is seen here standing on a truck bed in front of the Lerman Brothers store on the north side of Main Street. (MJG.)

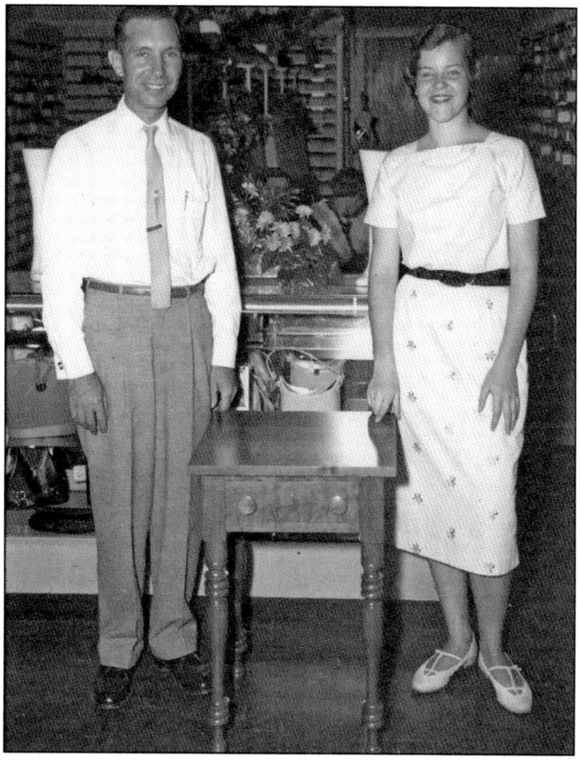

Richard McMahan stands by Oida Jean Wethington Rivers, winner of a table given away at the grand opening of McMahan's Shoes on Main Street. Located in the Puryear Building near the Campbellsville Hotel, McMahan's Shoes opened on August 7, 1958. As a promotional feature, McMahan offered a free pair of shoes to any one family who had purchased 12 during the year. (TCL.)

From 1954 to 1961, Redmon Turner ran Turner's Town and Country Restaurant at 204 East Main Street. The building previously housed Stephens' Drugstore before Turner opened Turner's Food Market in 1941. Turner moved the grocery to the back of the building in 1954 when he opened Town and Country Restaurant. The restaurant had additional dining space on the second floor. After a July 1961 fire, the restaurant closed. (TCL.)

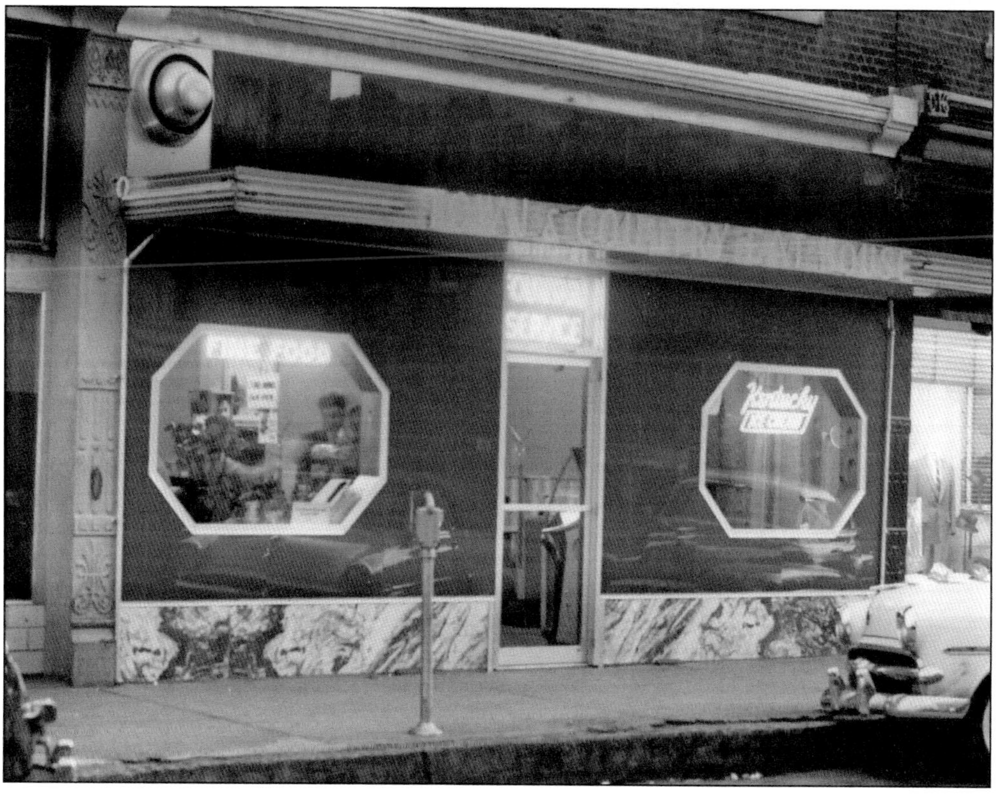

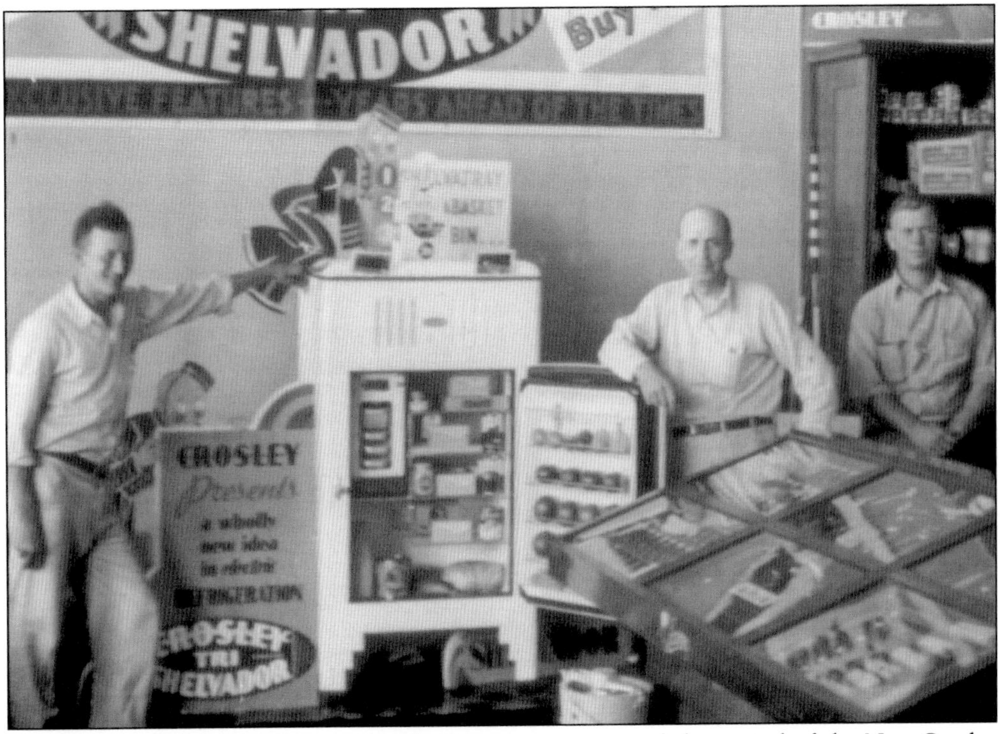

In February 1934, Taylor County Supply Company announced the arrival of the New Crosley Shelvador electric refrigerator. At the time of the photograph, the company was located on Main Street, near the present Citizens Bank. From left to right, Robert W. Buckner, John W. Ramsey, and Charles Newcomb show off the newly received refrigerator. (TCHS.)

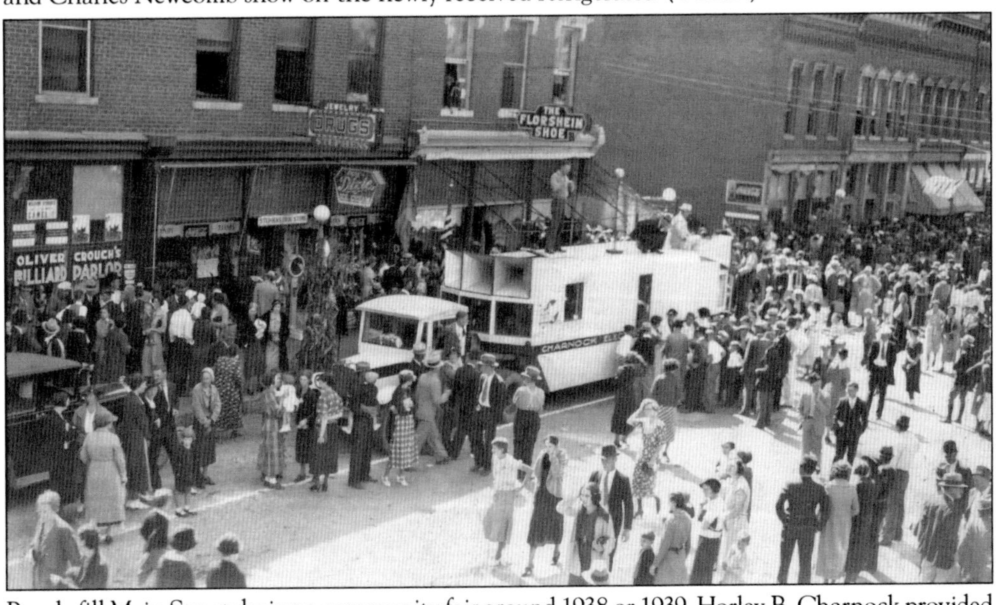

People fill Main Street during a community fair around 1938 or 1939. Harley B. Charnock provided a large, mobile sound truck to be used by speakers and performers. Charnock had an electrical business in Greensburg and had started an open-air theater there called the Old Fort Theater. While the buildings remain, all of the pictured businesses are gone. (FHB.)

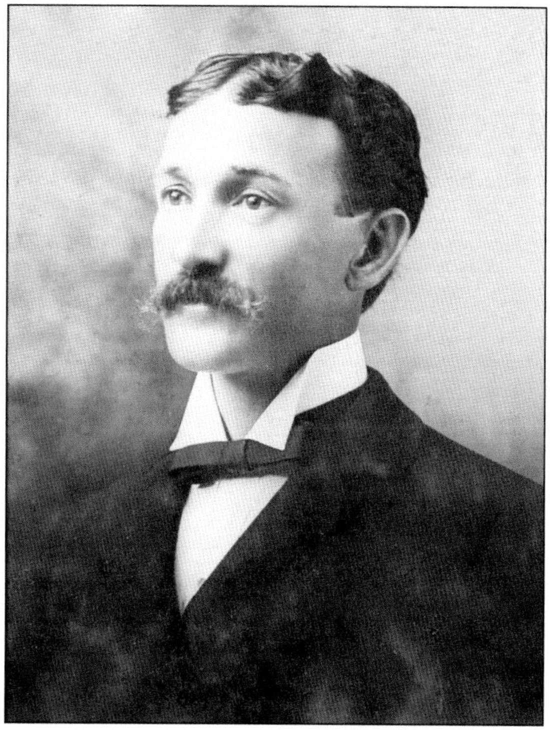

James R. "Hawk" Davis was a Campbellsville native who served as councilman and mayor of Campbellsville. He was a director of Farmers and Peoples Bank and served on the Board of Trustees for Campbellsville College. Davis and his brothers, Thomas W. and John E., established a successful mercantile business in a building on the corner of Main and Court Streets, now the location of Merle Norman. (TM.)

The probable location for this picture is the Green Cottage, owned by Ollie and Fannie Fawcett Phillips from 1932 to 1935. They are standing with an unknown waitress (left). In April 1935, T. O. Purcell purchased the business and remodeled it. A former employee of the *Taylor County Star* and deputy sheriff, Purcell promised changes after his remodeling that included no dancing except on special occasion "when an orchestra can be obtained." (TCHS.)

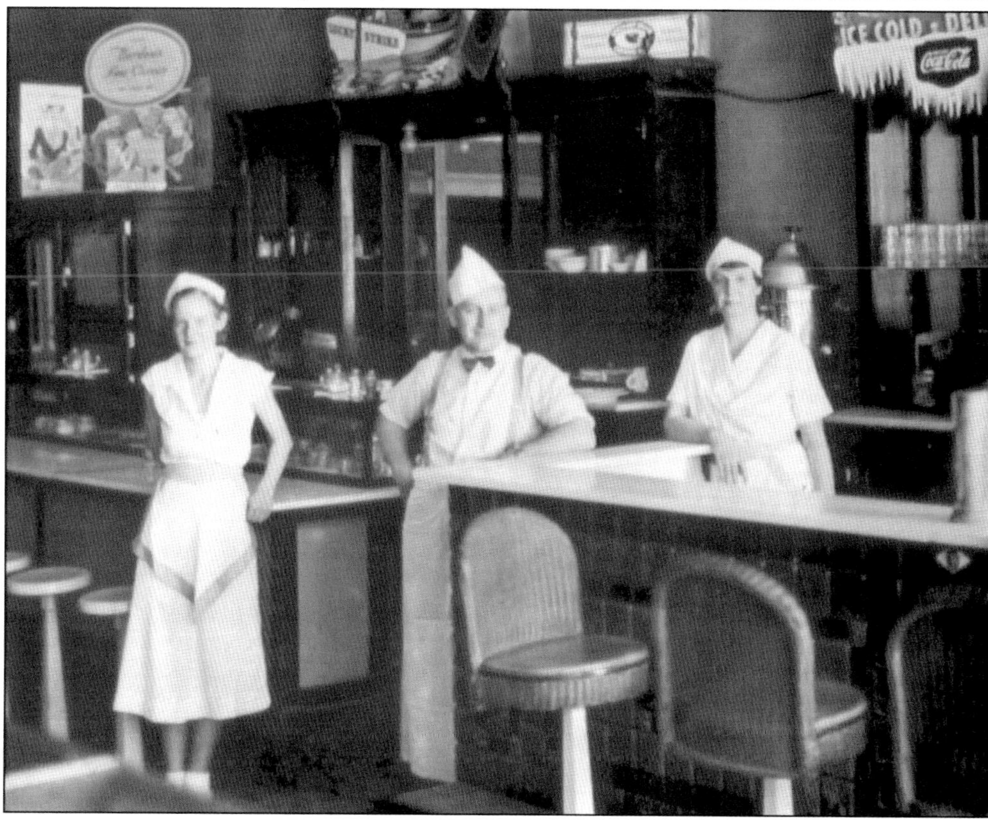

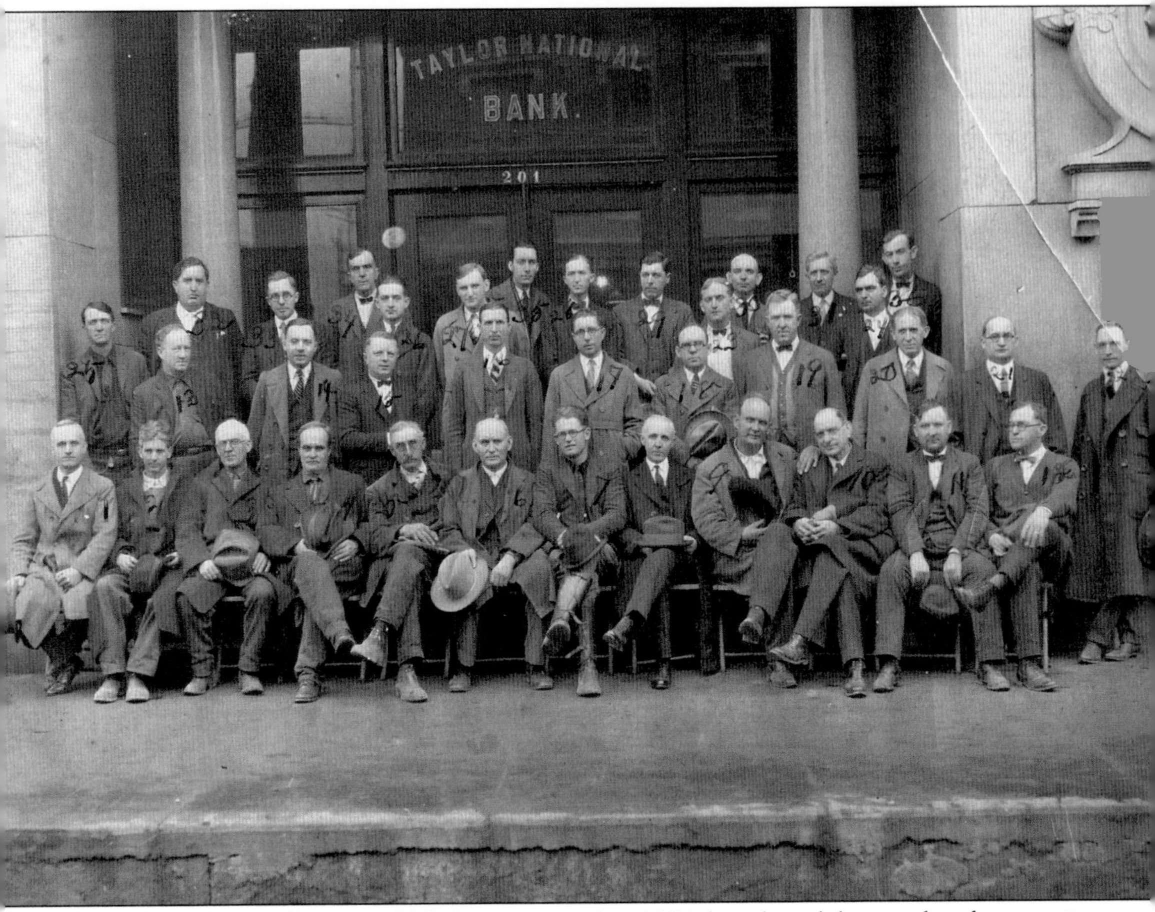

The Campbellsville Lions Club first organized in 1924, but that club ceased to function in 1935. Some of Campbellsville's most prominent businessmen joined and made the Lions' Club an active advocate for community projects. Members shown in this photograph taken in front of the present Citizen's Bank location are, from left to right: (first row) John H. Pickett, Tom Roots, "Tone" Buchanan, G. W. Ramsey, J. Hugh "Bud" Chandler, Judge William J. Rice, C. V. Bryan, M. W. Tucker, Col. Robert L. Faulkner, William R. Lyon, Fred Faulkner, and Henry T. Parrott; (second row) Towler Parrott, Chandler Wood, John McKenzie, Jodie P. Gozder, Lynn M. Mitchell, Thomas W. Callison, Rev. Hollis S. Summers, Frank Gabbard, Dr. Richard A. Sanders Sr., Reverend Arnold, and Oscar Kemper; (third row) Jim W. Kerr, unidentified, Dr. Edwin Lee Gowdy, George Turner, Joe Chandler, Travis O. Morton, Jim Durrett, Horace Massie, Omar Goode, Dr. C. V. Hiestand, Alexander Stuart Cole, and Ed Leachman. (TCHS.)

The Citizens Bank and Trust Company opened on Saturday, July 22, 1939, after more than 80 Taylor County residents subscribed $60,000 to the proposed bank as required by the State Banking Commission. The Citizens Bank replaced the 55-year-old Bank of Campbellsville after it failed to open on June 5, 1939. To secure the necessary federal insurance, the State Banking Commission required a $50,000 capital stock and $10,000 surplus for the new organization. The photograph on the right depicts a Citizens Bank fire on July 2, 1961, that resulted in the death of one occupant in an upstairs apartment. The photograph below shows the Citizens Bank after a remodel. Pictured are, from left to right, Robert S. Bailey, Hugh Colvin, Abb McKnight, Donald Gaines, Louise Coomer, Nora Lee Baldock, Virginia Rice, Mary Virginia Money, Gladys Roberts, Emily Ann DeSpain, Nancy Hunt, and Cary Matherly. (TCHS, top, EAD, below.)

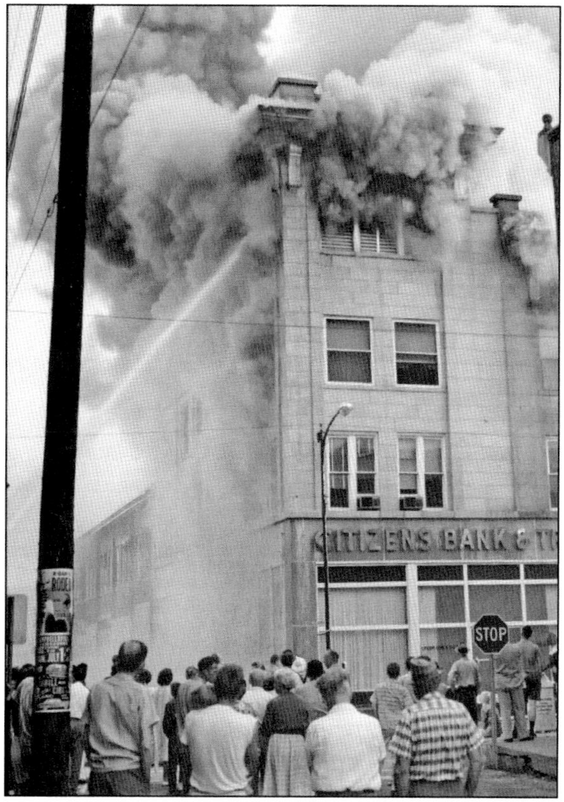

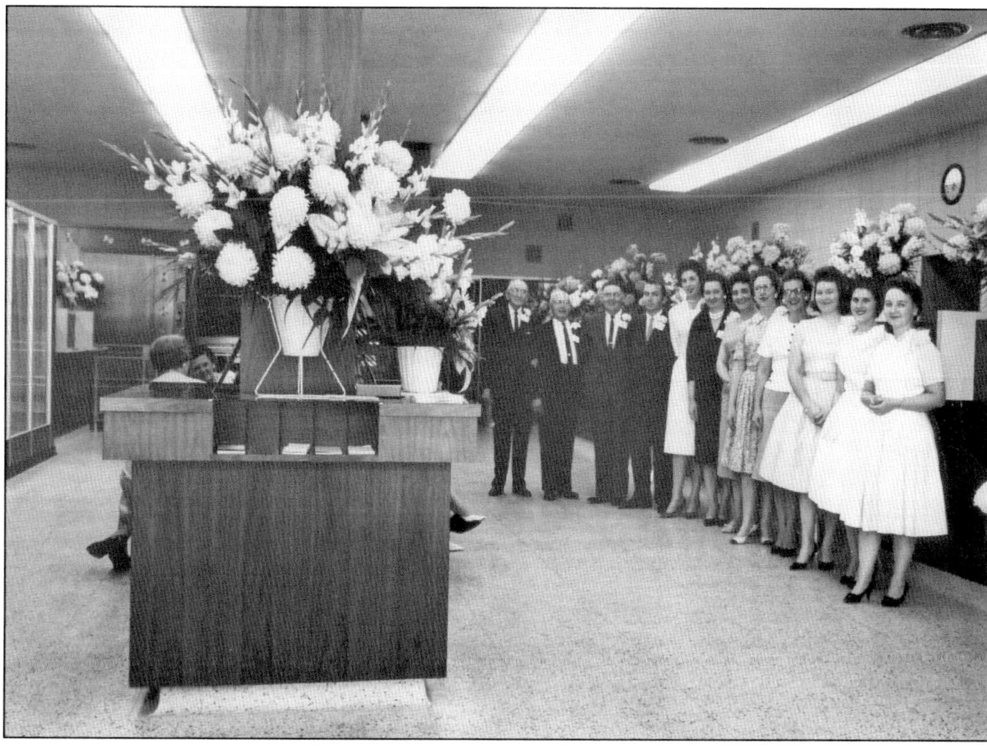

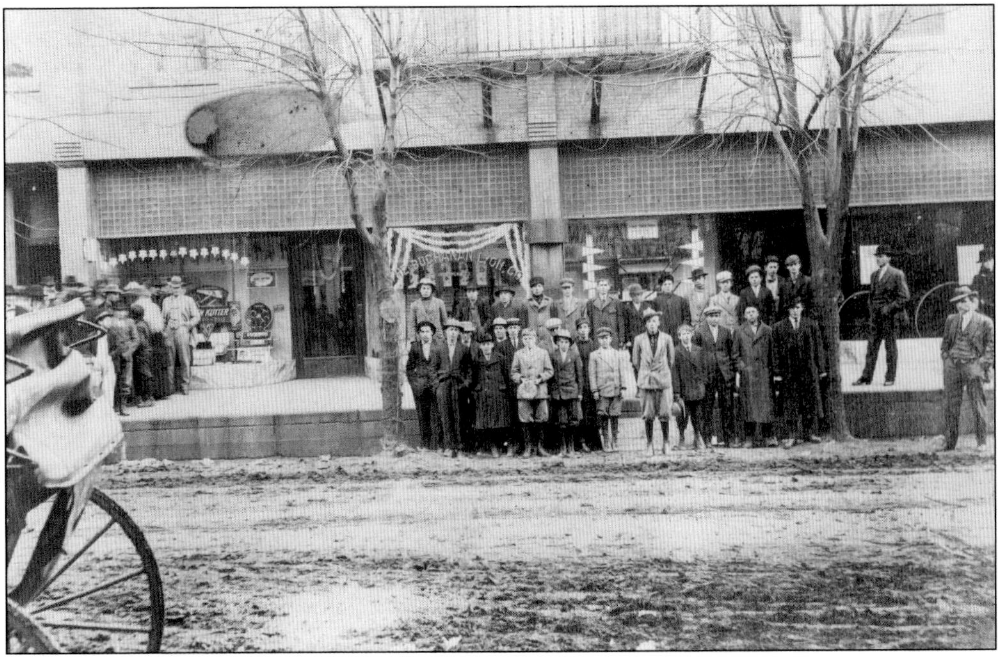

Above, an unknown group of people pose in front of the Willock building *c.* 1915. The Buchanan-Lyon Company hardware store displayed Keen Kutter cutlery and tools in the first floor window. For about four years, the second floor of the Willock Building shared space with a roller rink and the Star Theater. However, when the Campbellsville City Council passed an ordinance prohibiting movie theaters from being located on the second floors of buildings to reduce insurance rates, the Star closed. Taken about 20 years later, the photograph below shows the changing stores along Main Street. On the left, the Russell Stores occupy the space formerly used by Buchanan-Lyon. On the right, Kentucky Utilities has moved into the space. The iron balcony shown in both photographs was removed during World War II to help in the war effort. (TCHS, above and below.)

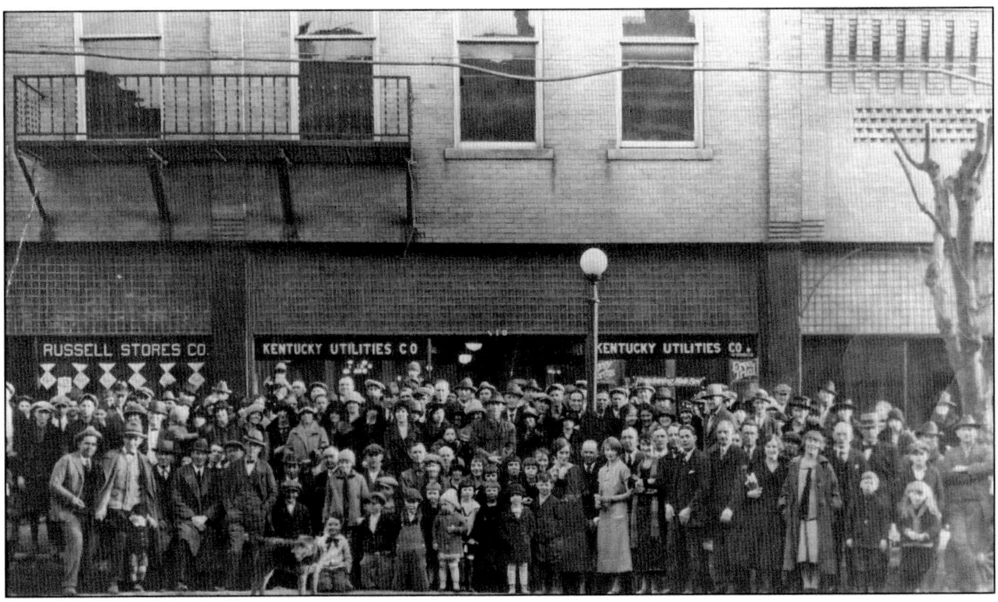

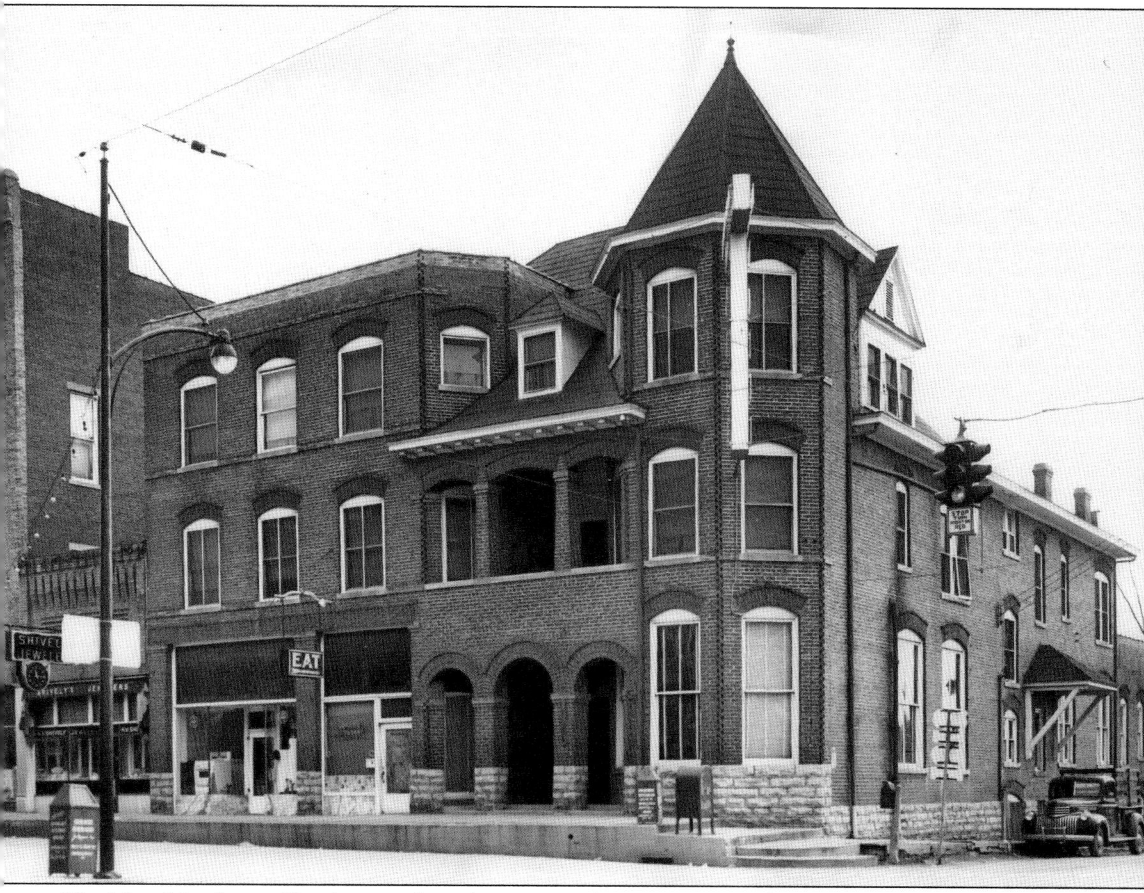

The New Merchants Hotel opened on the corner of Main Street and Columbia Avenue in 1910. Built partly on a corner lot that previously contained the Leet Hotel, the hotel became the most visible connecting point for travelers. In 1912, owners equipped the hotel with a water works system through a 2-inch line connected to the ice plant several blocks away, and so it became a stop for most 20th century transportation modes, including Greyhound. The hotel discontinued its restaurant in 1937 to add additional rooms. Eluding the damaging fires that affected many other Campbellsville hotels, like the Campbellsville Hotel and the Commercial Hotel, the Merchants Hotel survived as a hotel until the mid-20th century. The Merchants Hotel received its name from the 22 Campbellsville merchants who bought shares in the Merchants Hotel Company. Chief among them was its president, Joe Willock, former owner of the lot on which the company built the hotel. Willock owned 57 shares out of the 130 total. (TCHS.)

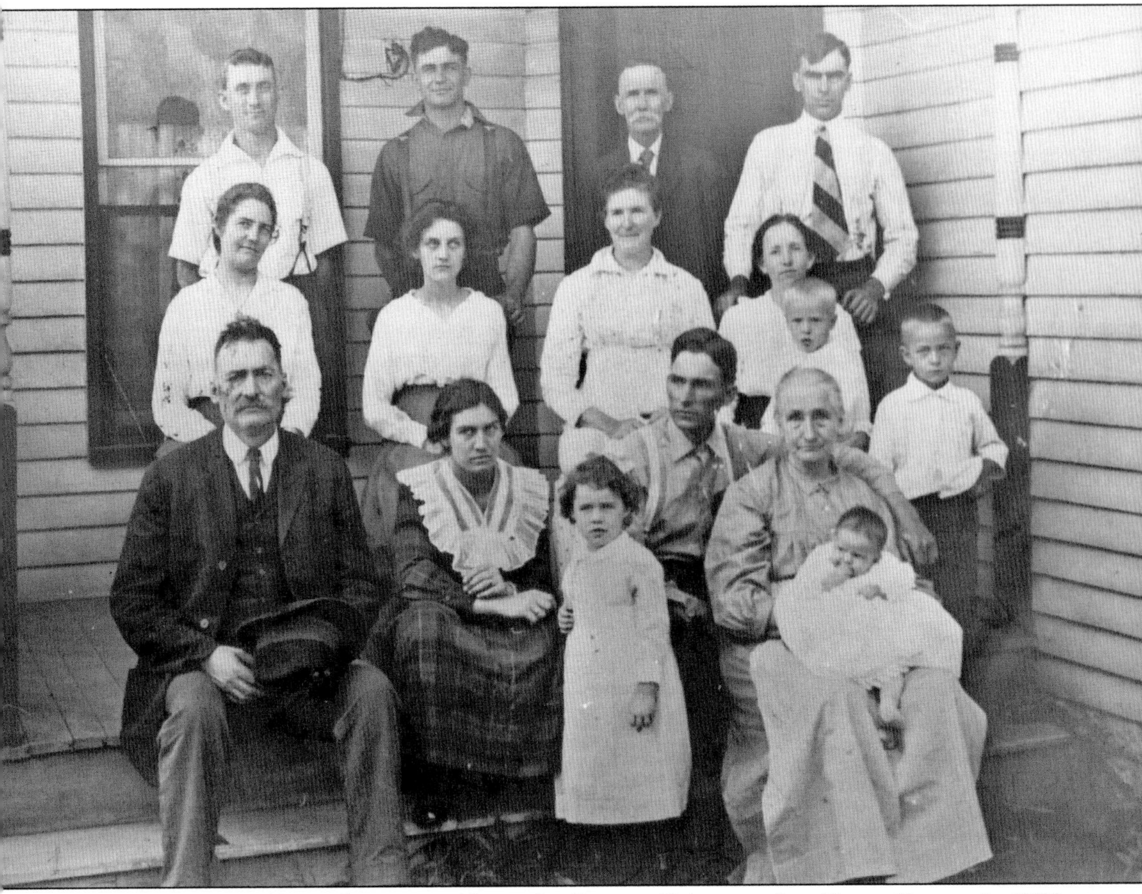

Mason County, Kentucky, native Alexander Stewart Cole moved to Green County in 1906 to teach. He spent ten years as a U.S. storekeeper-gauger, then went into the general insurance and real estate business in Campbellsville. He became active in civic affairs as a member of the Lions Club, a trustee for Campbellsville College, an organizer of the old Taylor County Fair Association, a proponent of the Burley Tobacco Pool in Campbellsville, a promoter of the York Trail, and a partner in the Campbellsville Coca-Cola Company. In 1938 he ran an unsuccessful campaign for Kentucky secretary of state. However, he served as chief accountant in the state treasurer's office under John E. Buckingham during the first Albert Chandler administration. Cole stands in the back row on the right in what is probably a family picture. (WS.)

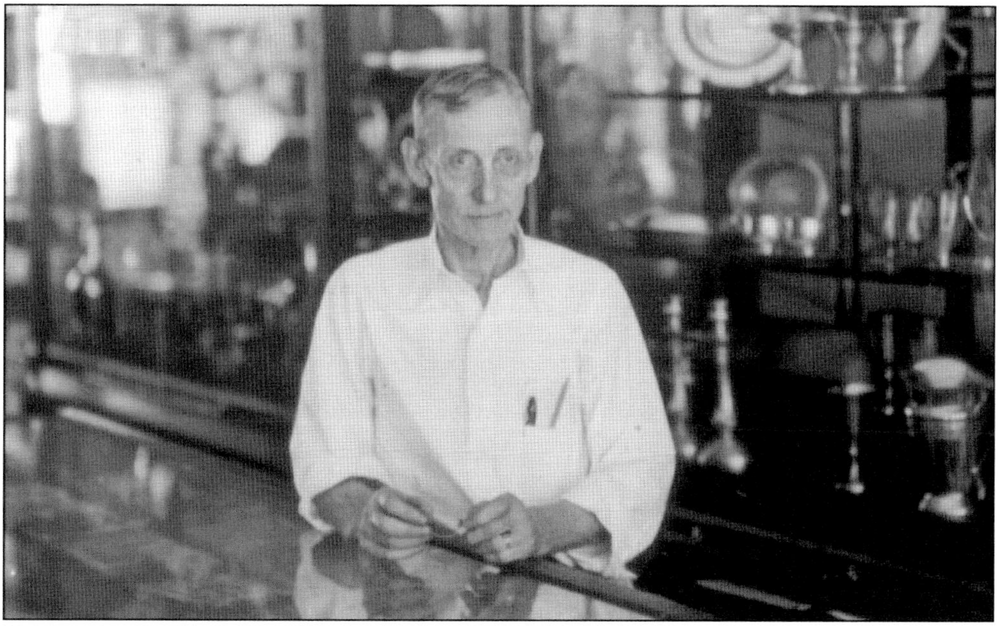

Herman V. Shively, pictured here, was an optometrist as well as a jeweler. Along with Elijah Bryant, he founded Shively and Bryant Jewelry in 1908. In January 1911, the business moved from the Campbellsville Hotel to the New Merchants Hotel, where it remained. Upon Bryant's death, Shively continued the business, which later passed to his son and daughter, Eugene B. "Zimmie" Shively and Elizabeth Shively Hall. (TCHS.)

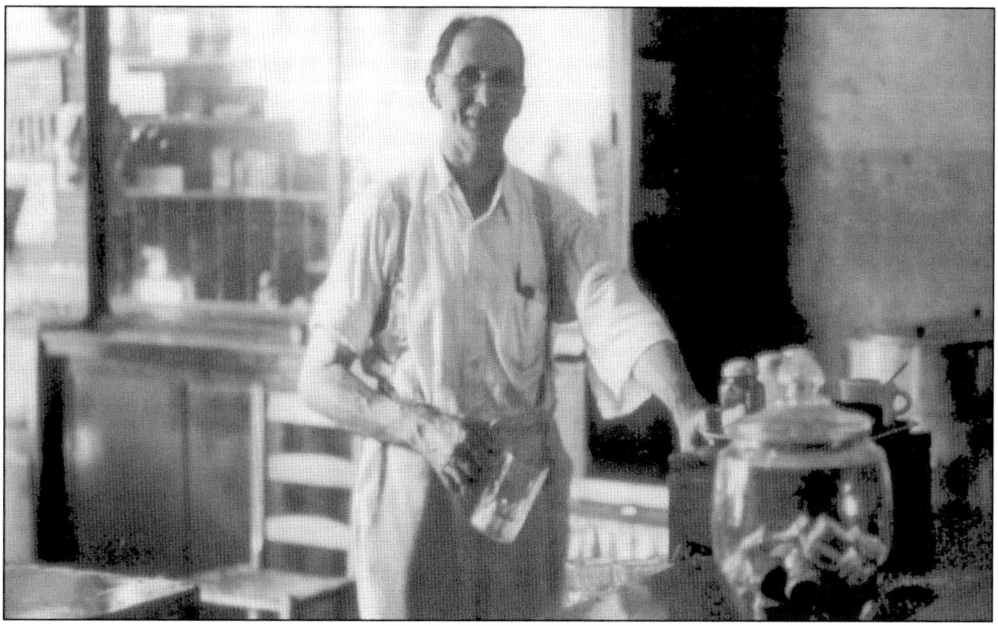

Dorah Lewis McCubbin was the manager of the Campbellsville Electric Company at the time of its sale in 1924 to Kentucky Utilities. McCubbin continued to work with Kentucky Utilities until 1930. Prior to coming to Campbellsville, he had been employed in the Revenue Service from 1903 to 1914 as a storekeeper-gauger and had taught in the rural schools of Hart County for many years. (TCHS.)

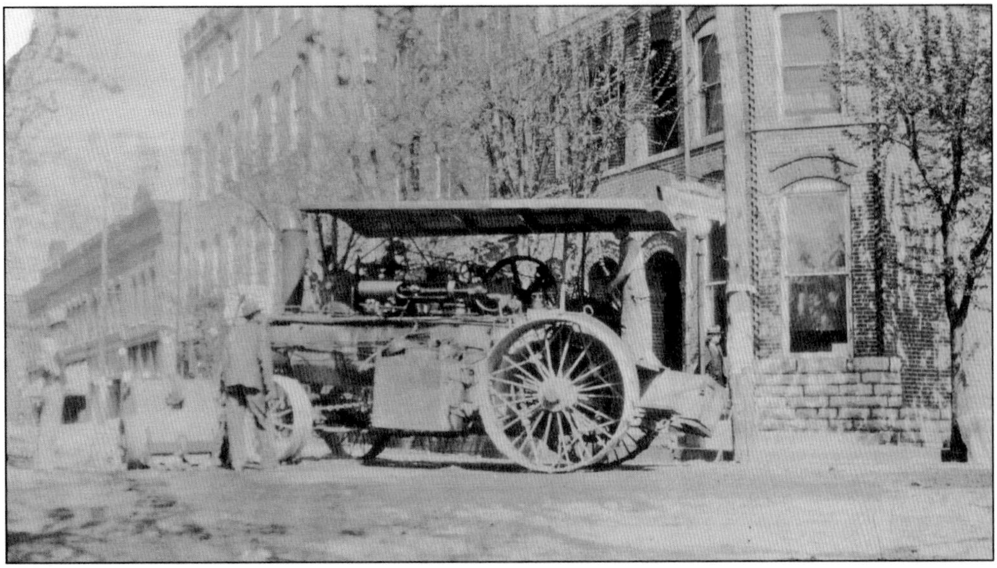

Before paved streets, Campbellsville had to maintain the dirt streets as best as possible. Work included grading and filling in holes to level the streets before oiling. The October 17, 1929, local newspaper noted, "Main Street is torn up." Under a city council contract, the R. B. Tyler Company, Louisville, had begun blasting the old concrete gutters and curbing between Central and Columbia Avenues in preparation for paving. (FHB.)

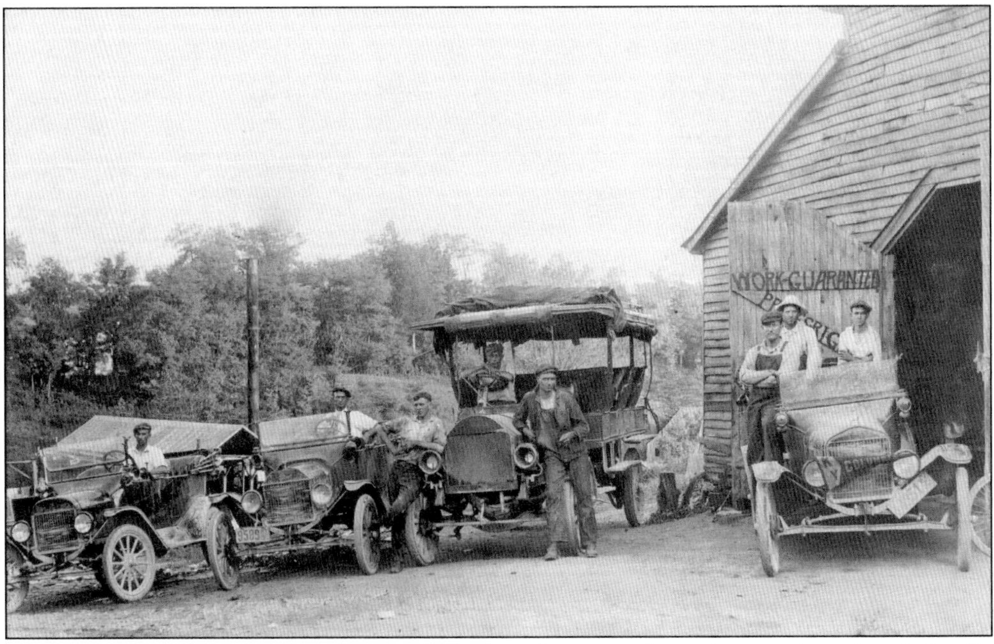

In 1911, Seymour Shaw, seated in the roofed vehicle in the center, drove the stage from Campbellsville to Columbia. A Columbia, Kentucky, pennant is on the front of the vehicle to the right. Prior to automobile travel, horse-drawn stages carried passengers between the two communities with at least one change of horses at the Green River Bridge. To catch the train in Campbellsville, Columbia passengers met the stage at 2:30 a.m. (SS.)

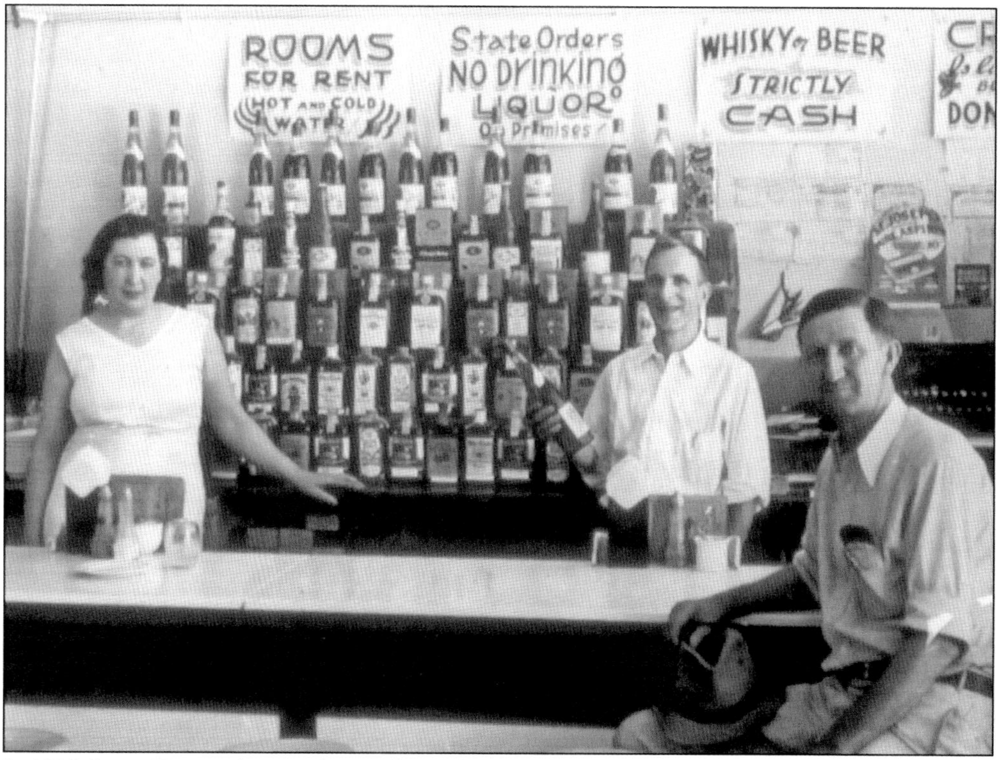

In 1933, Louis "Louie the Greek" Cordas and his wife Mattie ran the Eat More Restaurant at the corner of Main Street and Columbia Avenue, across from the Merchants Hotel. Within six years, Louie closed the restaurant, moved to Georgetown, and opened another restaurant there. They then moved to Lebanon, where Louie ran a tavern and where Mattie died in 1957. Following his wife's death, Louie returned to Greece. (TCHS.)

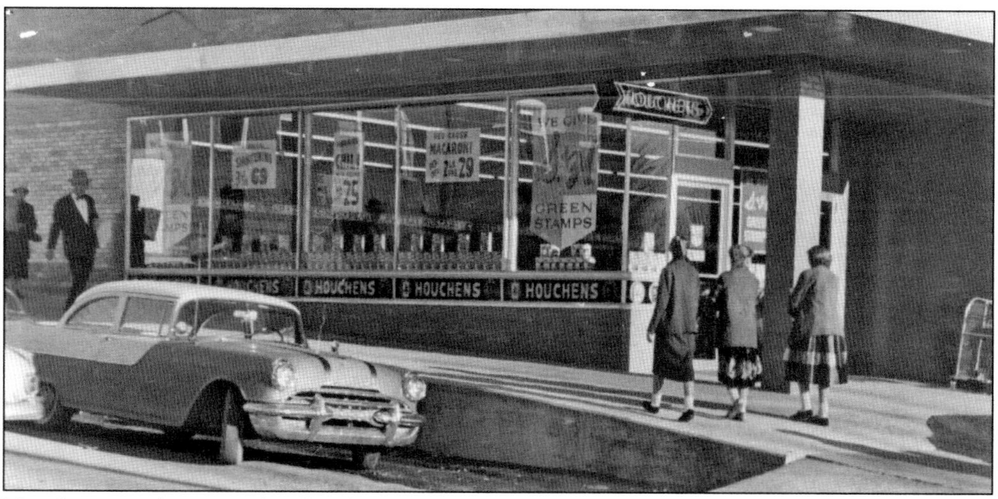

Houchen's Markets completed its first Campbellsville store adjacent to and abutting a Kroger store in September 1958. After removing two houses on West Main Street, which were known as the Knifley and the Anna Coakley properties, Smith and Fox of Glasgow, Kentucky, built the structure for owner Ray Taylor. A grocery chain based in Bowling Green, Houchen's eventually added a second Campbellsville store that remains open in the By the Station shopping center. (TCL.)

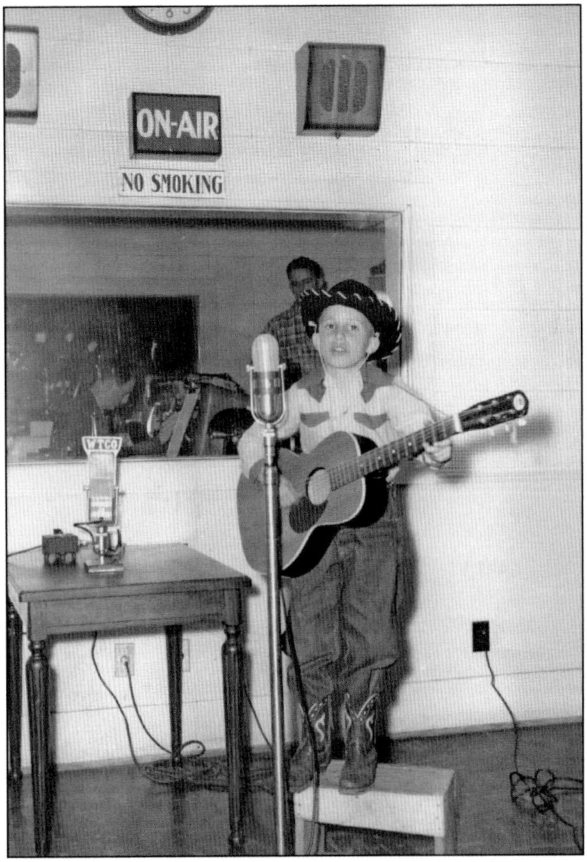

Campbellsville radio stations provided outlets for talented locals to be recognized and to develop their skills. Built in 1947, radio station WTCO provided a place for local talent, such as this unidentified youngster. With 1,000-watt power, the station began broadcasting from the second floor of the Hubbard building. On Tuesday, May 15, 1951, Campbellsville heard a new radio station when WLCK went on the air. Owned initially by local businessmen Dr. M. M. Hall, Raymond Thompson, and Ray Smith, under the name Taylor County Broadcasting Company, WLCK was located at 1450 on the dial and offered day and night programs. WLCK staff members included, from left to right, (first row) James Long, Tommy Kerr (farm news), "Sid" Sidebottom, and Keith Gabehart; (second row) Lindsey Harden (announcer), George O. Bertram (announcer), Elwood "Red" Jeffries, Turney Harding (sports), and Joe ?. (JBC, left and below.)

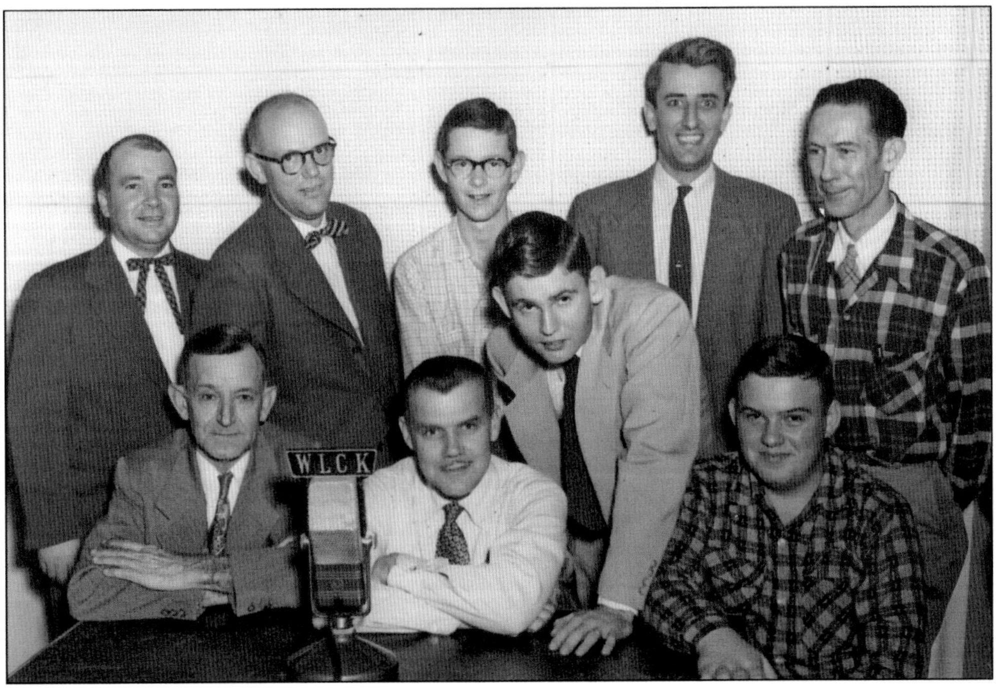

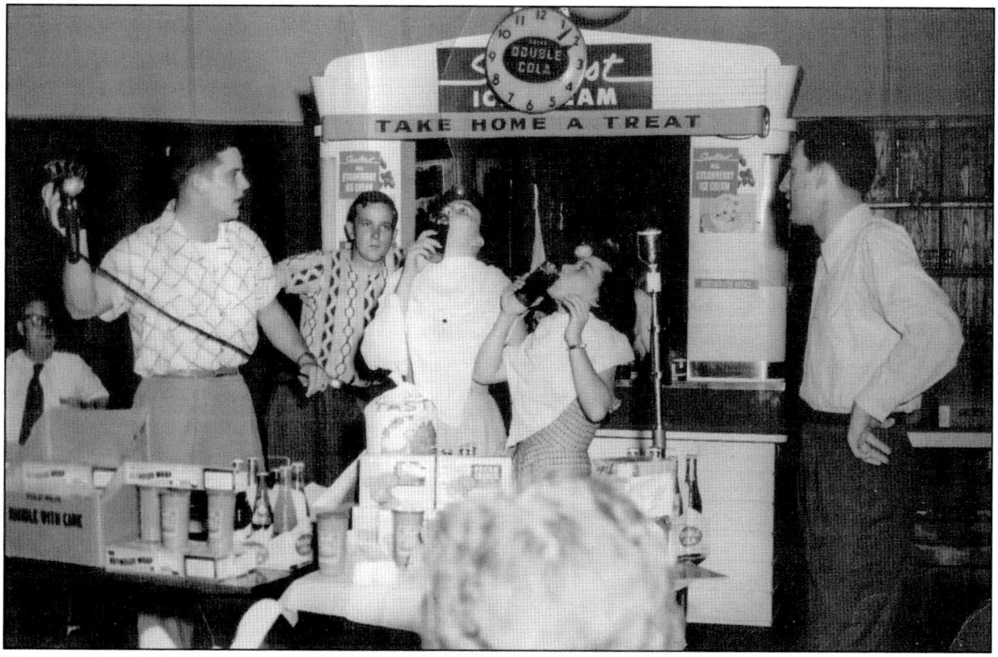

Ken Knight, Billy Cox, and Frank Hayden, pictured from left to right, watch as two unidentified women drink Double Cola during a promotion on WLCK, a Campbellsville radio station started by J. B. Crawley. In addition to Double Cola, the promotion included various other products such as Nesbitt's Orange, Pecan Crunch cookies, and Sealtest Ice Cream. (JBC.)

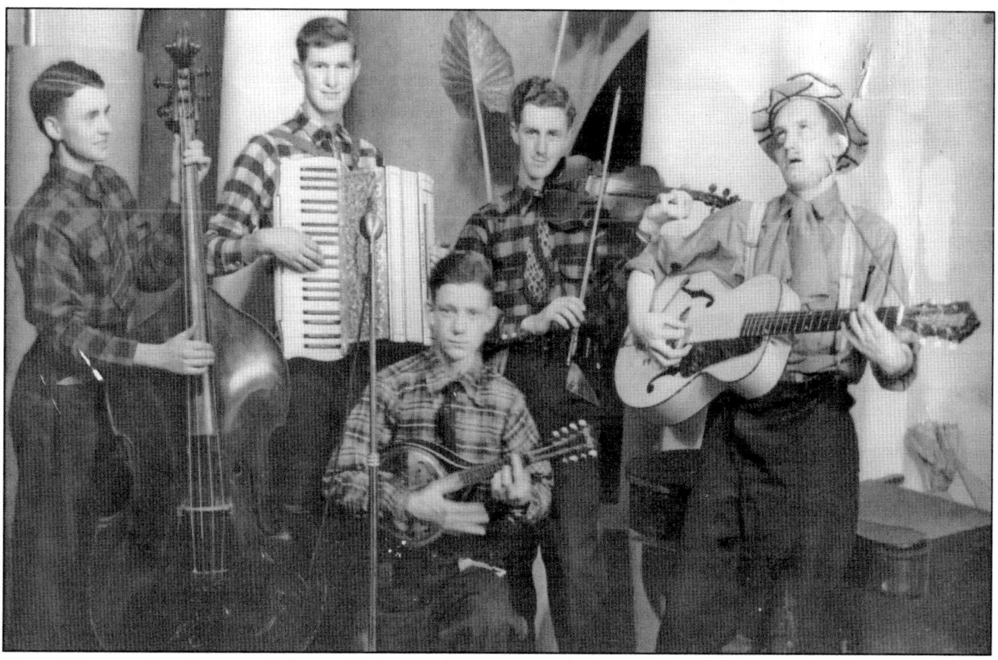

From left to right, Lynwood Gore, Herman Hubbard, Earl Fisher, J. B. Crawley, and Charles Watson (kneeling) formed a band that played on the local radio stations and other venues. Crawley started the Campbellsville radio station, WLCK, along with several others in Kentucky. Watson went on to become a professional musician, playing with Pee Wee King and others. (JBC.)

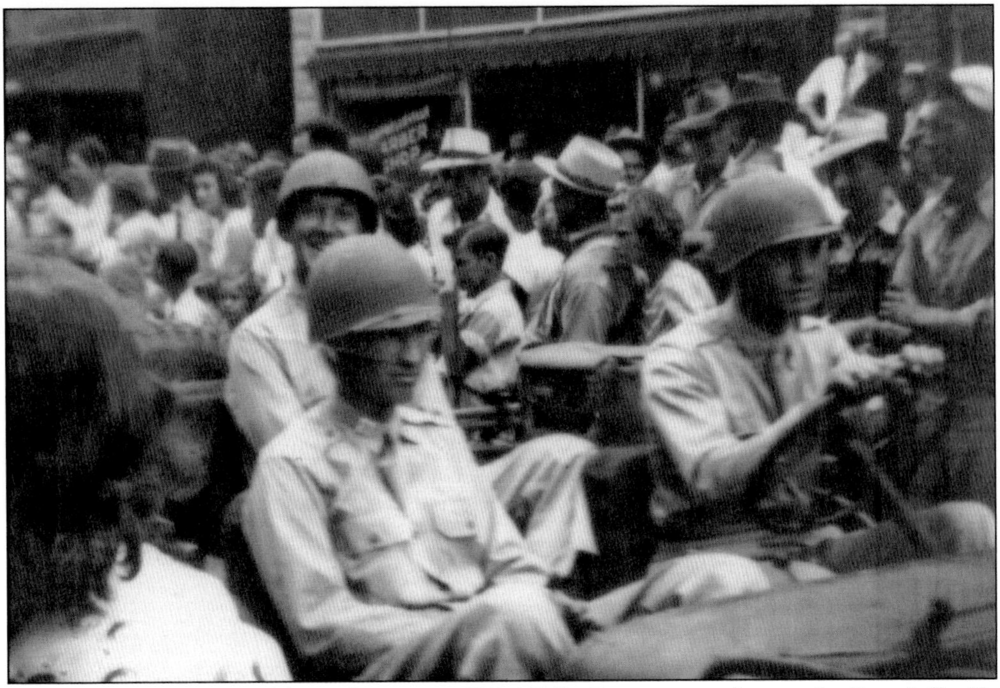

Taylor County residents celebrate the return of World War II veterans in this parade. Campbellsville and Taylor County have given their share of men and women to various war efforts. Over 43 Taylor County residents lost their lives in World War II, 14 in World War I, 5 in Korea, and 6 in Vietnam. (SN.)

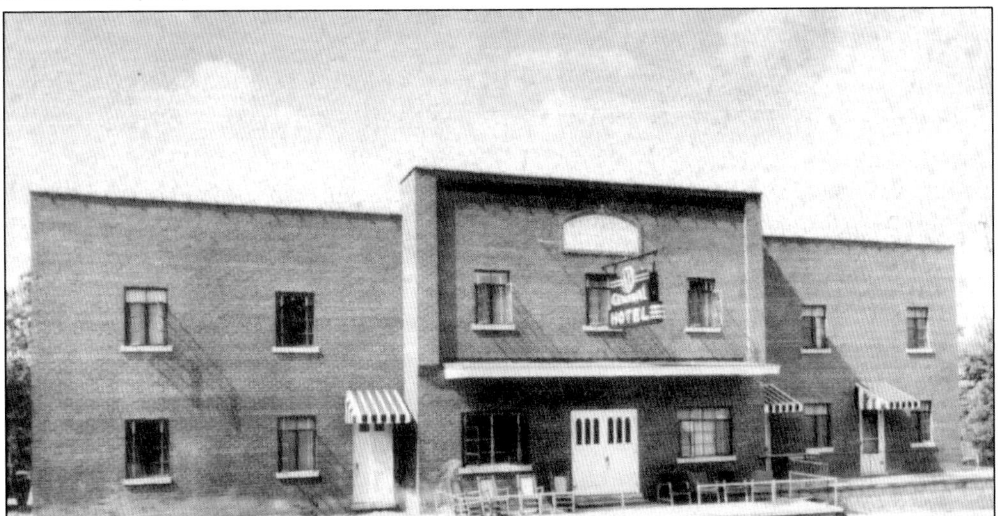

Thurman S. Curry built the Kentucky Central Motel in 1948. The two-story brick motel with a basement contained two five-room apartments and forty-eight rooms, each with a bath or shower and an outside view. The kitchen, dining room, laundry, and hotel garage were in the basement. Curry and Harry Fawcett supervised construction, with the Dix Brothers completing the brickwork. (F&CK.)

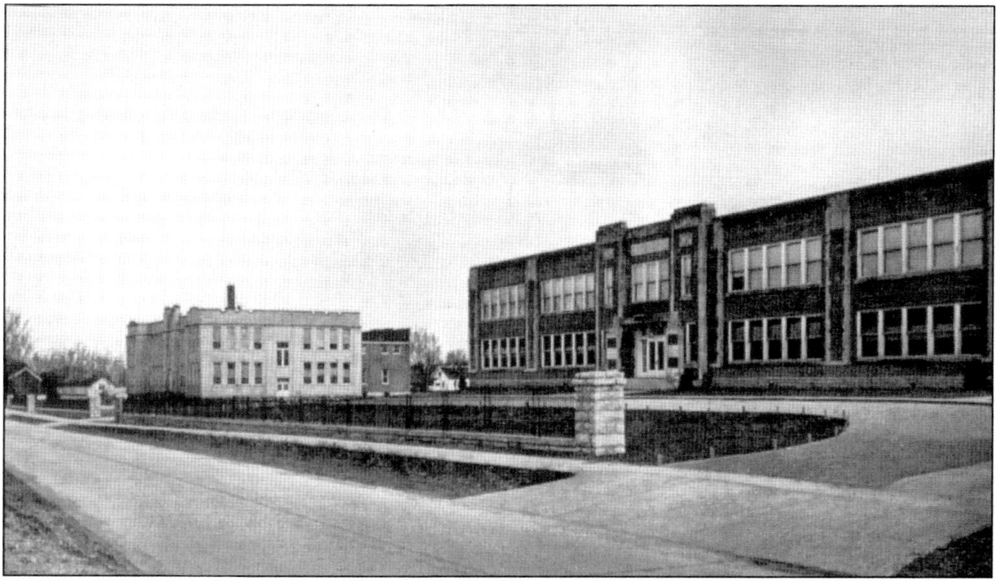

Built in 1919 and razed in 1982, Campbellsville High School (left) served both the Campbellsville Independent District and the Taylor County District until Taylor County built its own building in 1940. The building was known as Taylor County High until both local school boards discarded a unification plan in the 1930s. The Campbellsville School Board bought the Taylor County Board's interest in the building in March 1935 and renamed it Campbellsville High. (F&CK.)

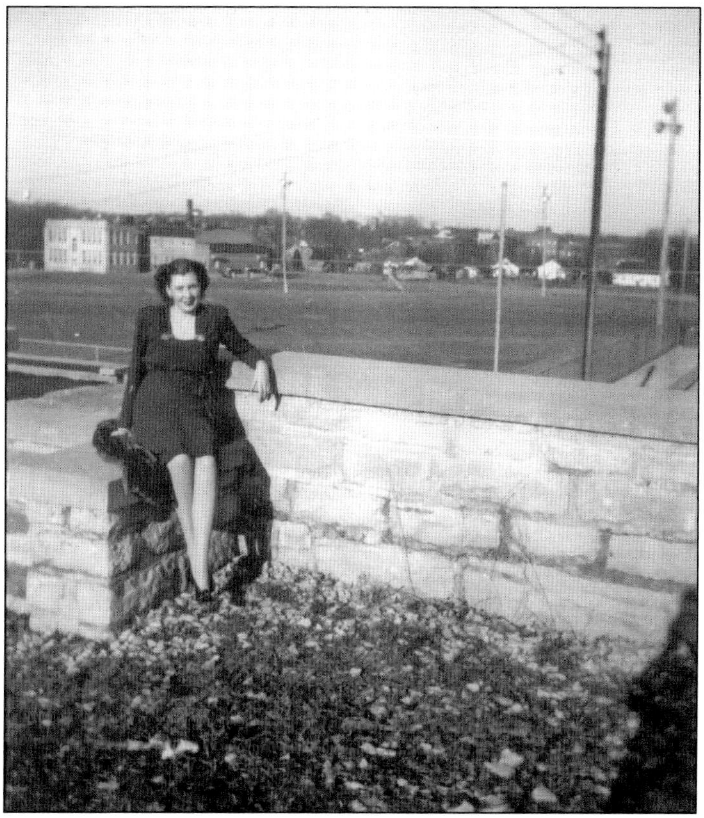

Virginia Newton sits on one of the WPA projects in Taylor County, the present Campbellsville High School stadium and field. Completed in 1936 and built of stone quarried from the Chandler quarry on Buckhorn Creek, the stadium sits on a natural slope and seats approximately 800 people. Locker rooms, showers, and storage rooms are located under the stands. Workers completed the stone wall in front of the school as part of the project. (TCHS.)

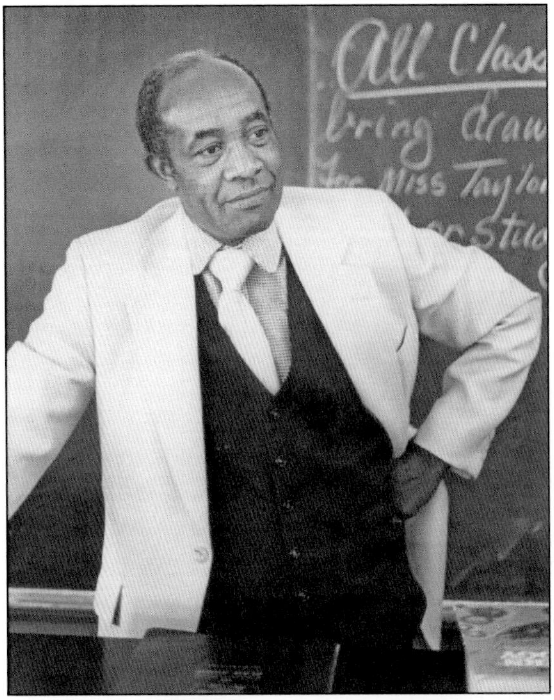

The first African American to teach in the integrated Campbellsville system, Henry Reedie Richardson taught in the Campbellsville Public School System for 36 years. After retirement, he taught biology at Campbellsville University. Following his service in World War II, Richardson completed a Bachelor of Science degree at Kentucky State University and a Masters in Animal Husbandry from Michigan State University. State and local organizations recognized his teaching and community service with numerous awards. (TCHS.)

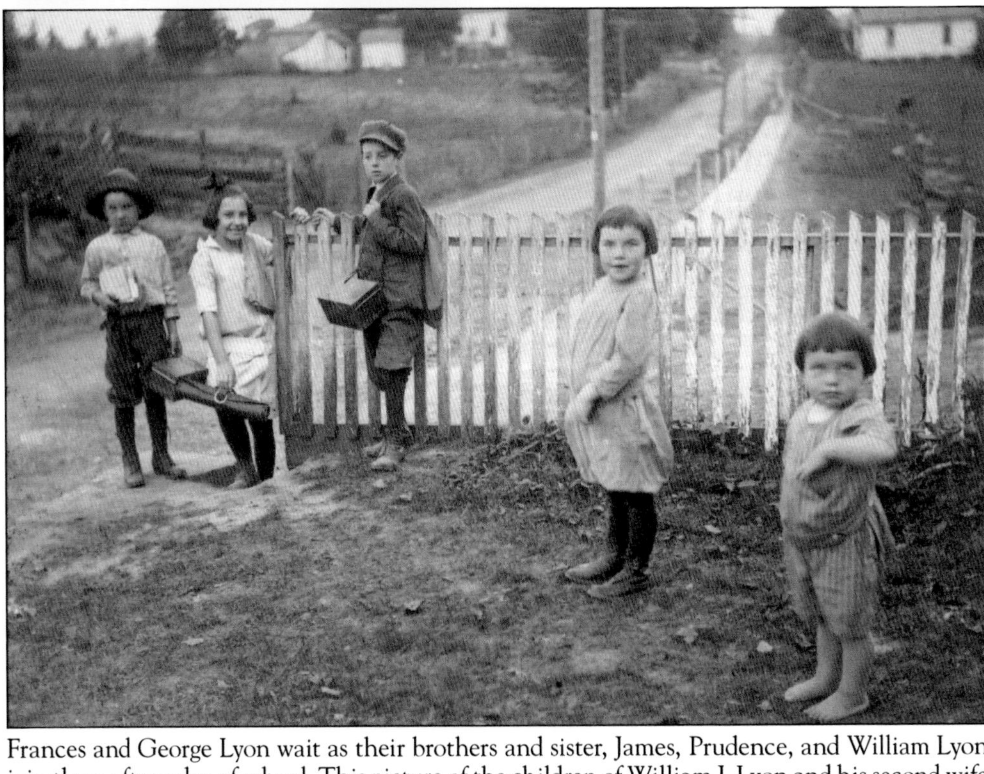

Frances and George Lyon wait as their brothers and sister, James, Prudence, and William Lyon, join them after a day of school. This picture of the children of William J. Lyon and his second wife, Ivy Yates Lyon, was taken in September 1913. At that time, William Lyon was actively involved in the Buchanan-Lyon grocery, automobile, and implements business. (TCHS.)

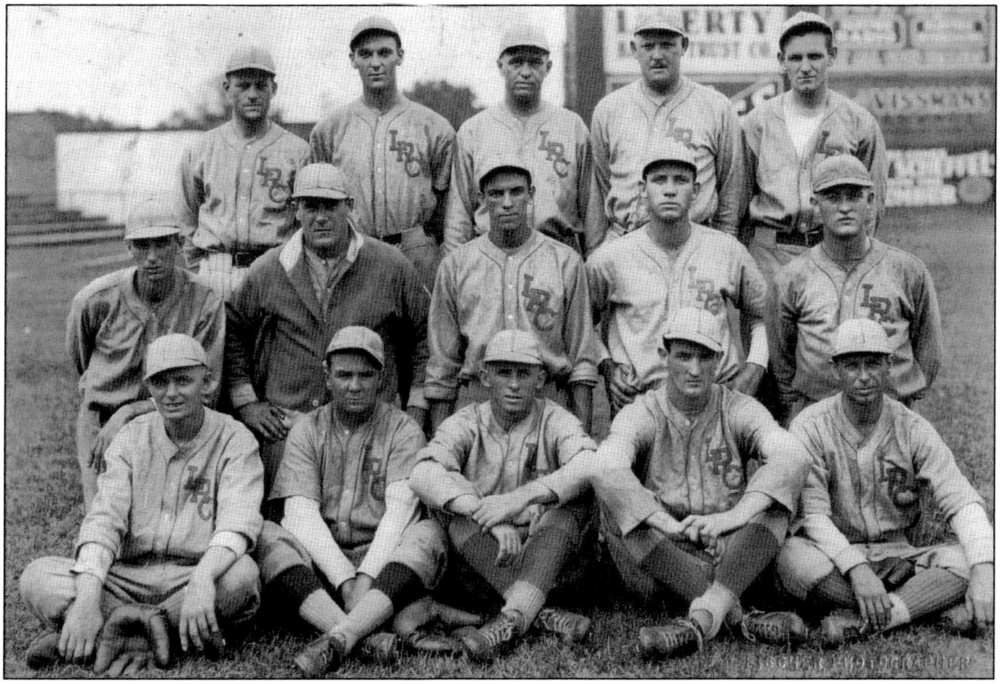

Cameron Wilson, son of W. H. Wilson, one of the former proprietors of the Campbellsville Hotel, played minor league baseball for the Louisville Colonels and the Eastern Pennsylvania League in Erie, Pennsylvania. Wilson, pictured in the front row second from right, was one of two Campbellsville players entering the minor leagues in 1932. Harold "Ole Head" Bailey played with the Hartford, Connecticut, team in the Eastern Connecticut League. (JW.)

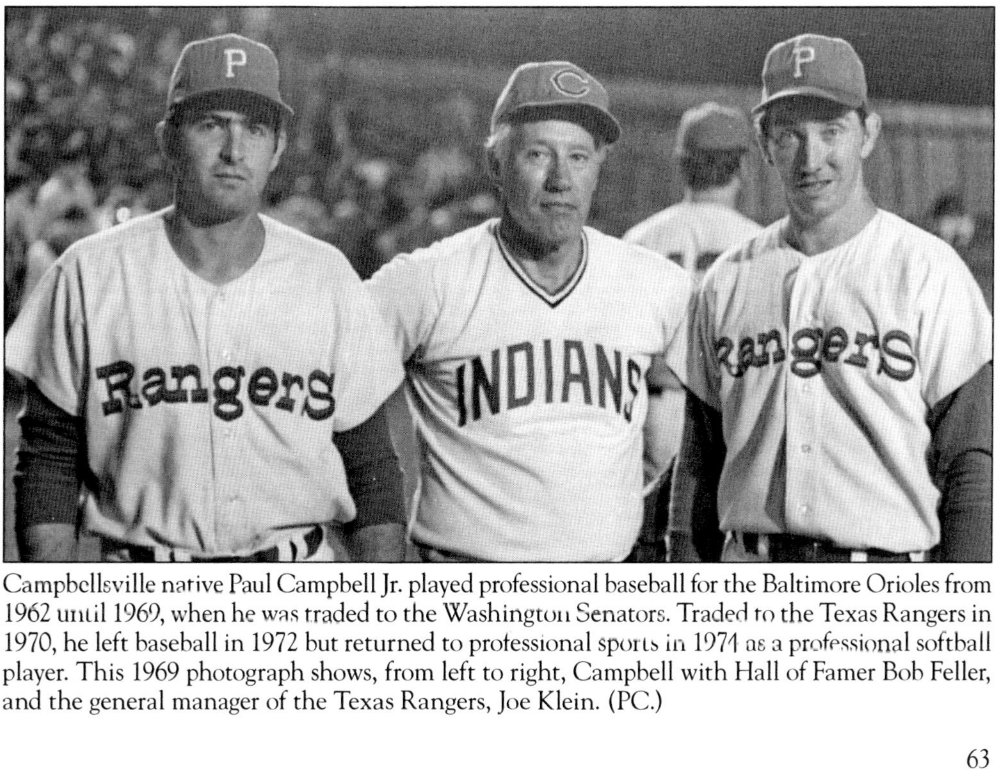

Campbellsville native Paul Campbell Jr. played professional baseball for the Baltimore Orioles from 1962 until 1969, when he was traded to the Washington Senators. Traded to the Texas Rangers in 1970, he left baseball in 1972 but returned to professional sports in 1974 as a professional softball player. This 1969 photograph shows, from left to right, Campbell with Hall of Famer Bob Feller, and the general manager of the Texas Rangers, Joe Klein. (PC.)

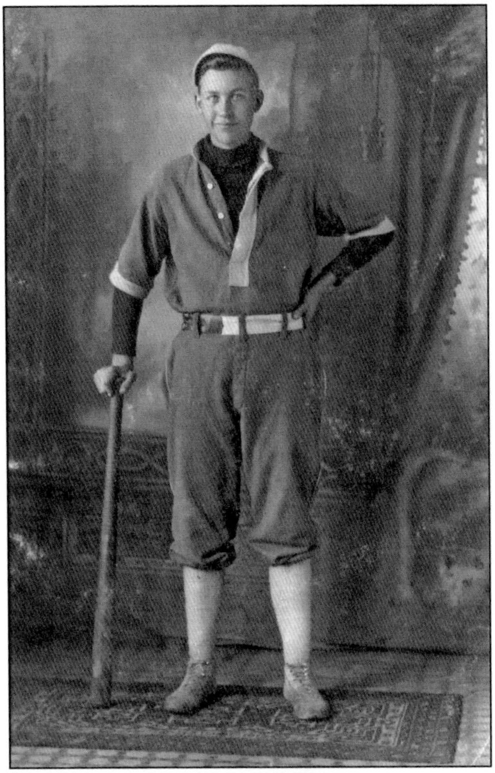

As the first Taylor County native to play professional baseball, Oliver Crouch moved from local teams to the Bluegrass League in Winchester, Kentucky, before being hired to play for North Carolina's Asheville Tourists in 1925. In succeeding years, he played with the Winston-Salem Twins and the Durham Bulls. Upon returning to Campbellsville, he remained involved as a player and coach, while managing Crouch's Pool Room on Main Street. (JH.)

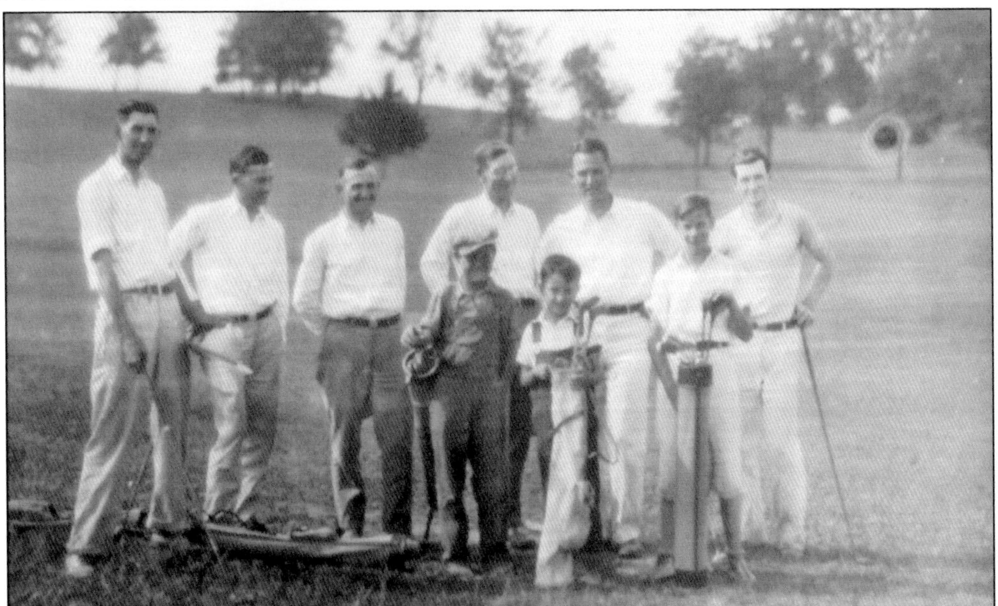

In 1927, Harry T. Edwards built Campbellsville's first golf course on a 45-acre tract that he owned on West Main Street, which is now covered by the Wilson Heights subdivision. Peter E. Pelchar, golf instructor at Louisville's Cherokee Park, helped Edwards lay out the course, and his brother Fred served briefly as an instructor. Pictured are Willie Cox, Bob Edwards, Dr. Frank Buckner, Frank Turner, William W. Durham, Sheldon Willock, and three unidentified boys. (TCHS.)

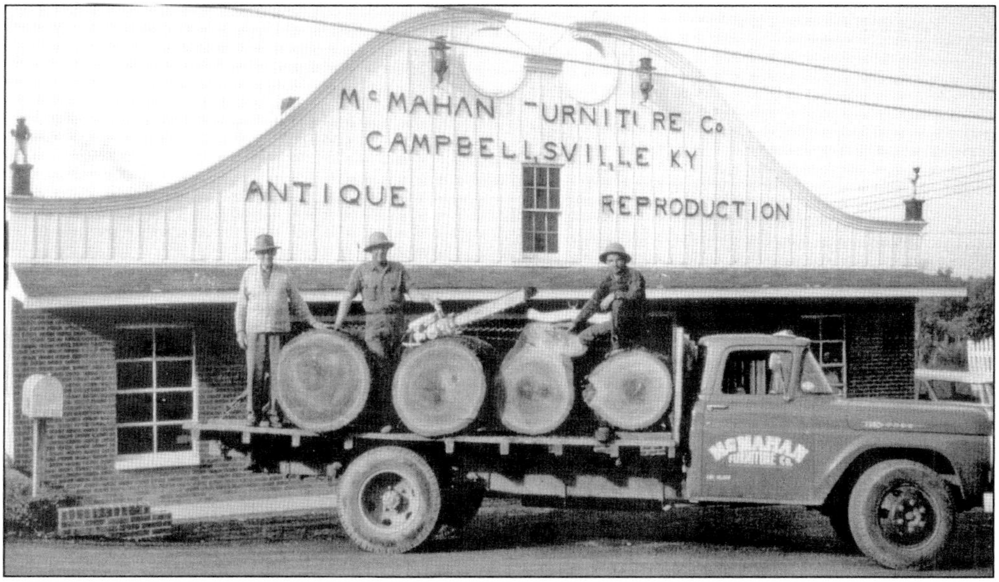

With access to abundant wood and skilled craftsmen, Campbellsville became a center of reproduction-furniture making in the 20th century. Started by Bruin McMahan and his brothers after World War II, McMahan Furniture became the largest company shipping reproduction cherry furniture across the United States. Other companies included the Cherry Shops, Pioneer Furniture Company, the Williams Furniture Company owned by Oscar Williams, Kearns Antique Furniture Shop owned by Joe Kearns, Coppock Old Fashioned Antique Shop run by Linnie Coppock, and W. M. Cox and Son in Acton. Individual furniture makers included Cyrus Skaggs, Tim Bradshaw Clark, and Fess Johnson. In the picture below, McMahan Furniture workers Leonard Johnson, Edgar Sexton, and Elbert Tarter finish chairs and a table. Starting about 1925, Charles Herriford of Herriford Furniture Company appears to have been the first to reproduce furniture on a large scale. (TM, above and below.)

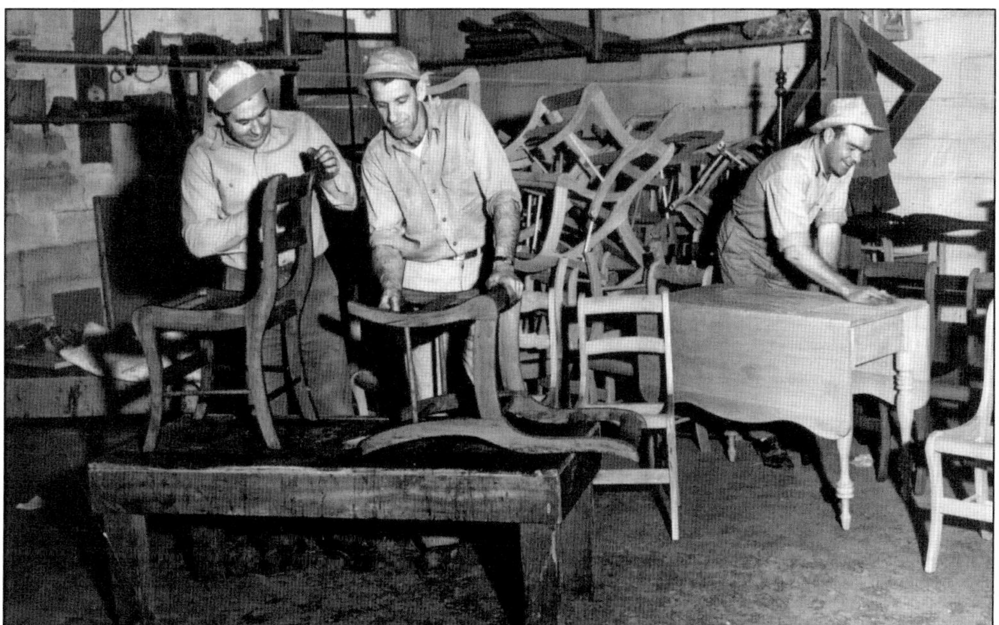

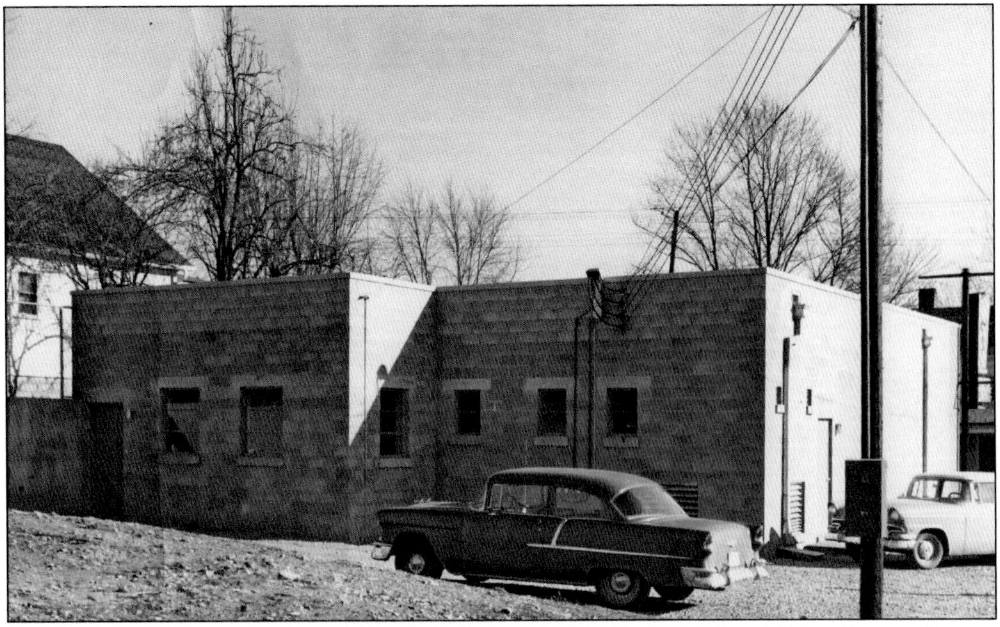

Kentucky Utilities became Campbellsville's electrical power source in April 1924, after purchasing the Springfield and Campbellsville Utilities Companies in January and acquiring the franchise rights for $67.20. Luther B. Smith bought the first Campbellsville Electric Light Company at public auction in February 1912 for $6,500. It included B. S. Kincart's bottling operation and the ice plant, and Kincart joined Smith in operating the facility. (KU.)

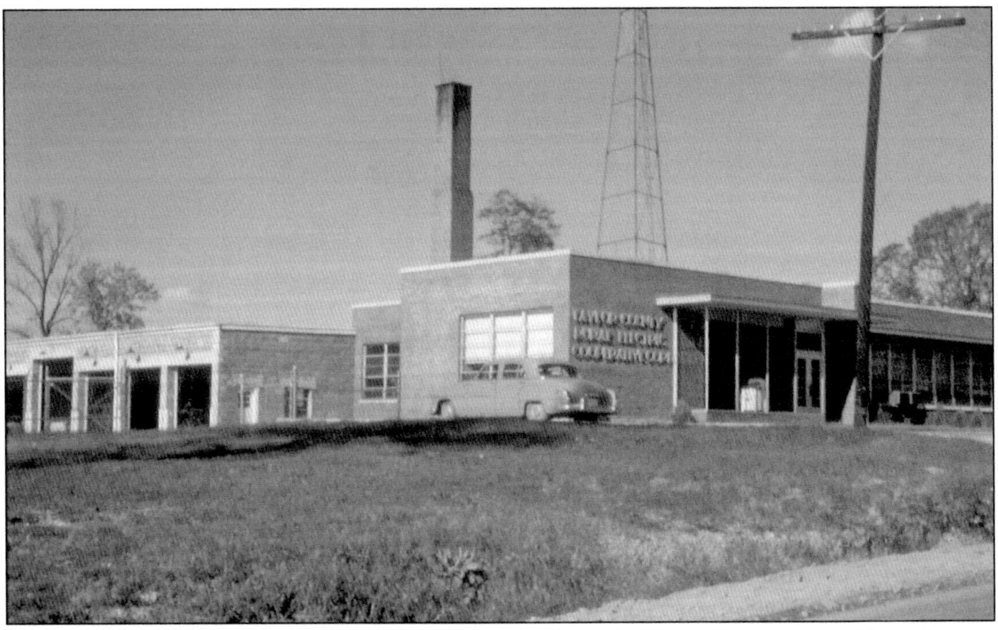

Approximately 120 rural homes first received electricity from the Taylor County Rural Electrification Administration on Monday, February 27, 1939. Lines to Columbia and Greensburg were the first to be energized through about 57 miles of line. Later the Taylor County Rural Electric Cooperative built an office on West Main. The company's building burned in 1952, but it rebuilt on the same site, with the same plan, in 1953. (TCL.)

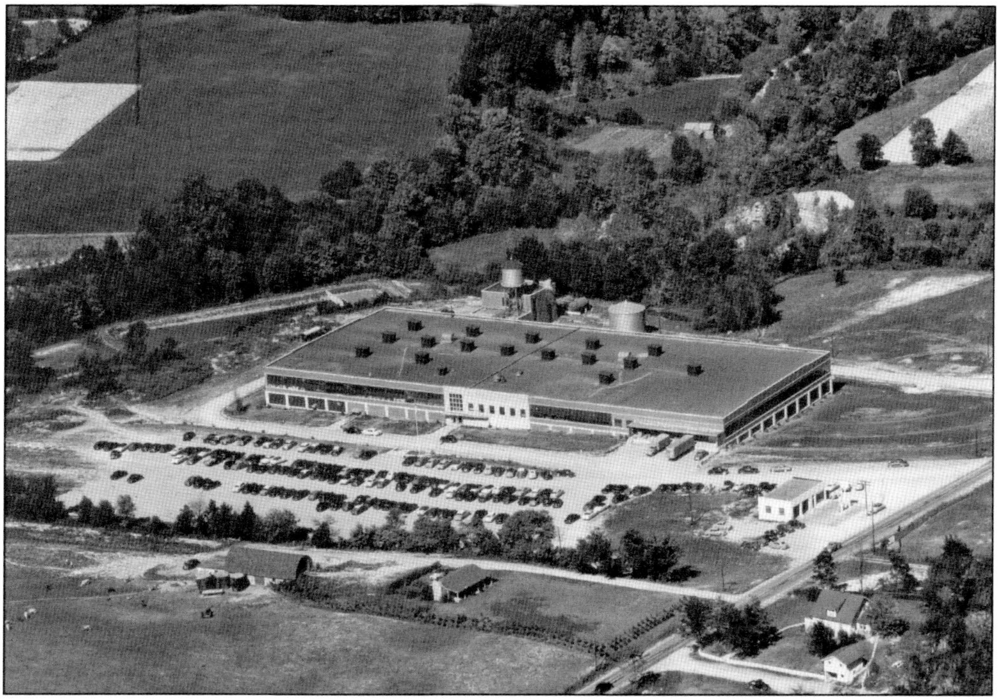

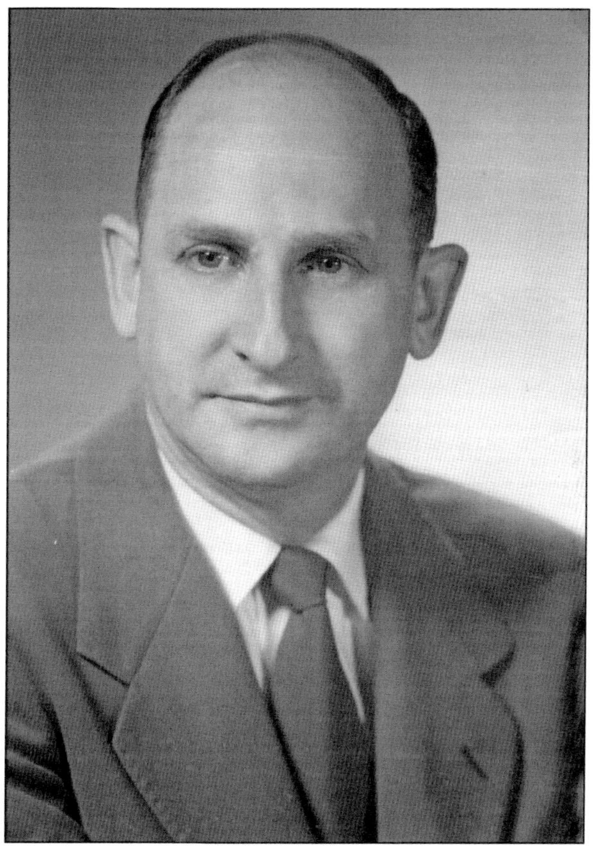

In December 1952, Union Underwear, maker of Fruit of the Loom garments, completed a new 160,000-square-foot building on the Campbellsville-Greensburg Highway and moved its operation and approximately 450 workers to that location. The company began its Campbellsville operations in 1948 through its division Taylor Manufacturing, managed by Monroe County native Albert G. Ross (right). Initially located in the Armory on the corner of Central Avenue and Broadway, the company began to outgrow its space. Consequently, it moved into Campbellsville's old woolen mill on South Court Street and placed some 125 employees in the basement of the Kentucky Central Hotel. Under the management of Ross and Executive Vice Pres. "Hamp" Baxter, Campbellsville's Union Underwear eventually grew to over 4,000 employees, becoming the world's largest producer of men's and boy's underwear. (TCL, above and right.)

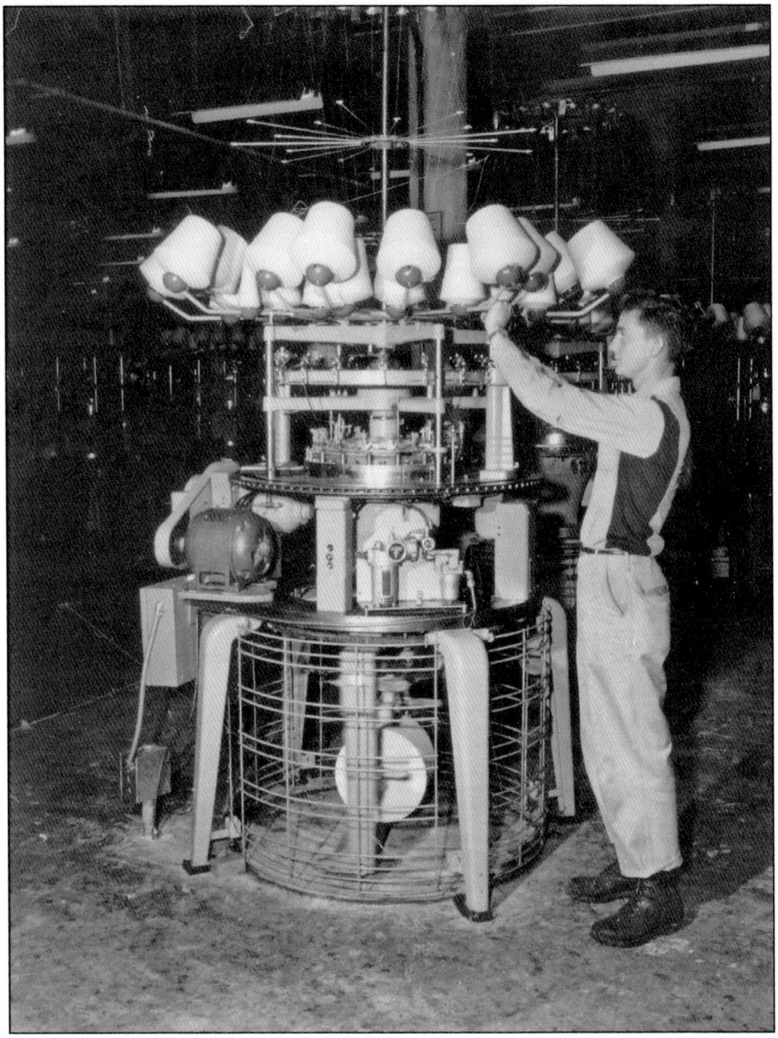

An unidentified worker sets up a knitting machine, one of the first of its kind to be used in Campbellsville. The machine produced rolls of cloth in 10- to 35-inch widths, with each roll weighing between 40 and 45 pounds. The knitting machine pictured may be a Philadelphia-made Britton or a Vanguard. (TCL.)

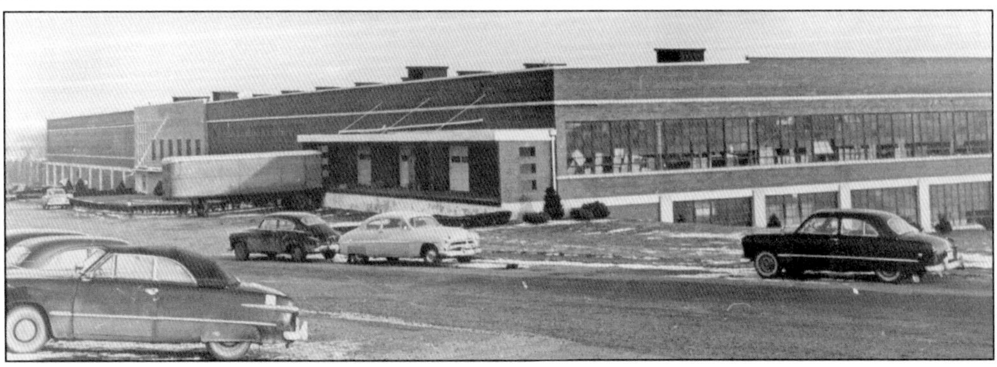

While the company was named Union Underwear, most people locally called it Fruit of the Loom, because Fruit of the Loom products filled the plant's major production demands. The Union Underwear Company also produced underwear, t-shirts, and activewear with brand names of BVD, Gitano, and Munsingwear. Fruit of the Loom closed its Campbellsville operation in April 1998. (TCL.)

Two

BEYOND MAIN

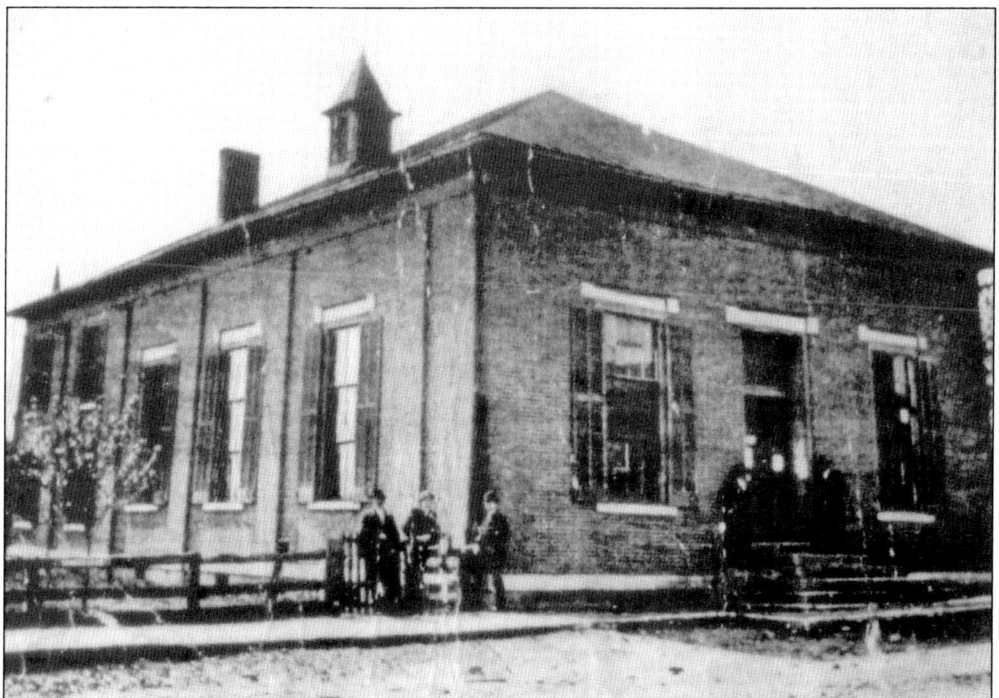

Confederate general Hylan B. Lyon burned the first courthouse on Christmas Day 1864. The county built a new courthouse, pictured above, eventually adding a clock tower and second floor. After installing a telephone in 1934 for a $4 monthly charge, the *Taylor County Star* reported: "an official can be had without asking some business house to get him on the phone." The county erected the current courthouse in the 1960s. (RR.)

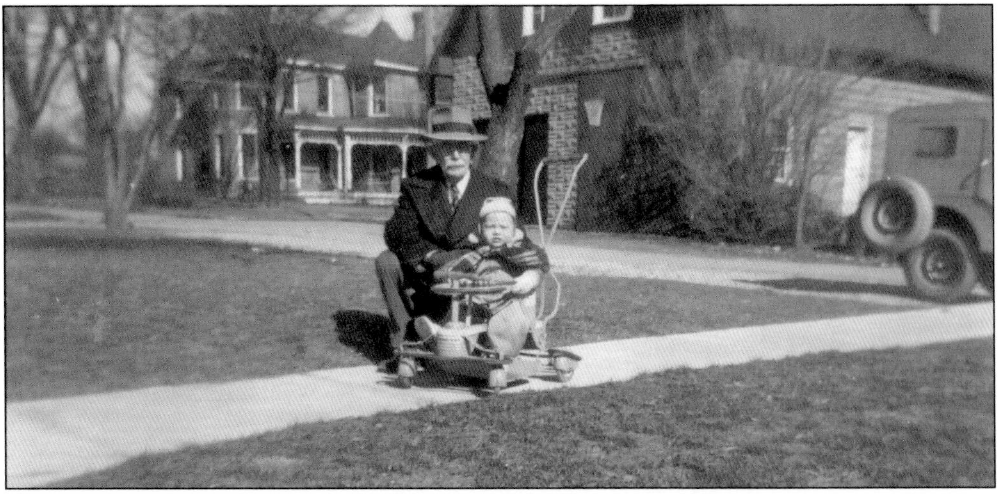

Throughout the 19th and 20th centuries, several funeral parlors existed on Campbellsville's Main Street. Edward P. Chilton, pictured above with his step-grandson, James Walker Bryant, joined first with Charles Redford Fleece. Later he and Fred Parrott established Chilton-Parrott on the second floor of the Davis Building, now Merle Norman. Finally, Chilton and James L. Nall formed Chilton-Nall and established their business on Central Avenue, across from the depot. (RG.)

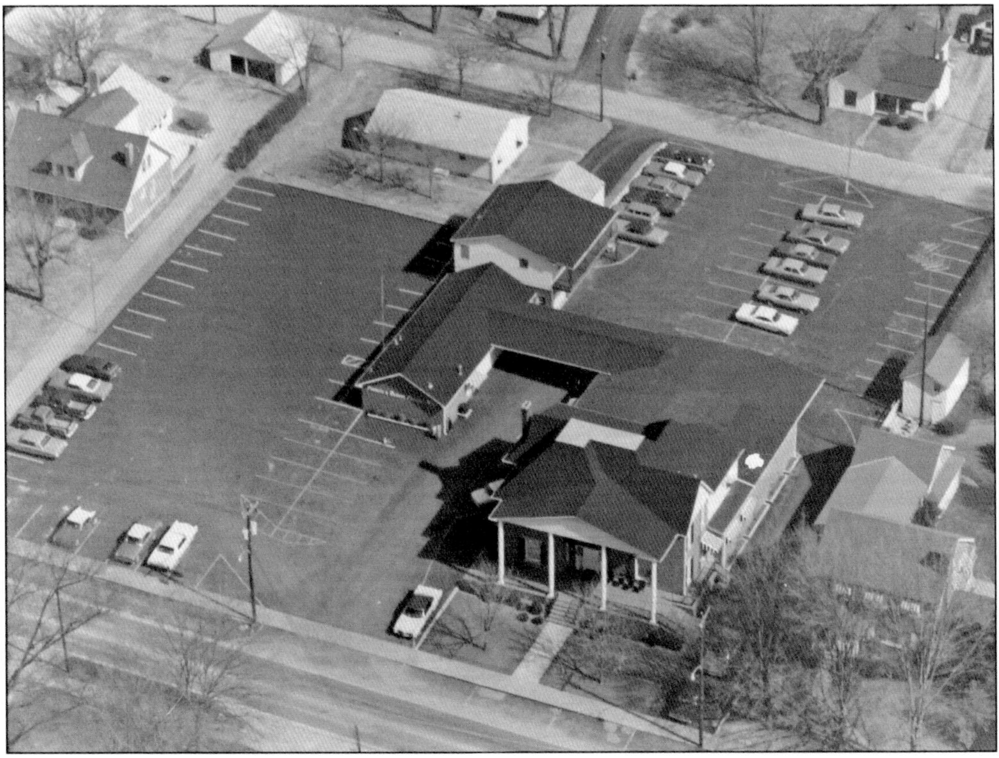

Fred L. Parrott, John W. Ramsey, and Robert W. Buckner initially opened Parrott, Ramsey, and Buckner Funeral Home in the Taylor County Supply Company store on Main Street, where Ramsey and Buckner were owners. Their equipment included a new 8-cylinder Buick combination funeral car and ambulance. Pictured is the Parrott-Ramsey Funeral Home, located on Lebanon Avenue and owned by Terry Dabney. (TD.)

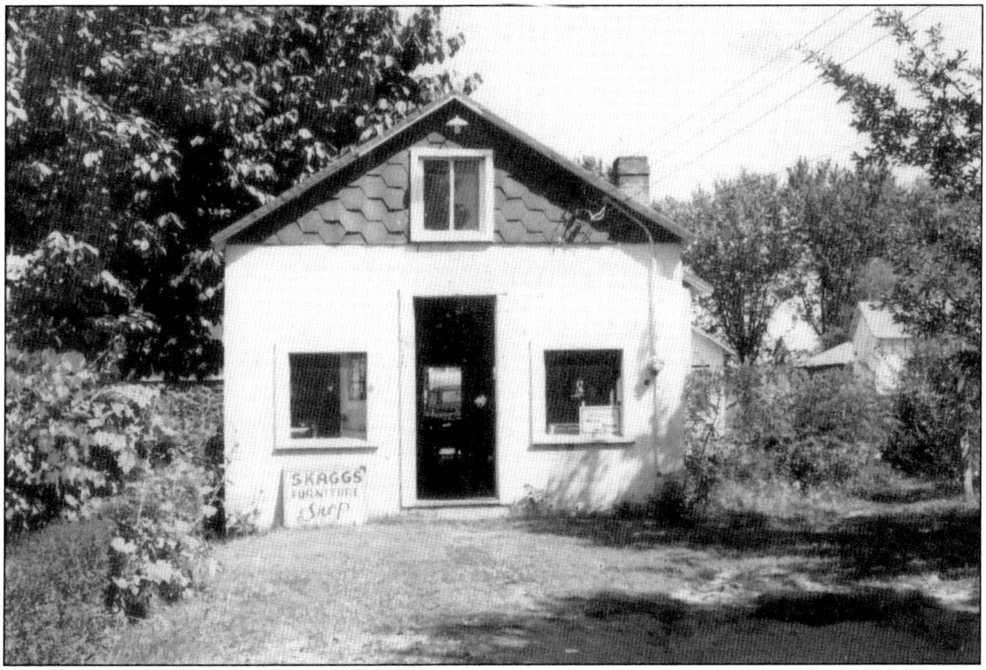

Woodworkers practiced their art in Campbellsville and Taylor County from early days. Cyrus Skaggs, whose Meader Street shop is pictured here, was among many small shops that produced quality cherry furniture. As a testament to the more personal and relaxed nature of business in previous years, the sign in the window reads, "Inquire next door." (VC.)

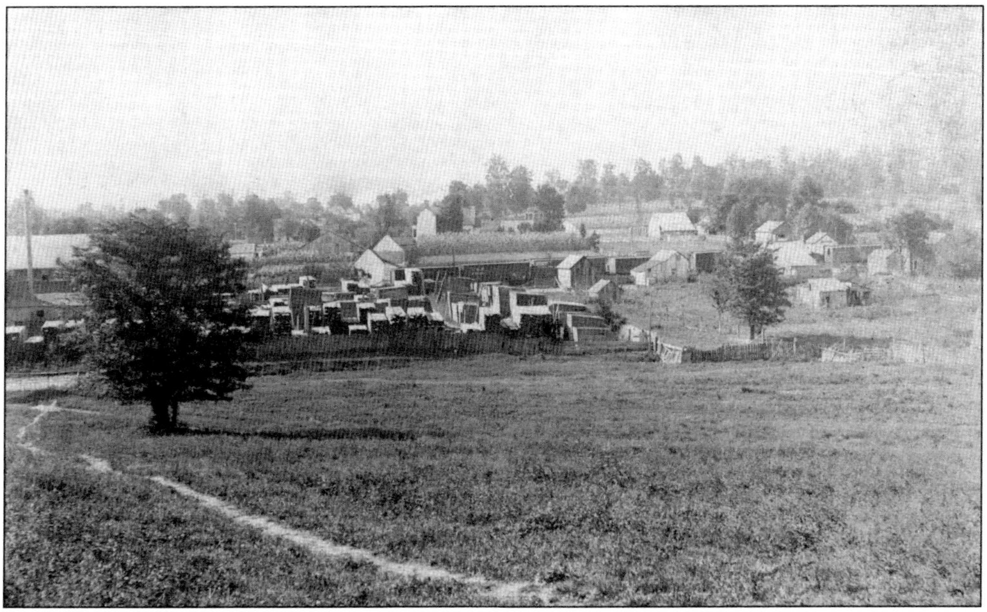

The Campbellsville Lumber Company sat near the Campbellsville Depot. Walter E. Wood and Ralph B. Wood began the company in 1887. Incorporation papers of January 1889 listed J. B. Stouffer, Levi Summers, Ulysses P. Walling, John S. Stults, and H. O. Wood as owners. However, Walter and Ralph Wood retained an interest in the company until it was sold to Henry T. Parrott and others in July 1924. (TCHS.)

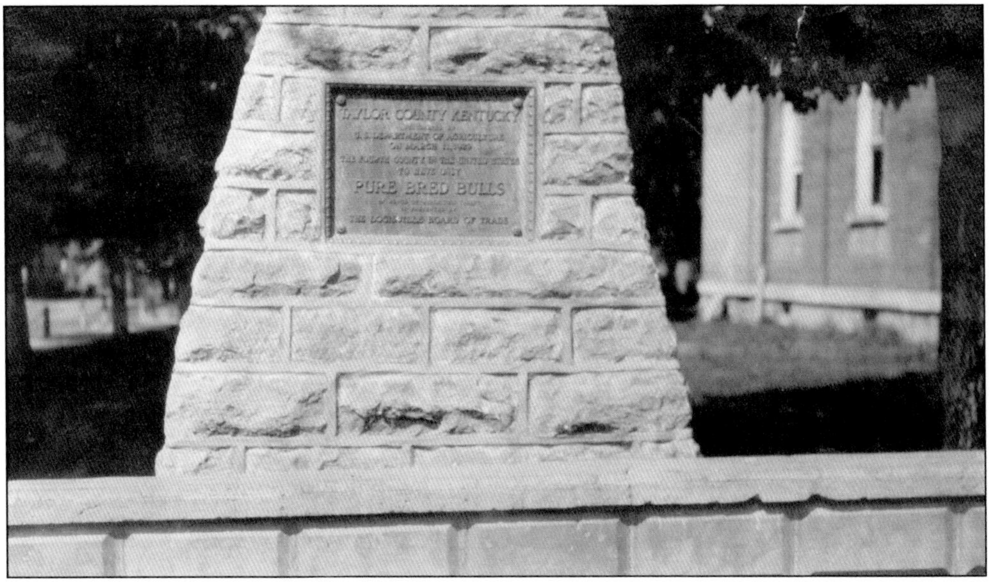

On October 18, 1929, approximately 100 representatives from the Louisville Board of Trade dedicated a tablet commemorating Taylor County's contribution to purebred bulls for dairy stock. The table reads, "Taylor County Kentucky / Contributed By / U. S. Department of Agriculture / On March 11, 1929 / The Fourth County In The United States / To Have Only / Pure Bred Bulls / In Honor Of Which This Tablet / Is Presented By / The Louisville Board Of Trade." (FHB.)

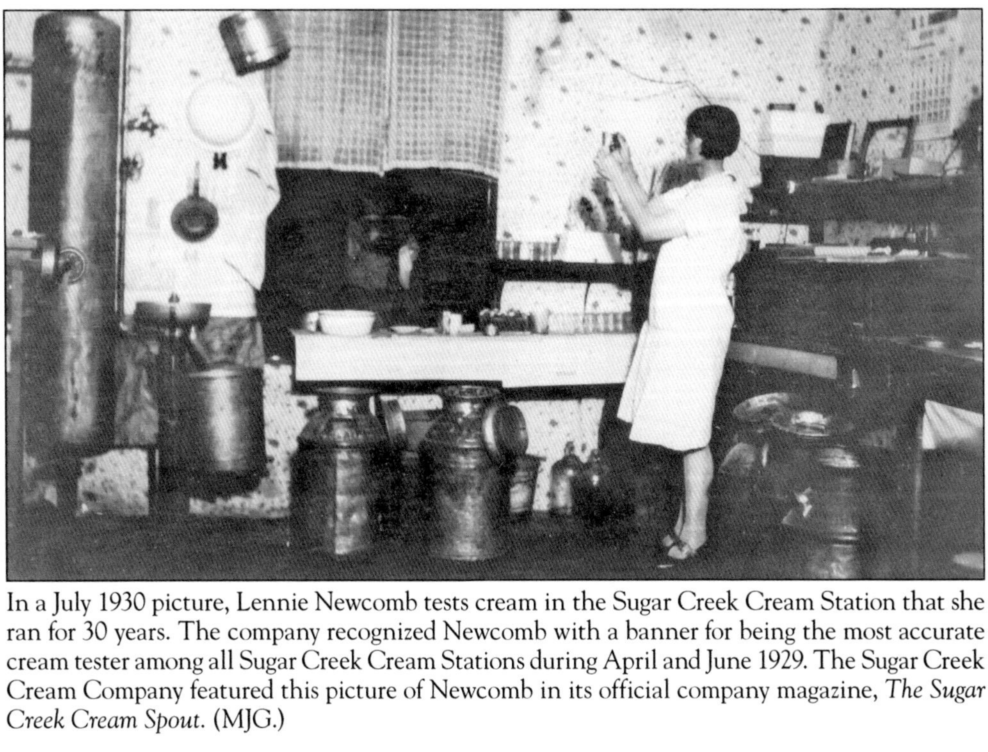

In a July 1930 picture, Lennie Newcomb tests cream in the Sugar Creek Cream Station that she ran for 30 years. The company recognized Newcomb with a banner for being the most accurate cream tester among all Sugar Creek Cream Stations during April and June 1929. The Sugar Creek Cream Company featured this picture of Newcomb in its official company magazine, *The Sugar Creek Cream Spout.* (MJG.)

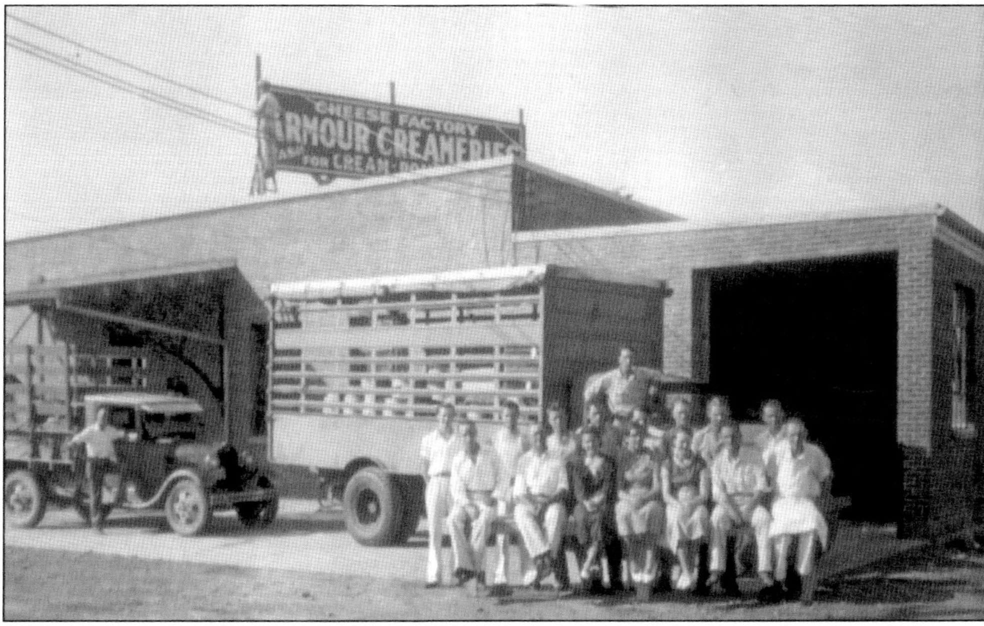

Armour located its first Kentucky cheese plant in Campbellsville in 1929. Prior to making the decision to locate in Campbellsville, the company assessed the road quality within an 8-mile radius of Campbellsville and surveyed farms to determine if there were a sufficient number of cows within that radius to provide the milk necessary for the plant's production. In February 1934, Armour occupied a new 10,000-square-foot brick building on the lot of the former Burley Pool Warehouse, near the railroad. The building housing the plant had the capacity to handle 60,000 pounds of milk daily, a cream buying station, and company offices. Not only did Armour buy local products and provide jobs, it also contributed to improvements in milk handling and production by educating local farmers through regular meetings. (TCHS, above and below.)

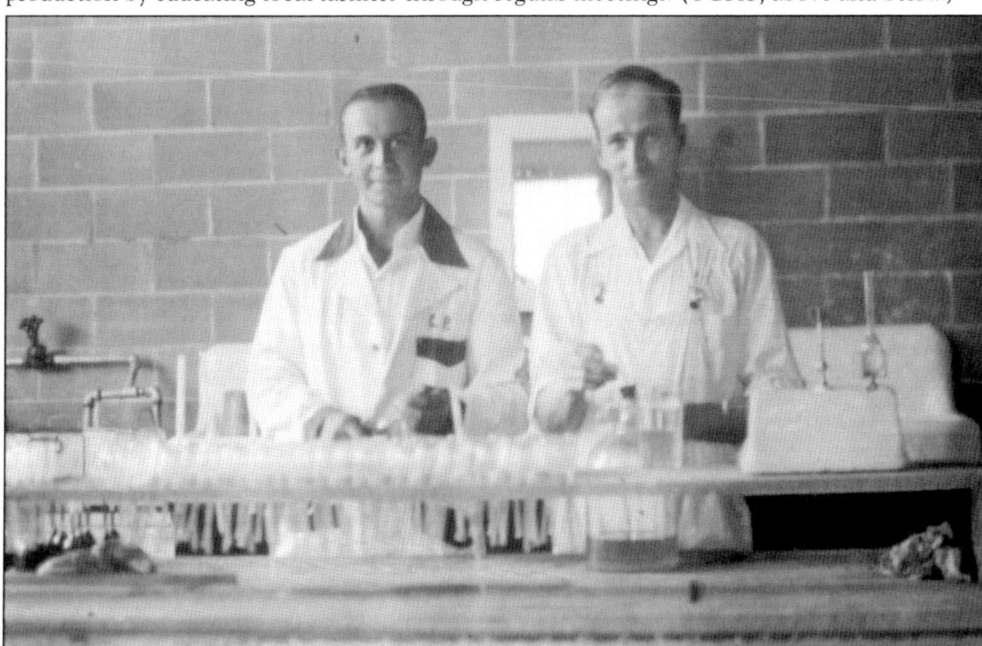

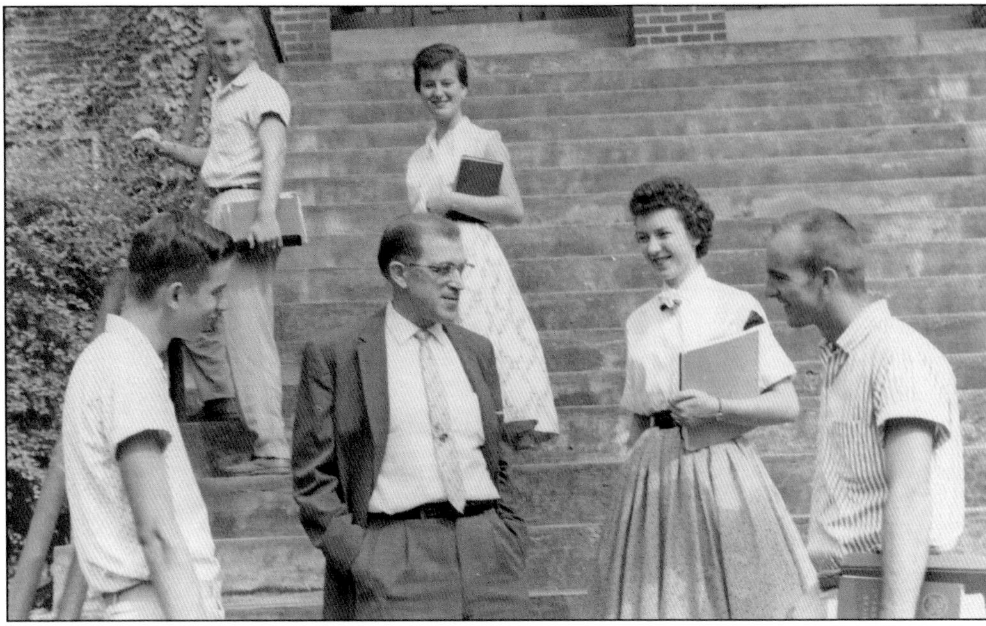

Taylor County native Dr. Auguston A. Page, in the suit, served as president of Pikeville College from 1940 to 1962. After completing undergraduate and post-graduate work and teaching at Western State College in Bowling Green, Kentucky, he became Pikeville College president. At their 125th commencement exercises, Centre College awarded Dr. Page a Doctor of Letters in recognition of his outstanding public service. (PCSC.)

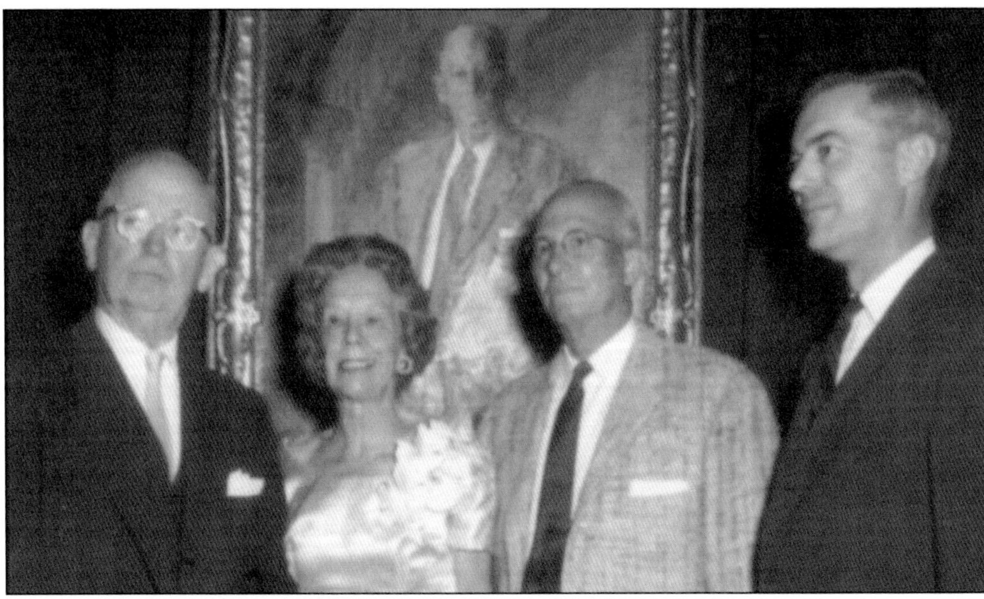

A Taylor County native, Frank Dewey Peterson, second from right, served in various state government posts for over 20 years including deputy commissioner of finance (1936–1941), during which time he organized Kentucky's National Youth Administration (NYA). In 1941, Peterson became the University of Kentucky's comptroller, later serving at various posts including the UK Athletic Association. His wife, Audrey Whitlock Peterson, second from left, coached two successive state champion women's basketball teams in 1931 and 1932. (UK.)

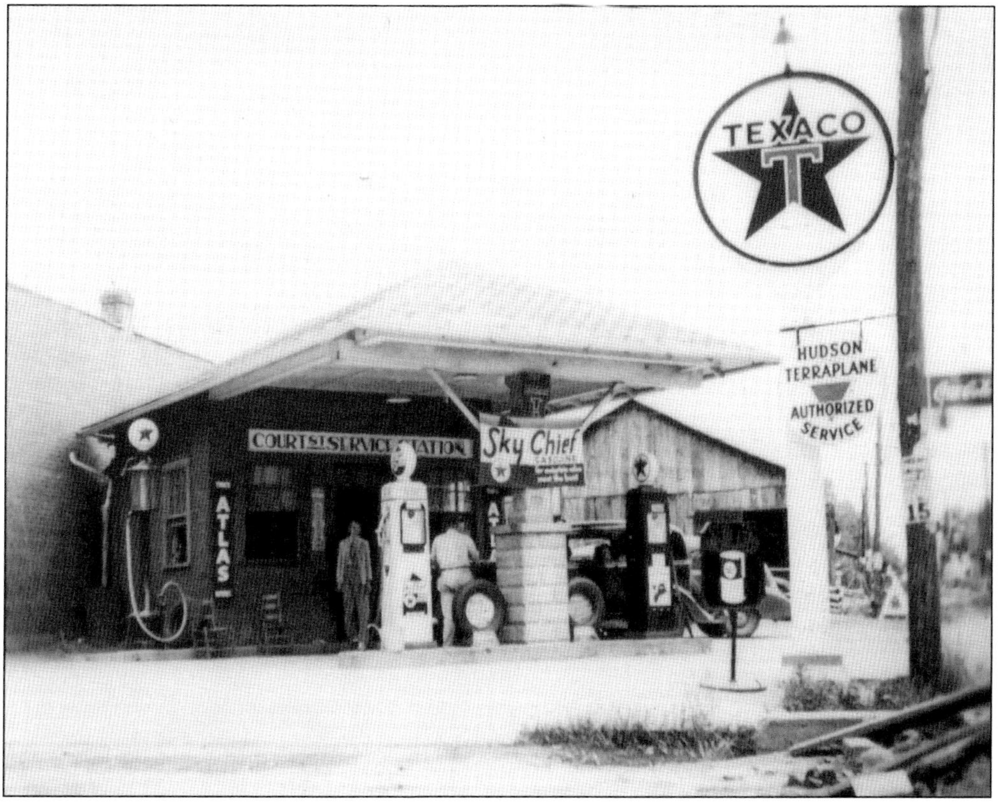

John Hugh Chandler and Henry Edrington opened the Court Street Service Station across from the courthouse on Monday, October 6, 1930. In April 1934, Jack Follis and Robert Arnold purchased an interest in the station, and operated it along with John Hugh's son, John Shelby. Follis and Arnold also brought with them two businesses, a taxi service and a U-Drive-It Service, that they continued to run at the Court Street location. (MJG.)

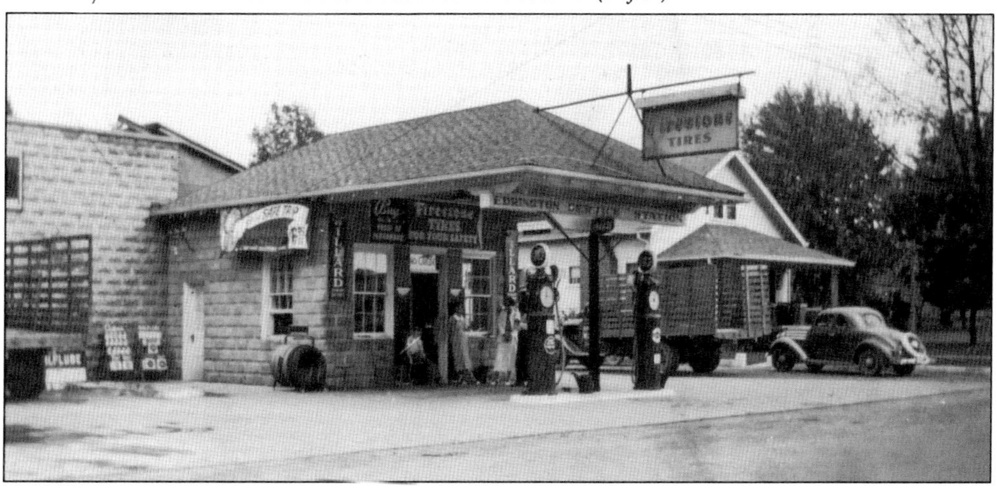

Henry Edrington built his first service station at the corner of Main Street and Lebanon Avenue. In 1930, he joined with J. H. Chandler to build the Court Street Station at the corner of First North and Court Streets. Less than a year later, in June 1931, on behalf of the City Service Station Company, he announced the opening of this station on Columbia Avenue. (BC&MWS.)

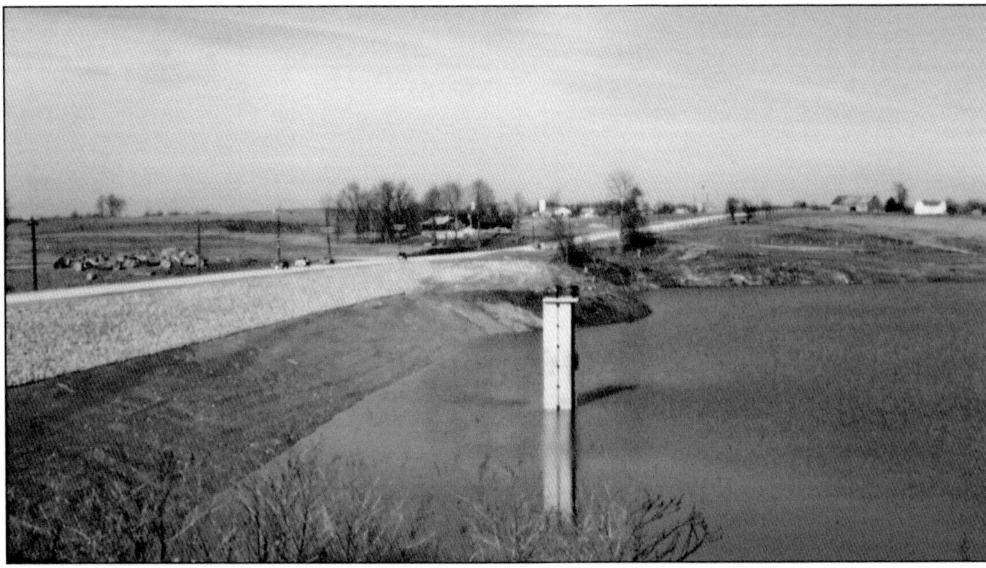

In preparation for expanded industry and growing population, Campbellsville reworked its water system in 1951. Construction for a new dam and increased reservoir size required rerouting the Lebanon road, currently State Highway 289, across the new fill and dam. Here the 15-unit Lakeview Motel is under construction. Built by Roy and Otis Wethington, it opened on Sunday, June 21, 1953. Roy Wethington also owned the eight-unit Lucky Vista Motel across town on the Campbellsville-Columbia Highway that opened in August 1951. In the photograph below, the old Lebanon Road, currently called North Shore Drive, can be seen across the newly created lake. To the right of the road lies the current Johnsport Subdivision. The barn, at top left, stands approximately where Lake Village Furniture and Ace Hardware are now located. (TCHS, above and below.)

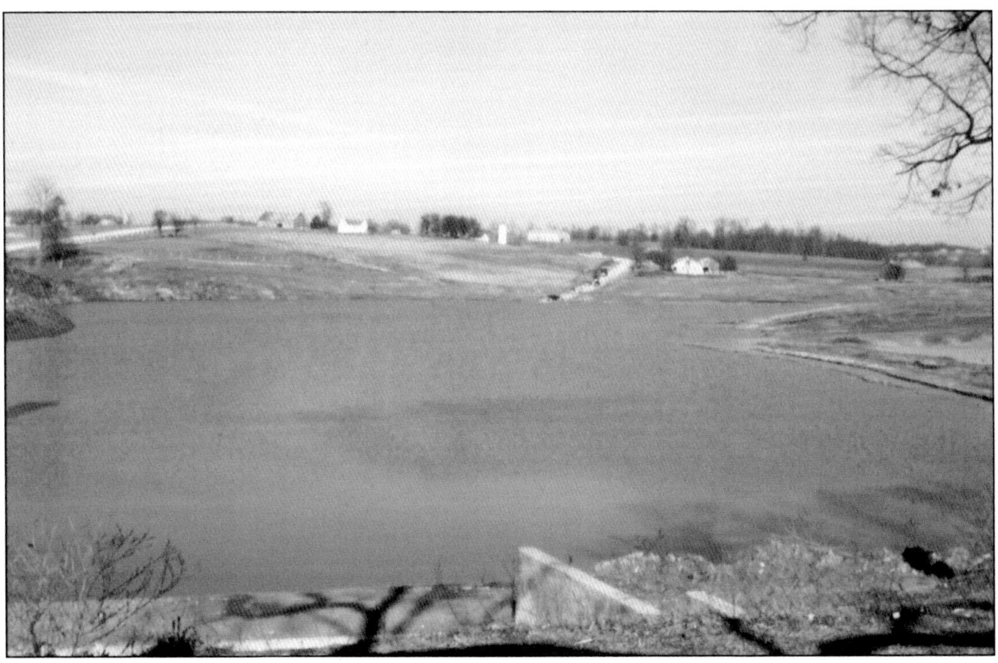

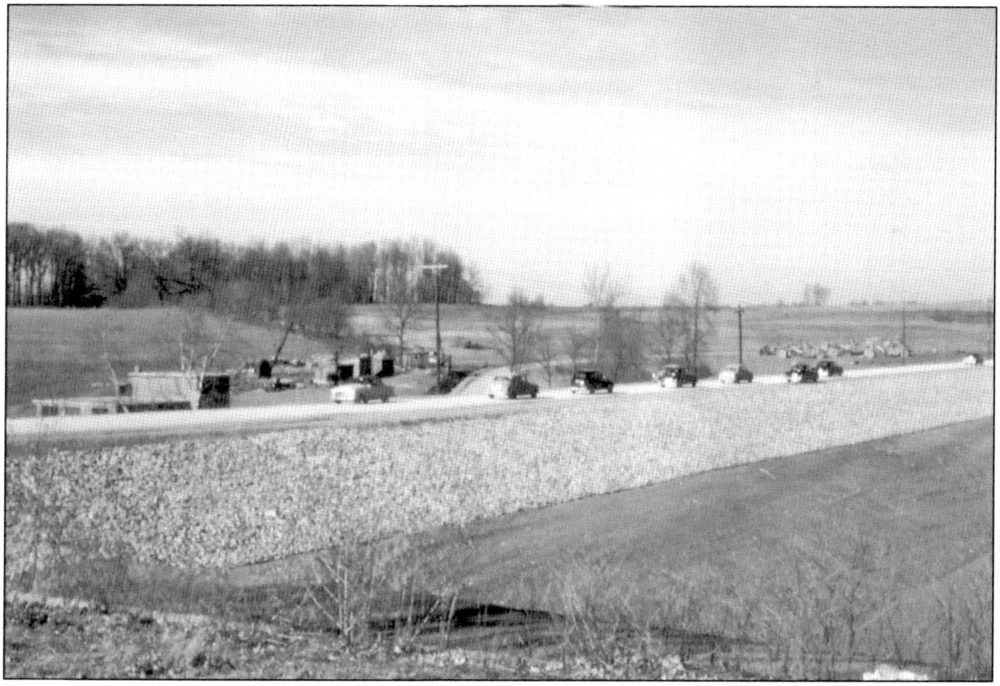

Beginning in 1951, the Campbellsville water system expansion included a new filtration building, which is seen at left. Private financing produced Campbellsville's first water system in 1913. In 1928, the West Virginia Water Company purchased the Campbellsville system and ran it until 1938, when the City Council voted to repurchase the system for $100,000. In this photograph, the lake has yet to reach a full pool. (TCHS.)

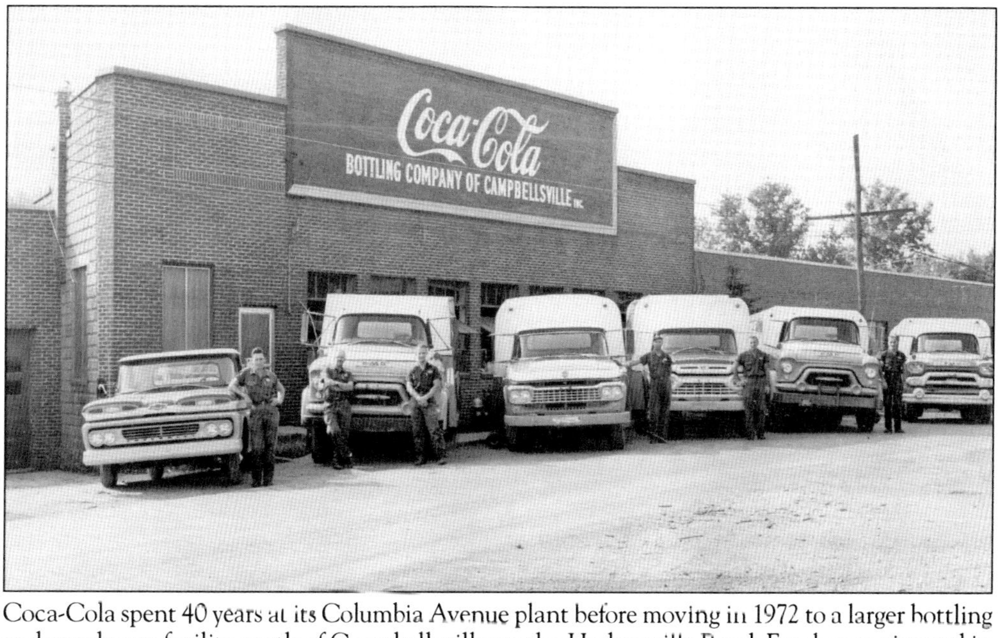

Coca-Cola spent 40 years at its Columbia Avenue plant before moving in 1972 to a larger bottling and warehouse facility north of Campbellsville on the Hodgenville Road. Employees pictured in this 1960 photograph include, from left to right, Albert Long, Paul Coakley, Russell Montgomery, Lawrence Parsons, Jessie Brummett, and Clarence Colvin. (RuM.)

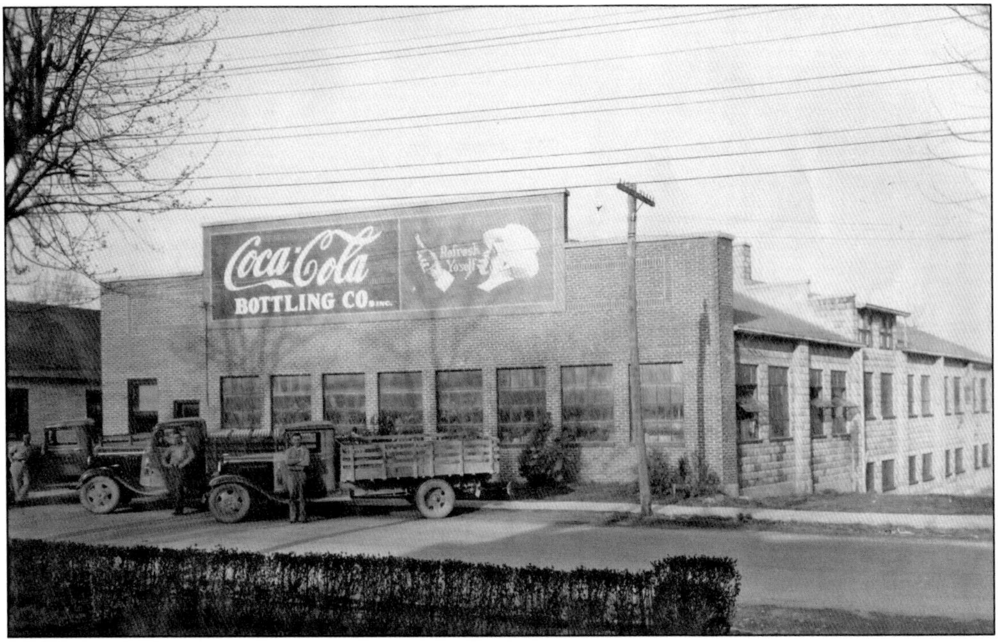

Joe Willock opened the first Coca-Cola Bottling Company on Main Street in 1905, eventually selling the business in 1914 for $10,000. In 1927, under different ownership, Coca-Cola moved to a new building on Columbia Avenue, pictured here. However, Coca-Cola was not the only Campbellsville bottling operation. Soon after Willock started the Coca-Cola plant, William Ottley and Walter Hobson promoted their Grape and Dope-Cola. In 1915, L. E. McKinley began the Gay-Ola Bottling Works and advertised its Orange Smash. In 1927, the Campbellsville Bottling Works bottled Eppings Carbonated Drinks. Finally, in 1930, the John G. Epping Company opened a plant just north of the Columbia Avenue Coca-Cola plant producing products that included a mixer called 4%, that was made with "pure fruit of lime, lemon and grape fruit juices." (RuM, above and below.)

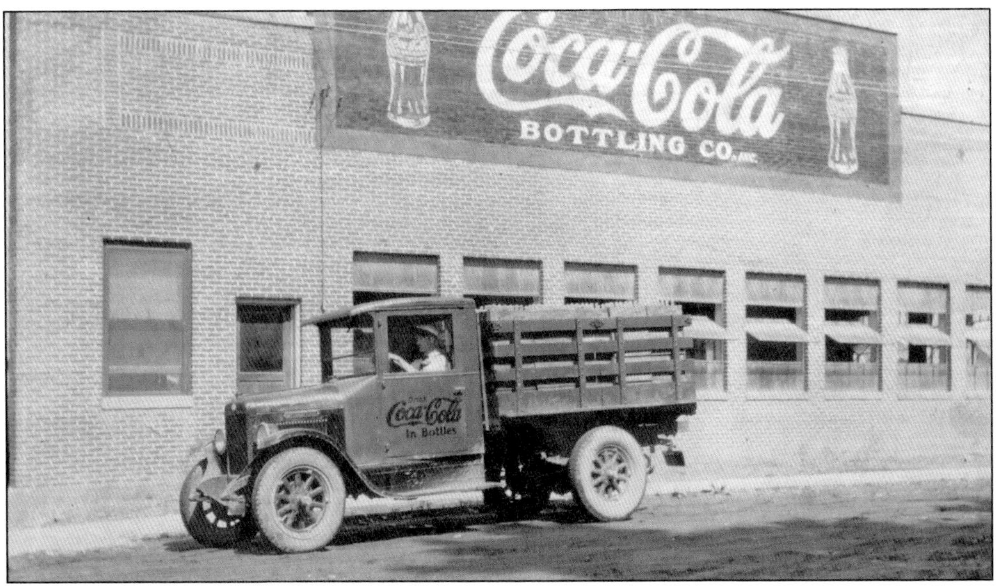

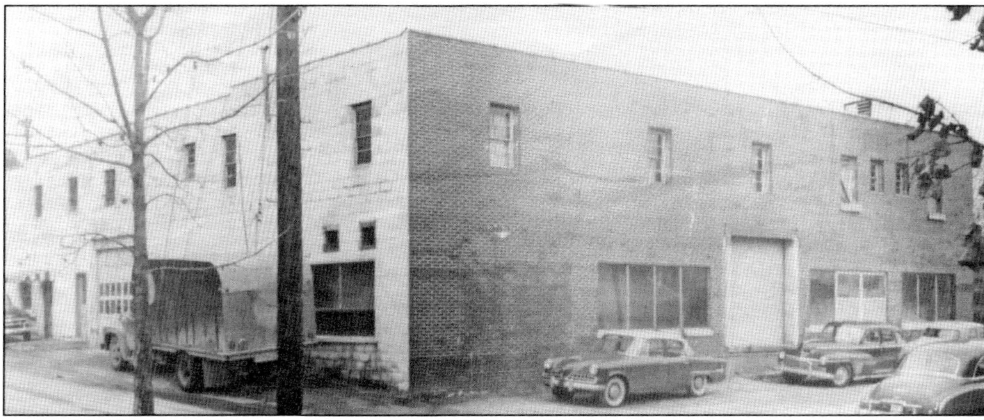

Pictured above, Harlan, Kentucky's Chappell's Dairy began its Campbellsville receiving and pasteurization operation in 1952. A $1 million Grade A production facility added in 1957 processed milk and produced cottage cheese. At its peak, Chappel's Dairy had 19 routes and employed 90 people. The addition of the Grade A market added approximately $1 per 100 pounds for farm producers over the second grade market. In 1947, the Carnation Milk Company, shown below, began purchasing milk for shipment to its plant in Maysville, Kentucky. Soon the plant began evaporating milk in Campbellsville, and in 1958, its initial floor space was tripled with a 17,800-square-foot addition. Carnation received, cleaned, and evaporated 25 to 30 million pounds of milk annually. Beginning in the 1920s, the arrival of these companies resulted from the early twentieth century community effort to improve the dairy herds. (TCL, above and below.)

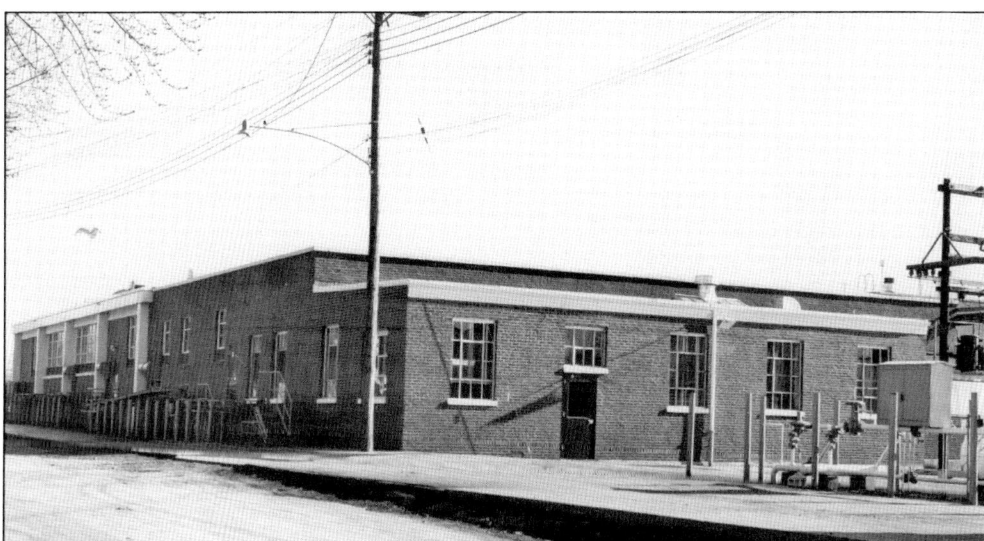

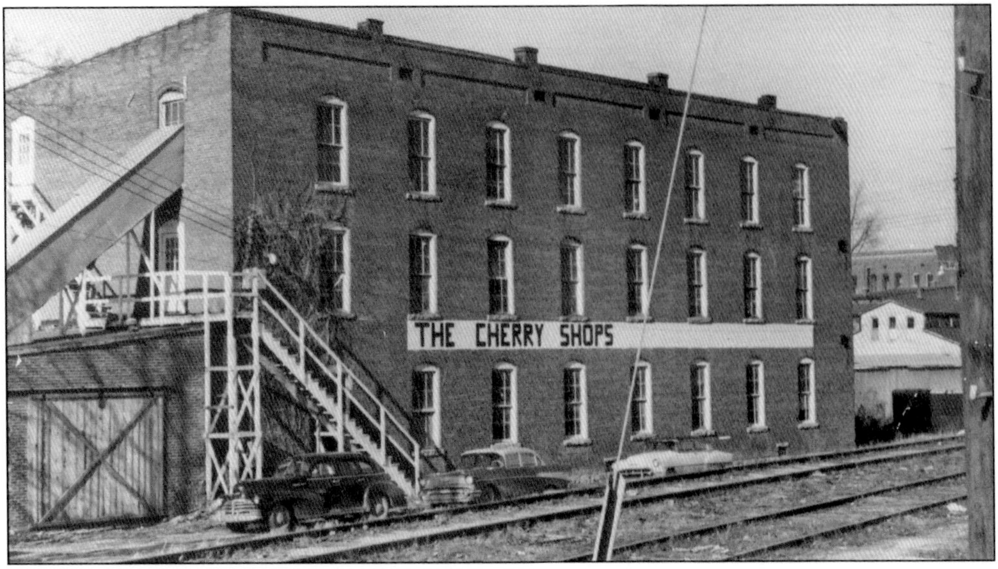

Built about 1885 by Luther Baker Smith and used as a carding mill, the building known as the Old Woolen Mill housed Taylor Manufacturing for two years, before Taylor moved to new facilities on West Main. Following Taylor Manufacturing, Merlin Christie moved his reproduction furniture company from Yuma into the building. Christie called his company the Cherry Shops. By 1960, Christie created another company, Pioneer Furniture, and moved to Lebanon. (TCL.)

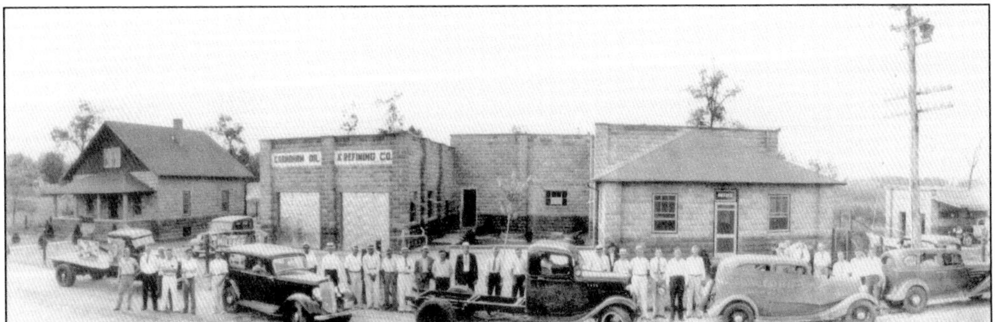

In 1934, Carnahan Oil and Refining built an oil storage and compounding plant at a reported cost of $10,000, located about a half mile south of Campbellsville's city limits on the old Columbia Road. The construction included a warehouse, compounding plant, and a one-story residence for the warehouse operator, all of which replaced a smaller operation built in 1926. Taken during the grand opening, this picture shows the new 1934 Ford models. (TCHS.)

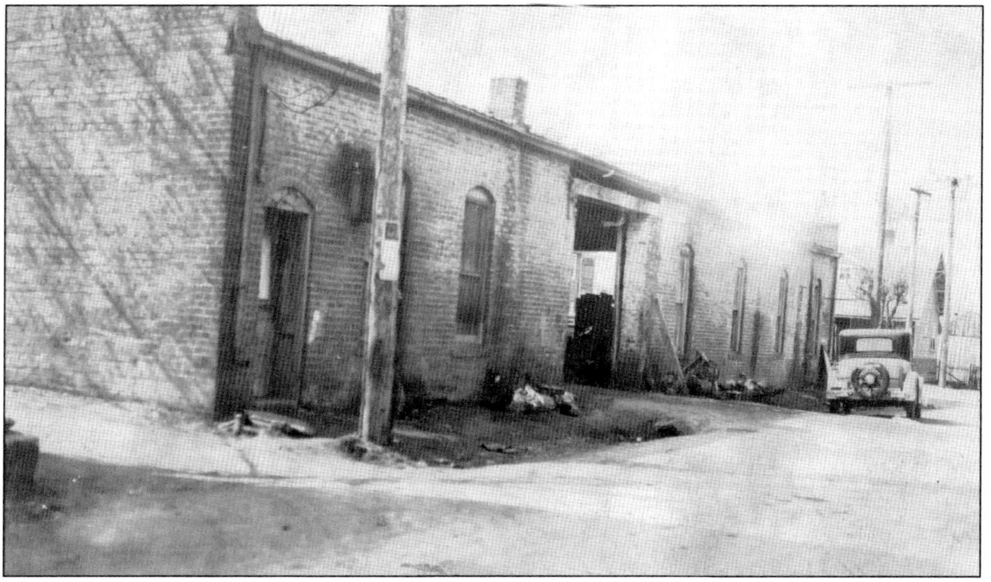

Buchanan-Lyon initially sold its automobiles in a Main Street building currently used for display and storage. By 1915, the company had completed its first garage behind the Main Street building, with floor space for 30 cars. Later the building was home to Super Save Gas, Warren Radiator, and David's Barbershop. The sign at the door advertises Simplex Piston Rings. The building no longer exists, having been replaced by a parking lot. (FHB.)

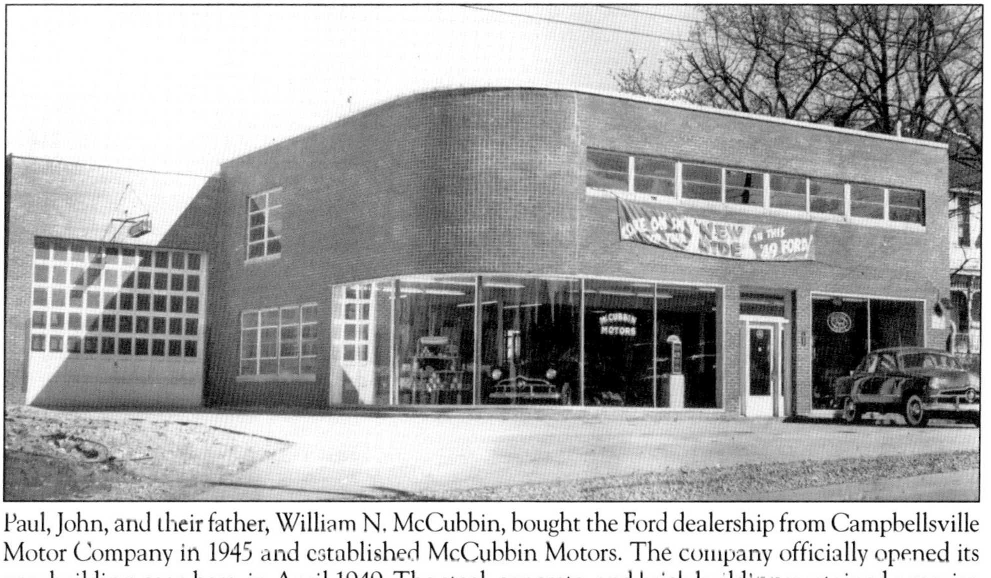

Paul, John, and their father, William N. McCubbin, bought the Ford dealership from Campbellsville Motor Company in 1945 and established McCubbin Motors. The company officially opened its new building, seen here, in April 1949. The steel, concrete, and brick building contained a service department, parts and store room, and a large showroom. At present, the Campbellsville City School Board maintains its central offices in the building. (TCL.)

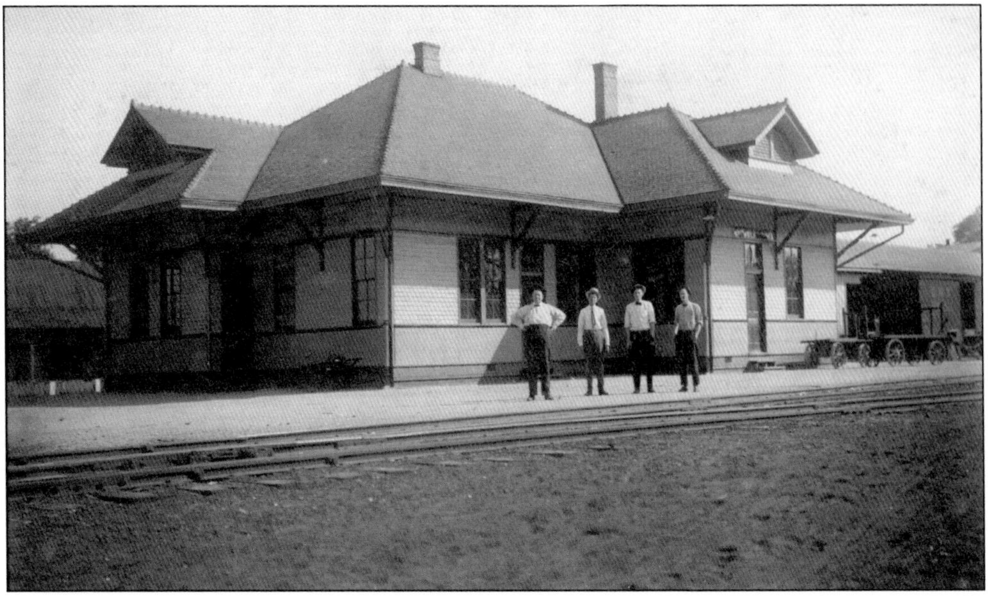

Located on South Central Avenue, formerly Depot Street, this *c.* 1910 Campbellsville Louisville and Nashville Passenger Station replaced an earlier board and batten station. The red-tiled-roof depot contained two waiting rooms and a freight office. The reconstructed board and batten freight office built alongside the depot remains. Standing on the left is J. A. McRoberts, L&N station agent from 1907 to 1927, and on the right is Fred H. Buchanan. (FHB.)

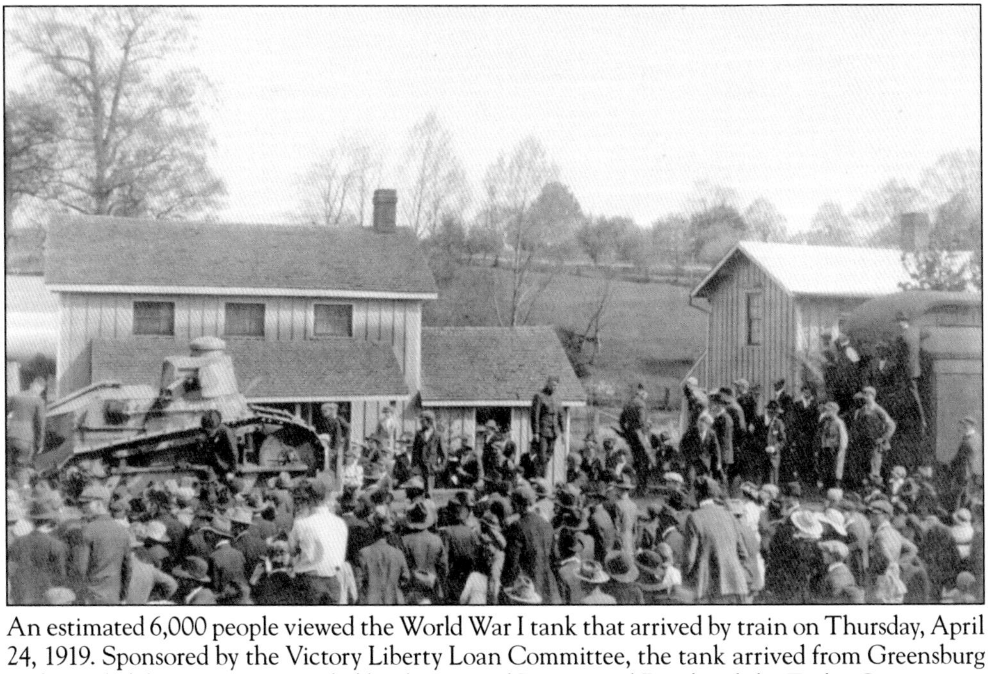

An estimated 6,000 people viewed the World War I tank that arrived by train on Thursday, April 24, 1919. Sponsored by the Victory Liberty Loan Committee, the tank arrived from Greensburg and paraded down Main Street led by the Second Regimental Band and the Taylor County men who served in World War I. (MJG.)

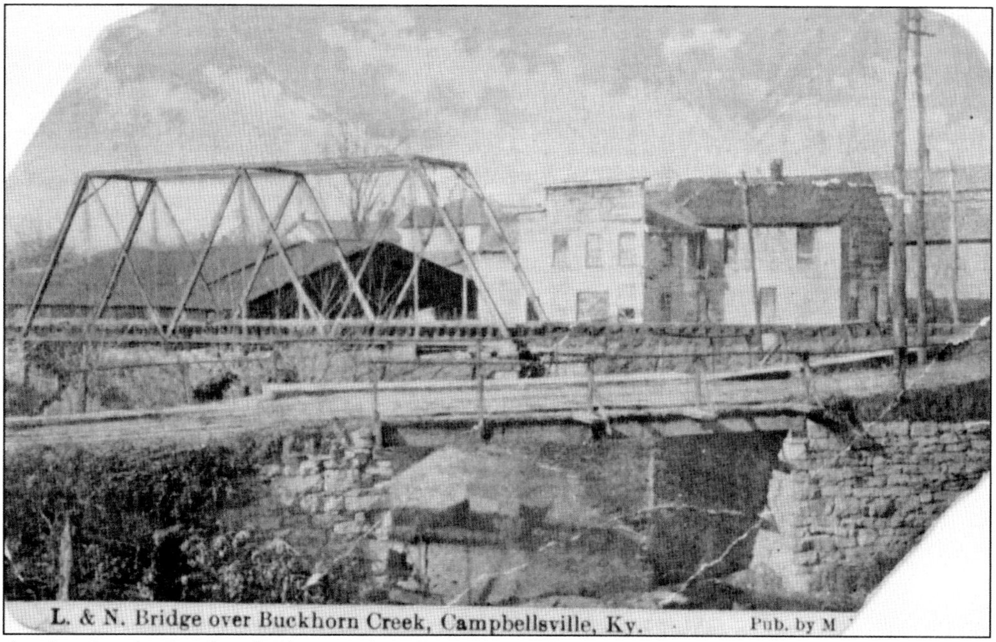

As the Cumberland and Ohio Railroad constructed its line to Greensburg, it began working on the bridge across Campbellsville's Buckhorn Creek in February 1874. When completed, the 75-foot span carried the first train for Greensburg on February 25, 1880. The C&O was eventually absorbed by the Louisville and Nashville Railroad Company. L&N ceased all service to Campbellsville by 1982. (SS.)

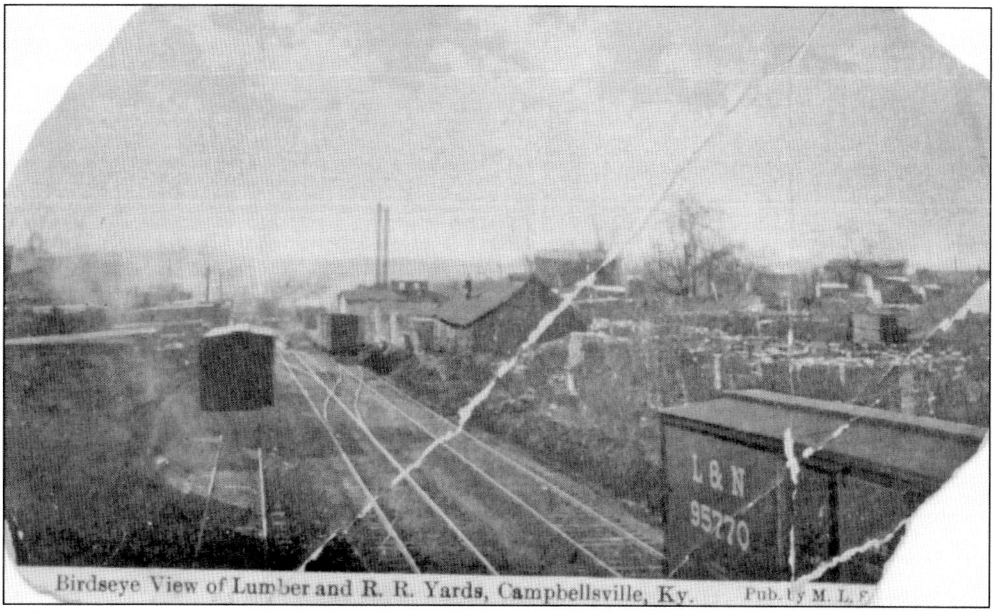

In October 1929, the C. A. West Realty Company of Campbellsville advertised for sale the Log Yard "located near and rear of the Taylor County Milling Company and the Campbellsville Ice Company, at the switch of the L&N." The lot contained approximately two acres with three one-room office buildings, one warehouse, one blacksmith shop, and a residence. This postcard view shows the area being auctioned. (SS.)

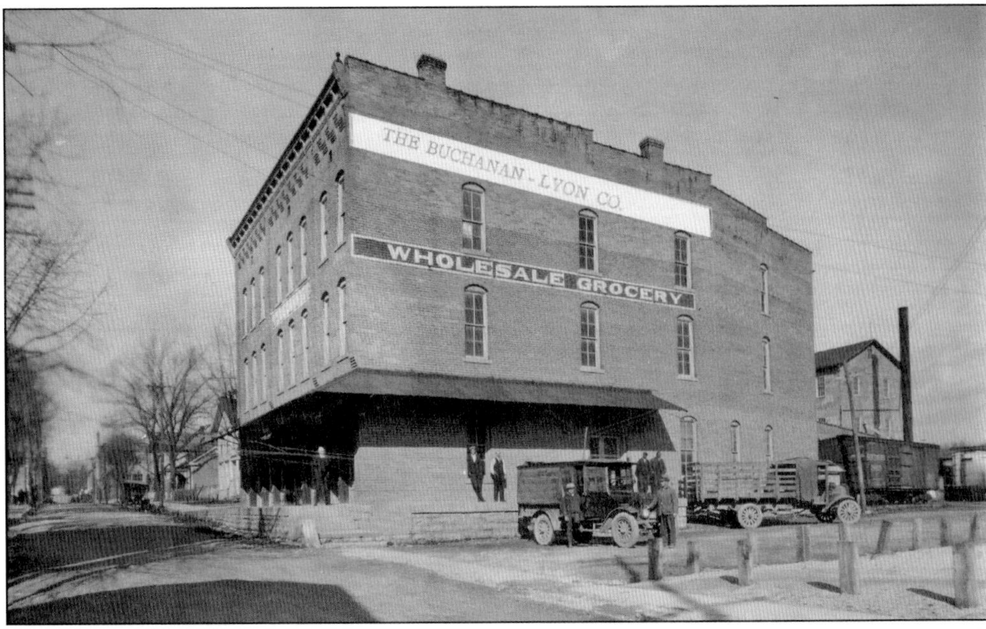

Vance Moore Gowdy built this three-story building on Depot Street in 1912 for his wholesale grocery business, which he moved from a building he owned directly across the street. In addition to his grocery business, Gowdy sold Star and Durant automobiles in Adair and Taylor Counties. He advertised "closed automobiles" that "will keep you warm in the Winter, and keep the dust out in the Summer." (TCHS.)

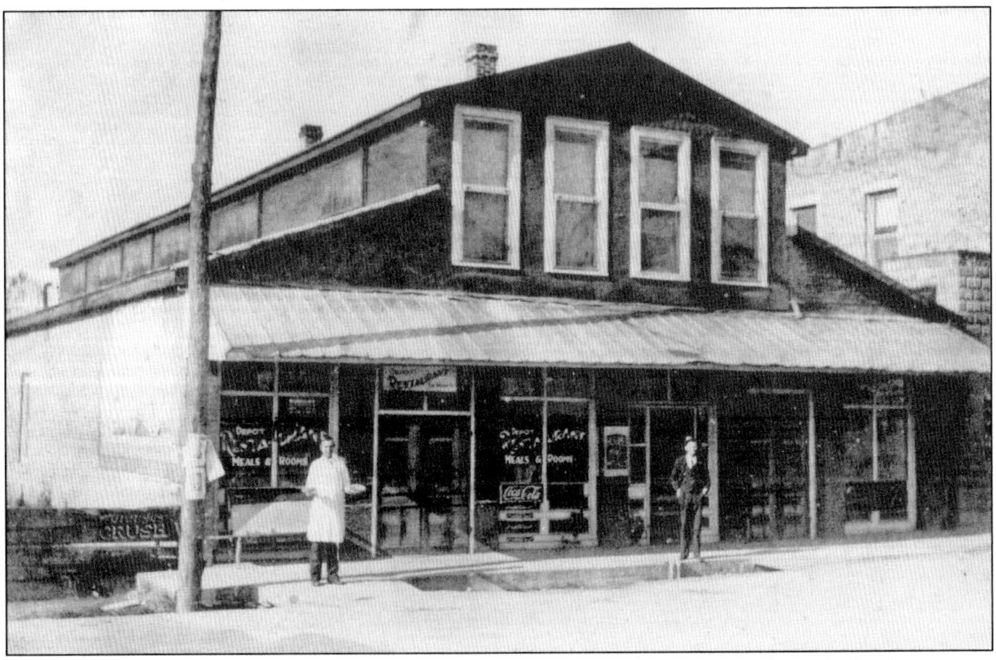

Prior to the Depot Restaurant, this building housed Vance Moore Gowdy's wholesale grocery and the Campbellsville Bottling Works that bottled Eppings Carbonated Drinks, Vichy waters in siphons, and charged water in soda tanks. Various people ran a restaurant in this location including J. W. Moss and Ed Osborn, with William S. Wooley as cook. (TCHS.)

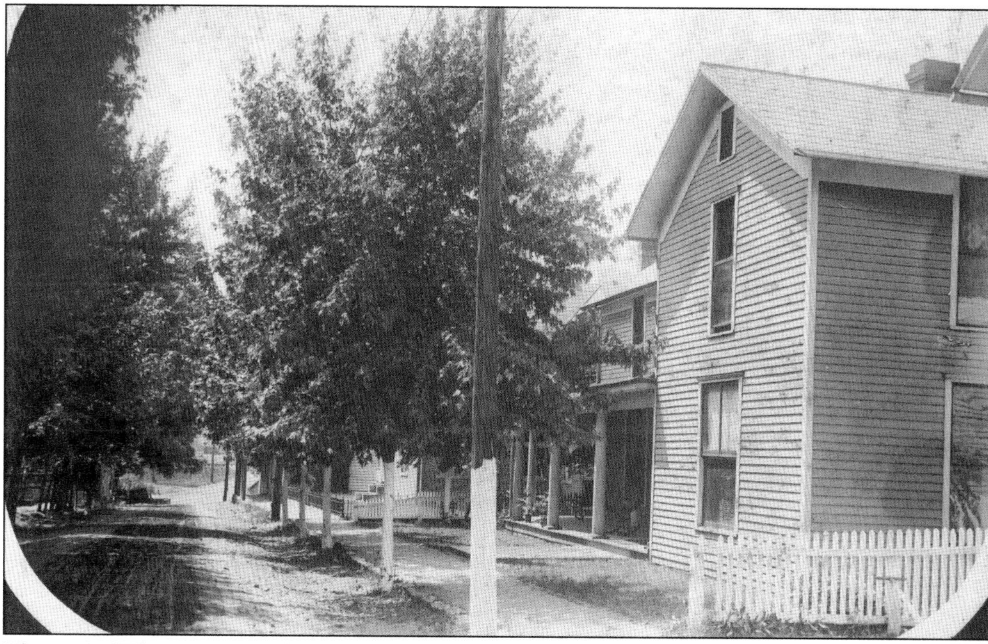

The c. 1916 Thomas W. Buchanan house sat on the west side of South Court Street. Buchanan was part owner of Buchanan-Lyon Hardware and Wholesale Company. In 1924 the firm divided, with the Buchanan family taking the Ford agency and hardware business and renaming it Central Sales. William Lyon took the wholesale grocery business, which eventually moved into the Vance Gowdy building on South Depot Street. Buchanan-Lyon later became Marcum Wholesale. (FHB.)

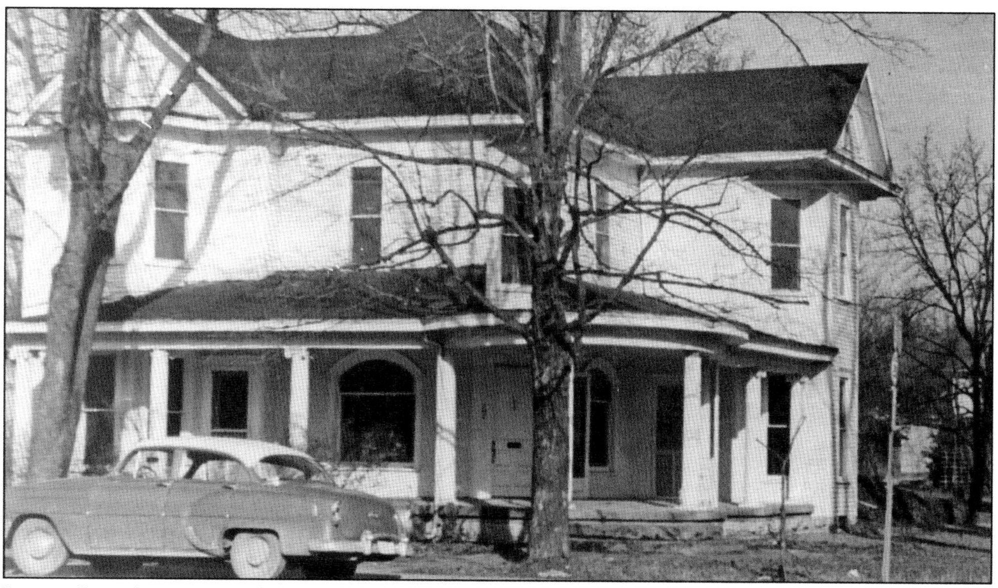

Located on the corner of Main Street and Lebanon Avenue, John Q. Alexander built the house that later became known as the J. A. Hubbard Home. A Metcalfe County native, Hubbard conducted successful businesses in Green County before moving to Campbellsville in 1916, where he remained an active businessman and citizen until his death. A Sunoco station replaced the house, and a Firestone store currently sits on the lot. (SS.)

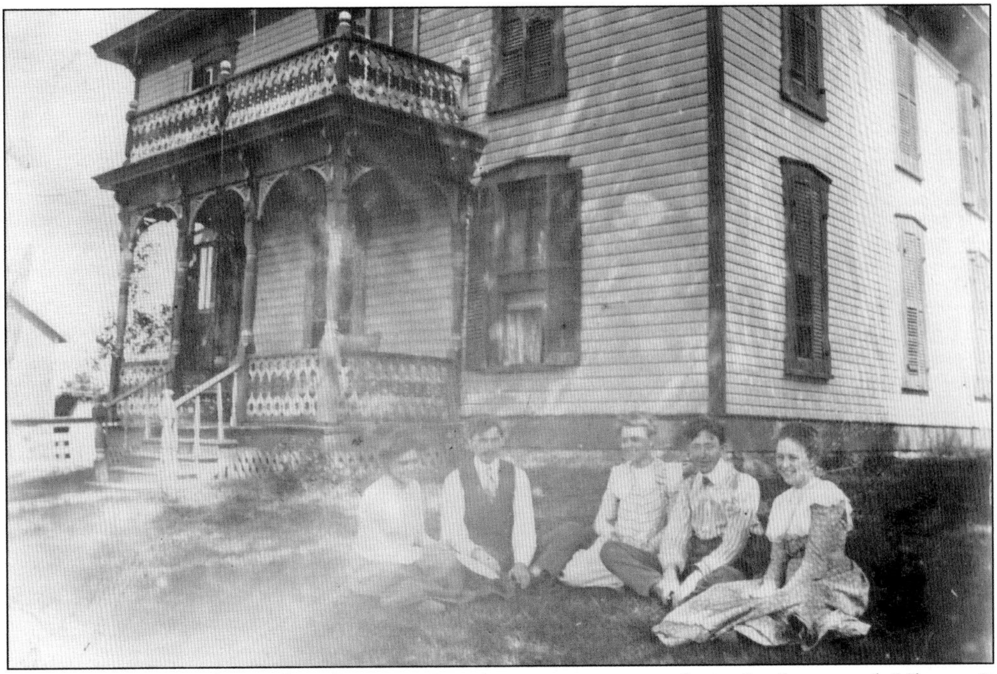

The picture shows the Walling home with unknown young people in the front yard. Ulysses P. Walling was part owner of Campbellsville Lumber Company. A Parkersburg, West Virginia, native, he moved to Campbellsville about 1887, where he became a partner in Campbellsville Lumber. Prominent in the community, he served as Campbellsville's mayor for three years. (GS.)

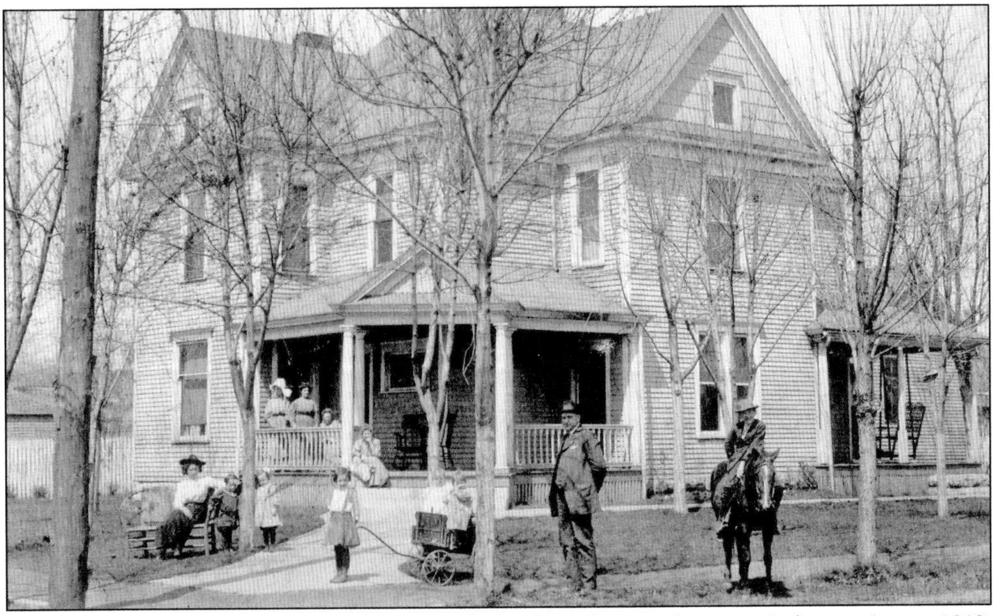

This photograph shows a family gathering at the William R. Lyon home on Lebanon Ave. c. 1912. Pictured are William's family and his brother Robert's families, from left to right: (on the porch) Lucy Lyon, Hattie Shirley, Ivy Lyon, and Hattye Gowdy; (in the yard) Ruth Lyon, James Lyon, Elizabeth Lyon (Robert and Lucy Lyon's daughter), Prudence Lyon, William Lyon Jr., Martha (Robert and Lucy Lyon's daughter), William R. Lyon, and Alvin Lyon. (TCHS.)

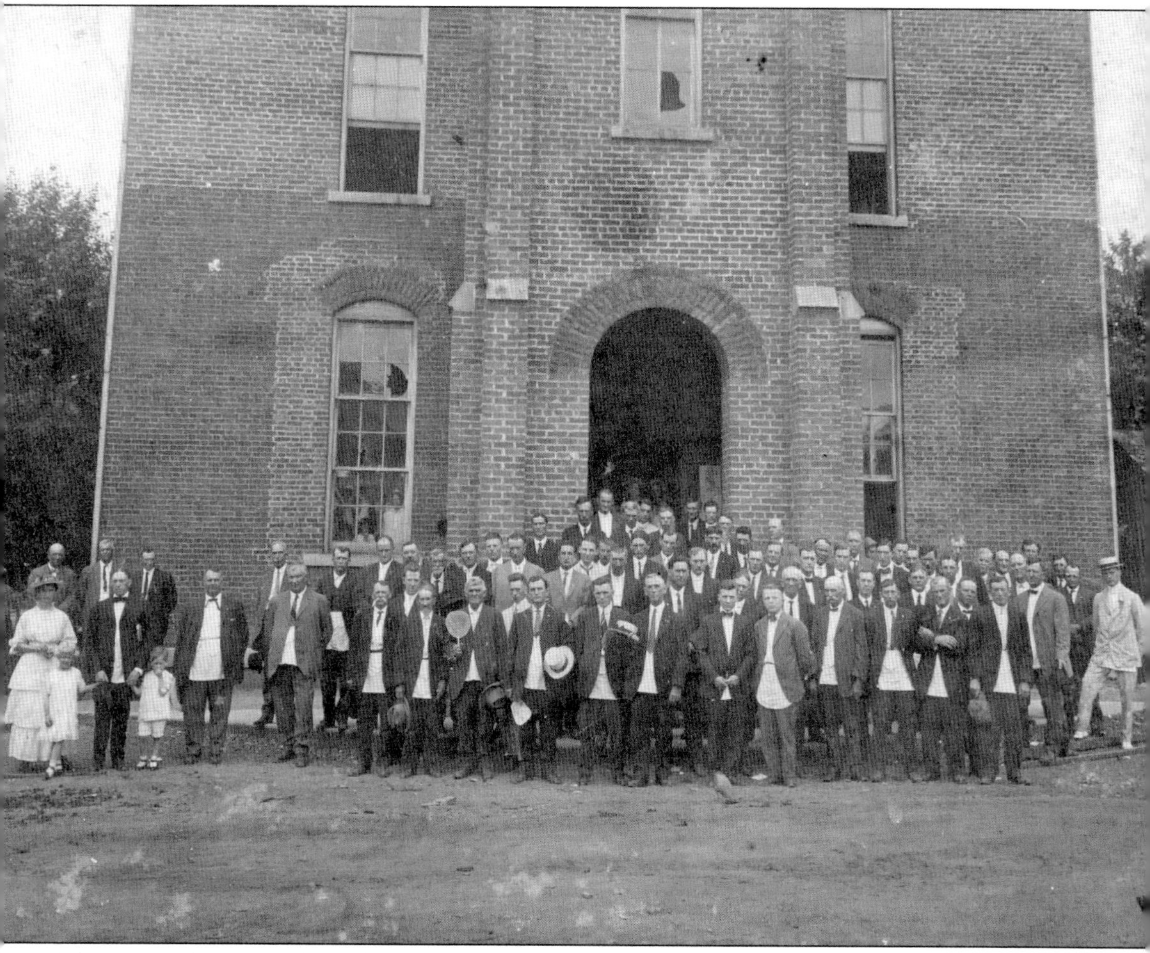

This image shows members of the Pitman Lodge No. 124 Free and Accepted Masons in front of an early courthouse. To the left is Rev. Wyatt G. Montgomery, at that time pastor of the Christian Church, with his wife Ida and unidentified daughters. They were passing by and were invited to be in the picture. While not all of the faces are identified, the picture is known to include Martin L. Spurling, Chris Smith, John Rhinehart, Johnnie Rickets, Jodie Gozder, Frank Rice, Guy Lindsey, G. C. Flora, Isaac T. Bomar, W. L. Hall, Alf Wade, Herman V. Shively, Ed Hill, Eugene Rice, Samuel E. Kerr, W. T. Hendrickson, John R. Durham, Ernest Smith, Robert Borders, George Giles, E. L. Bain, Bid Rice, W. J. Arvin, John R. Hubbard, George Whitlock, Frank Risen, Grady Risen, William Lyon, John McRoberts, Dave Thurman, Marvin Rice, Tom Turner, and Frank Gabbert. The lodge held meetings on the third floor of the Willock Opera House. (TCHS.)

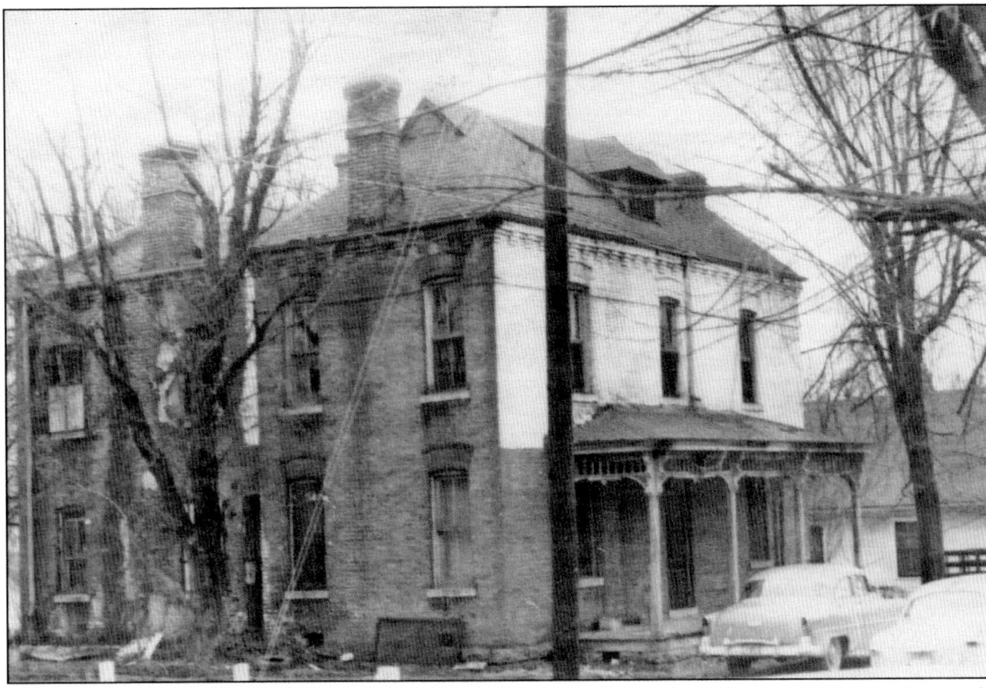

The City of Campbellsville began work in July 1958 to take down the old county jail it had recently purchased. The city offered the jail cells for sale, along with the bricks. Built c. 1899 during John W. Cloyd's judgeship, it replaced a log jail that had been sold and moved. The County Court replaced the old jail with a three-story structure that was built to handle 40 prisoners. (TCL.)

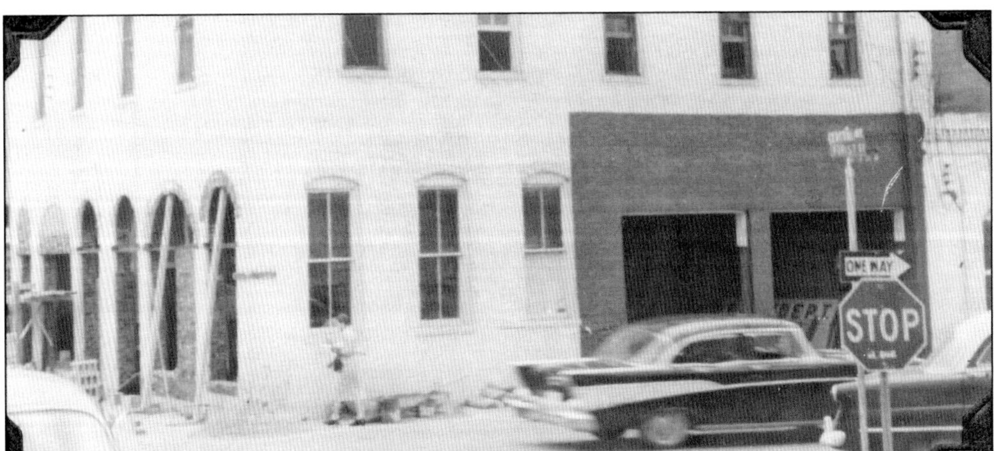

On May 12, 1960, the City of Campbellsville sold the former city building on the corner of First Street and Central Avenue, which had been purchased for city offices and a fire department in September 1938. Cain Realty moved into the building in 1967 and began a remodel that covered the arched windows facing Central Avenue. An upstairs apartment currently exists in the building, but the first floor is vacant. (TCL.)

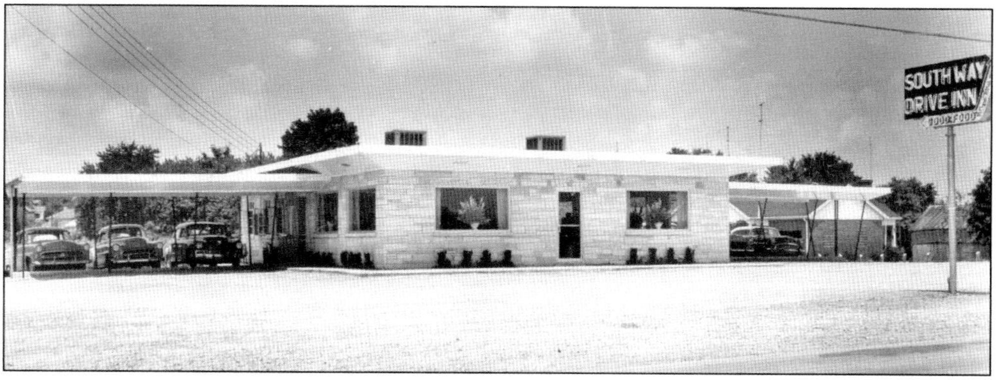

One of Campbellsville's most popular mid-20th-century restaurants opened in July 1955. Built by Fletcher Phillips, the Southway Drive-In on the Columbia Road featured curbside service and air-conditioned dining. A Taylor County native, Phillips operated a hotel in Marion, Ohio, before returning to Campbellsville and starting the U.S. Highway 68 Drive-In on Lebanon Road in 1953. Phillips's Southway was larger and more attractive, with its Bedford stone exterior. (TCL.)

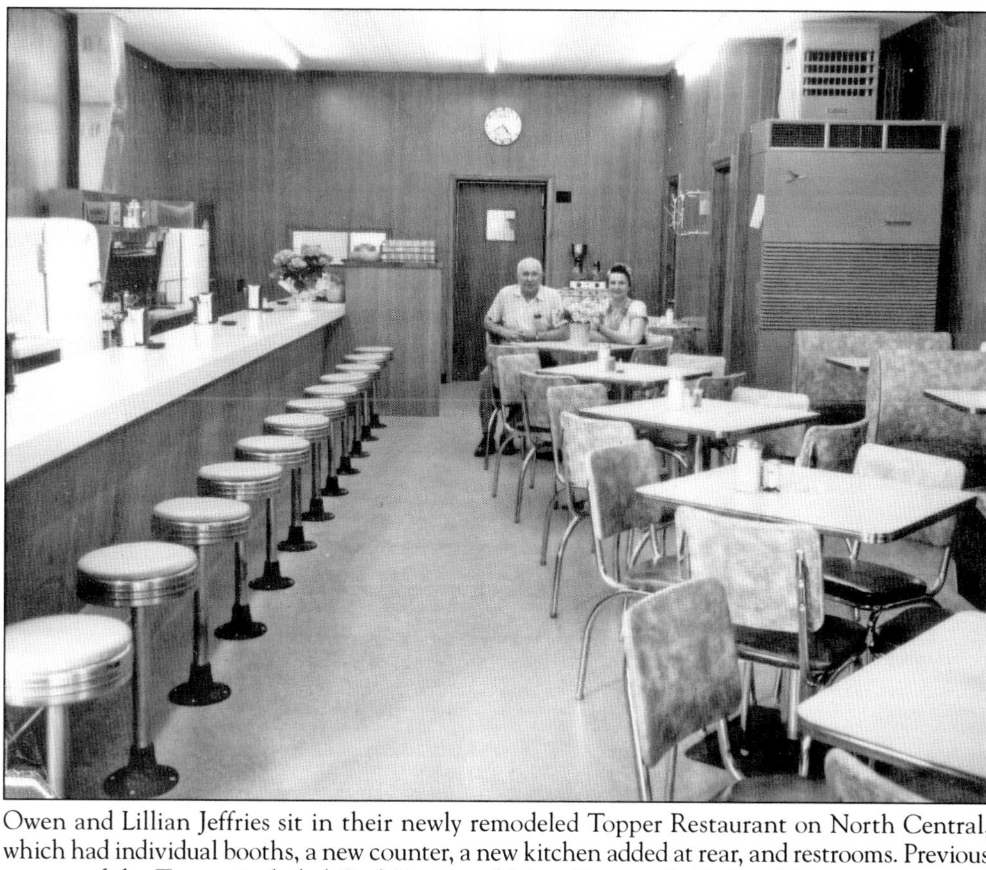

Owen and Lillian Jeffries sit in their newly remodeled Topper Restaurant on North Central, which had individual booths, a new counter, a new kitchen added at rear, and restrooms. Previous owners of the Topper included Carl Davis and Mazy Benningfield. In addition to its regular restaurant service, the Topper served as a meeting place for various local clubs. The building has been replaced by a United Methodist Church annex. (TCL.)

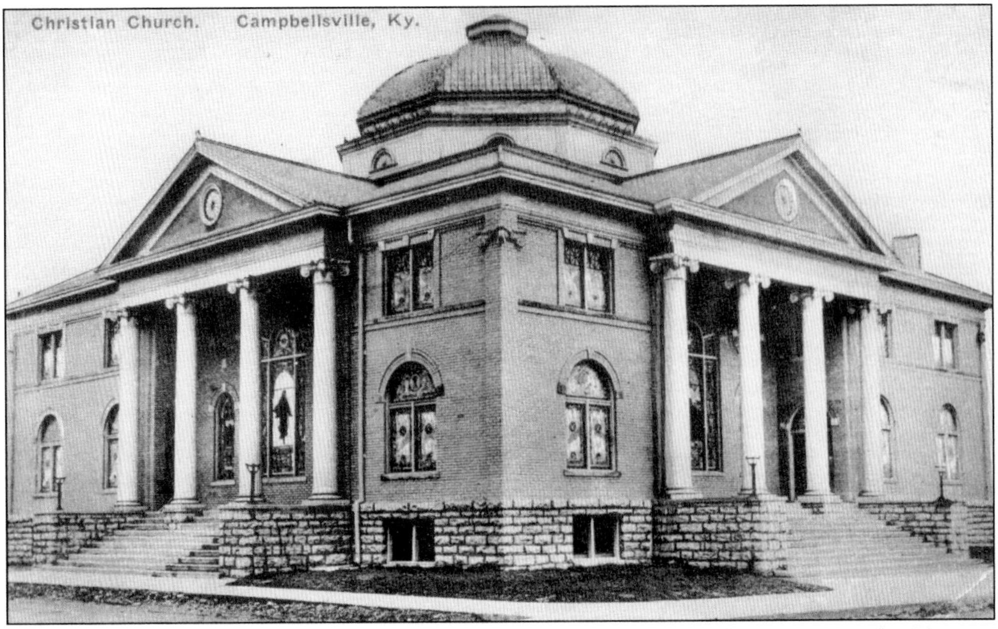

According to tradition, Campbellsville's first Christian church held services in a building in present day Brookside Cemetery. However, the building was so damaged from use as a hospital during the Civil War that the church ceased meeting there. In 1915, the congregation contracted with James C. Miller Sr. to build the present Campbellsville Christian Church, replacing an 1884 frame church across the street. (F&CK.)

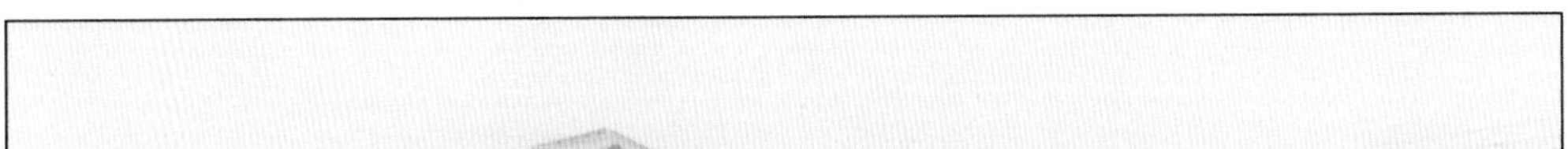

Tracing its roots to the Robinson Creek and Pitman Creek congregations, the Campbellsville Baptist Church first held services in town on the site of the present Taylor County Library. In 1915, the congregation built the brick church pictured here. The picture also shows the beginnings of an educational wing being added to this, the third permanent church building. This building burned in 1962. (TCL.)

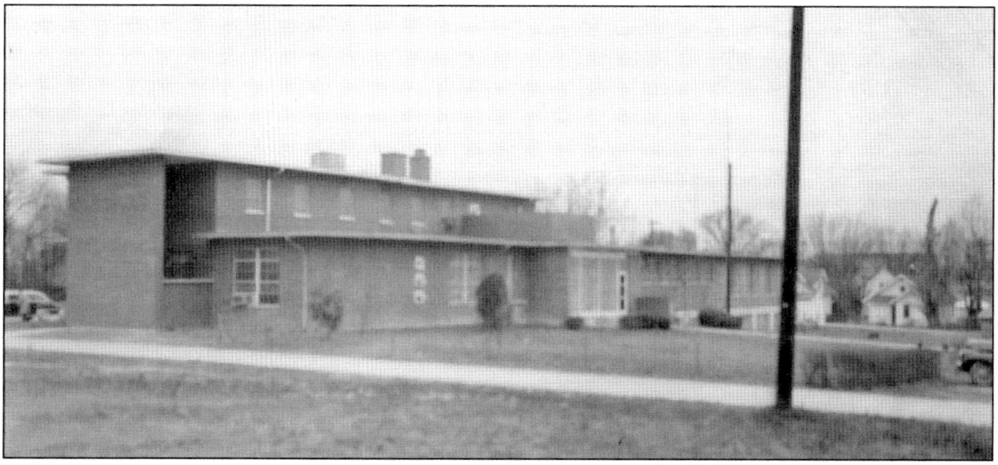

The Dominican Sisters of St. Catherine built Rosary Hospital in 1947 on Central and College Streets. With funds raised by the community, about $60,000 of the $156,000 needed went to complete a basement and the first floor. The initial plans by Thomas J. Nolan and Sons of Louisville called for 33 rooms. Federal funds matched local contributions to build a second floor in 1953, allowing the hospital to handle 50 patients. (TCL.)

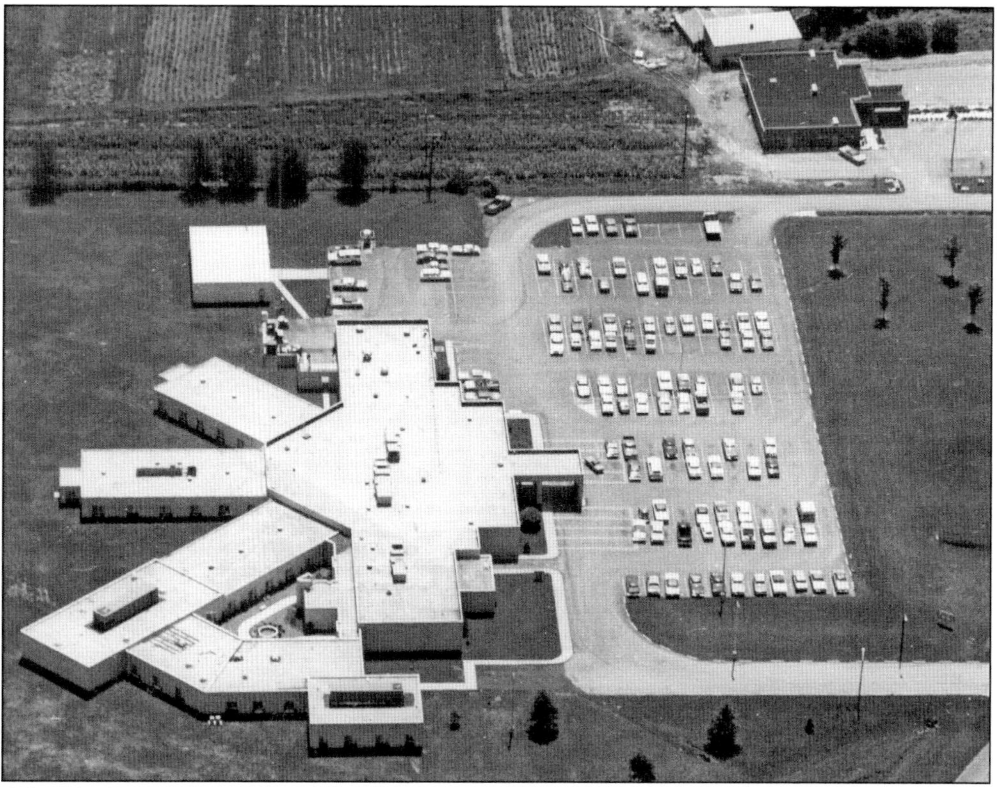

After the Dominican Sisters announced that they would no longer be able to support Rosary Hospital, a 1968 study by a Dayton, Ohio, consultant recommended a new 60- to 65-bed public hospital for Taylor County. The new hospital came to fruition when Taylor County Hospital, above, began receiving patients in 1973. Early efforts for a public hospital began in 1923, when William R. Lyon offered $500 and a location. (TCHS.)

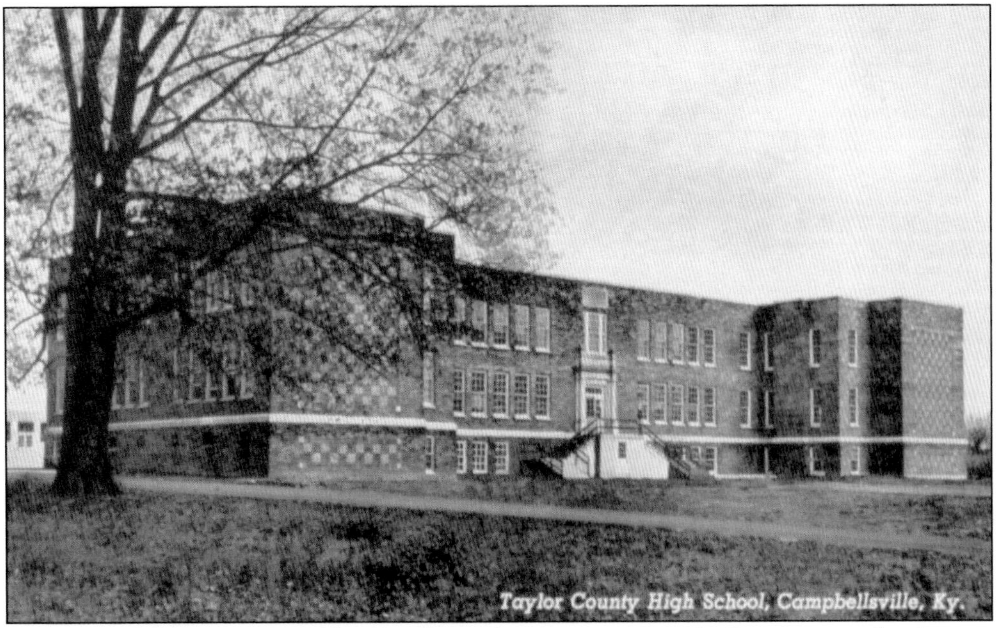

The Taylor County Board of Education located a 10-acre site on the Turner estate for the new Taylor County School building in 1939. The building was constructed in 1940, with students occupying the building in October 1941. An elementary addition was added in 1956. The building is used at present for the Taylor County Elementary School, with a high school located on East Broadway. (F&CK.)

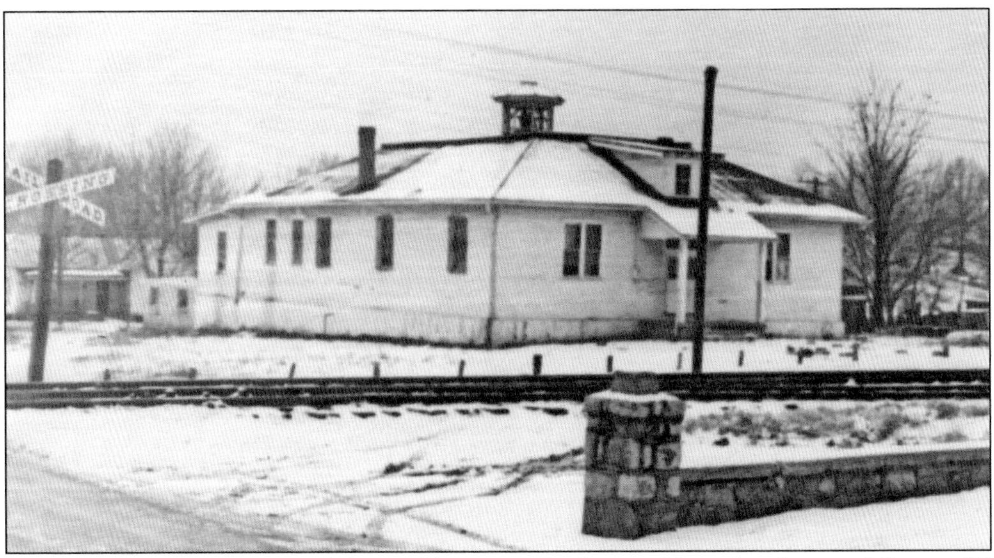

Durham School began on land donated by G. W. Buchanan. Named in honor of George W. Durham, one of the school's first trustees, the building in this picture was one of 158 African American schools built with matching funds provided by Julius Rosenwald, president of Sears and Roebuck. In 1939, Durham Graded and High School opened with a four-year program, the first high school for African Americans in the county. (MS.)

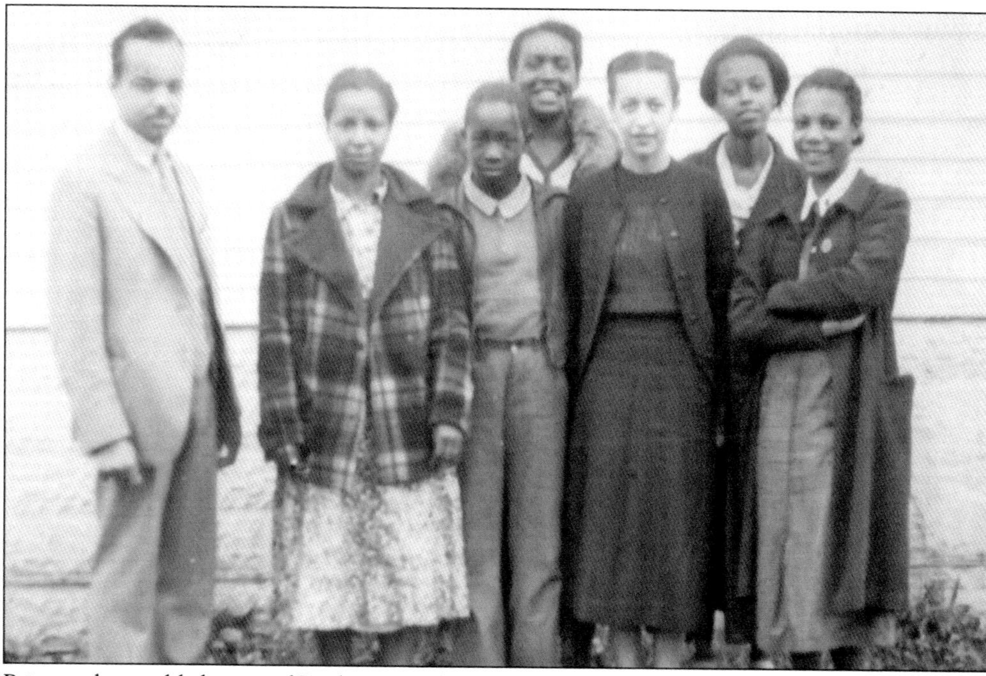

Prior to the establishment of Durham Graded and High, African American students attended six one-room schools in the county and one elementary in Campbellsville. Durham traces its roots back to land purchased in 1867 that was "to be used for church and school purposes forever." In about 1935 or 1936, Durham students include, from left to right, Principal A. Clinton Bishop, Vanetta Turner, Henry R. Richardson, Lena Durham, Christine Hodgen, Geneva McClair, and Catherine Robinson. (TCHS.)

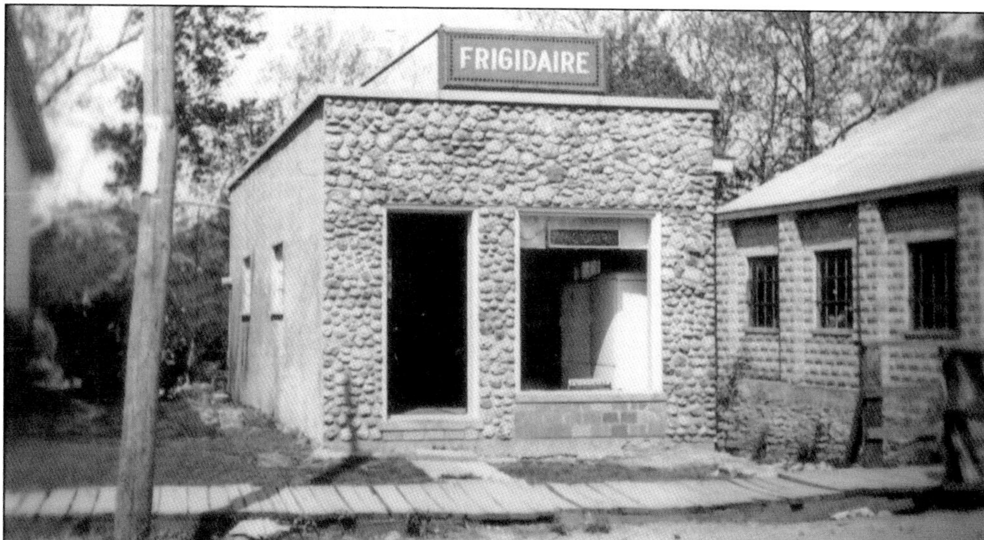

Ernest W. "Petey" Willock operated an appliance store on South Columbia Avenue adjacent to Buckhorn Creek, from which he sold Frigidaire appliances. Prior to his entrance into the applicance business, Willock sold Indian motorcycles and ran a skating rink. Partially visible in this picture across the creek to the right is Alvin C. Watson's garage, which later became the John G. Epping Bottling Company. (MJG.)

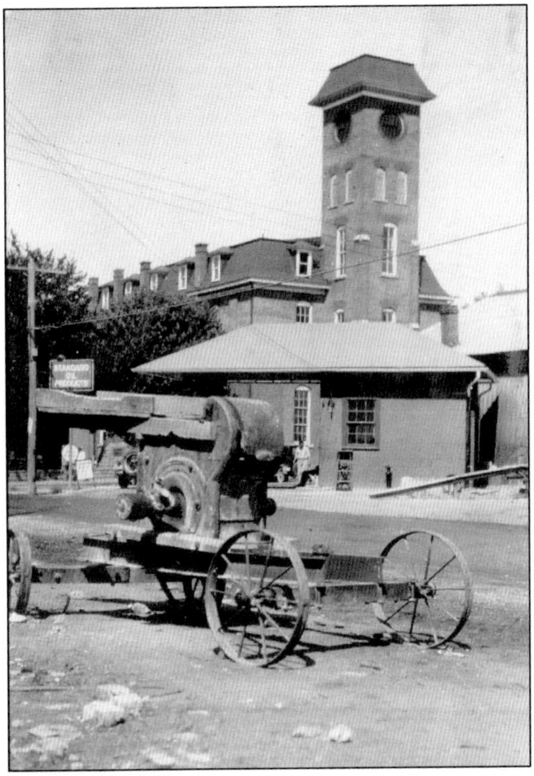

In 1935, at a cost of $1,392, Taylor Fiscal Court purchased a trailer-crusher to crush stone for roads. Machine-crushed stone hastened improved roads and replaced the previous method of crushing stone by hammer. The tractor-powered rock crusher pictured here across from the Taylor County Courthouse in June 1931 had been furnished by the state Highway Department. (FHB.)

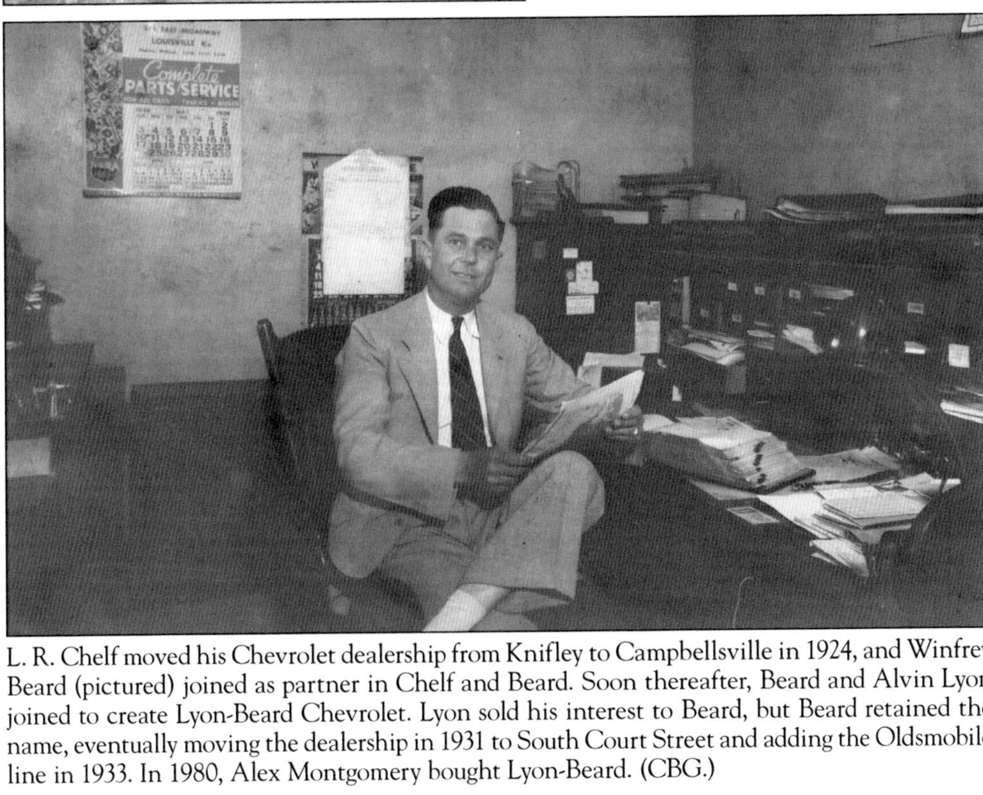

L. R. Chelf moved his Chevrolet dealership from Knifley to Campbellsville in 1924, and Winfrey Beard (pictured) joined as partner in Chelf and Beard. Soon thereafter, Beard and Alvin Lyon joined to create Lyon-Beard Chevrolet. Lyon sold his interest to Beard, but Beard retained the name, eventually moving the dealership in 1931 to South Court Street and adding the Oldsmobile line in 1933. In 1980, Alex Montgomery bought Lyon-Beard. (CBG.)

An accomplished singer and instrumentalist, Mary Dixie Wade studied at Campbellsville College and the Cincinnati Conservatory of Music, often performing on Louisville's WHAS radio. In 1929, she coauthored with Mary Margaret Sanders *Phi Chi Girl*, a song dedicated to the Phi Chi Medical Society, of which her husband, Dr. Henry H. Moody, was a member. She is pictured here with Dr. Richard Felts, who spent his life serving patients in Texas. (JFM.)

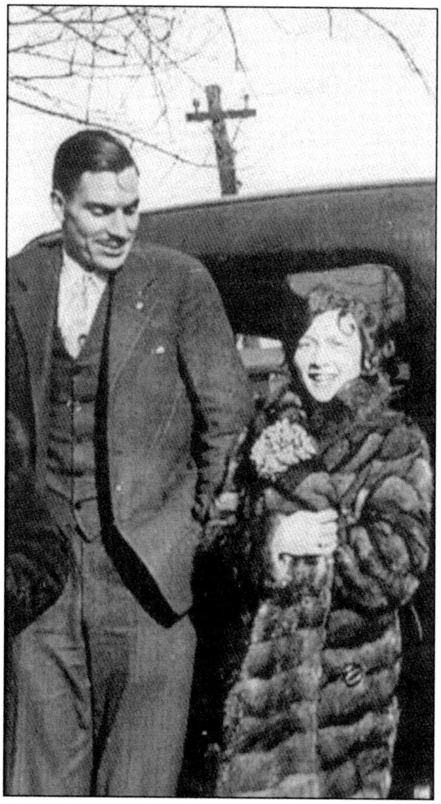

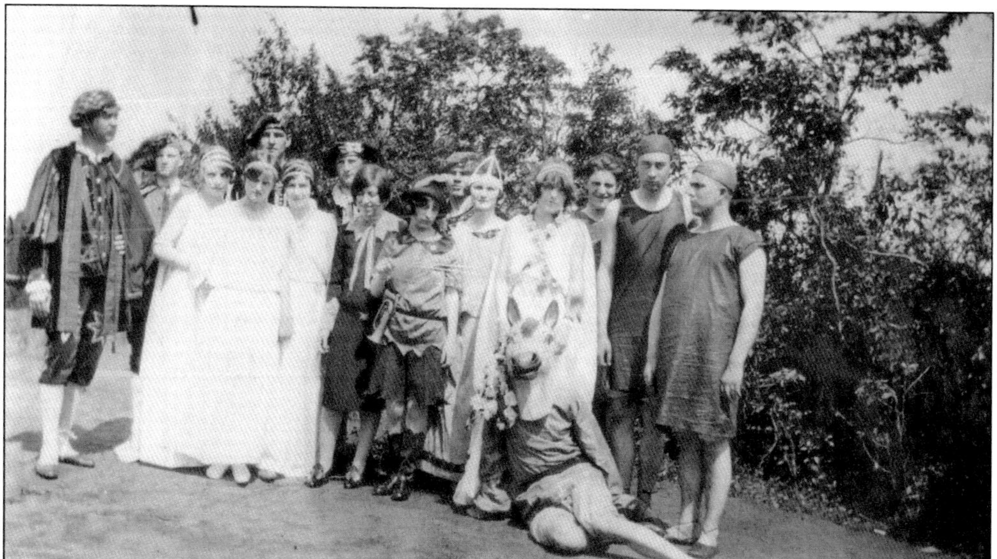

Announced as the first Shakespearean play to be presented in Campbellsville, Campbellsville College sophomores offered their version of *A Midsummer Night's Dream* at the college gymnasium on May 20, 1927. Though the individuals in this photograph are unidentified, the cast included many Campbellsville residents such as Cyrus Skaggs, William Lyon, James Bailey, Martha Lyon, June Mitchell, Mary Frances Hackley, and Mary Lois Harding. Reserved seats sold for 75¢. (JFM.)

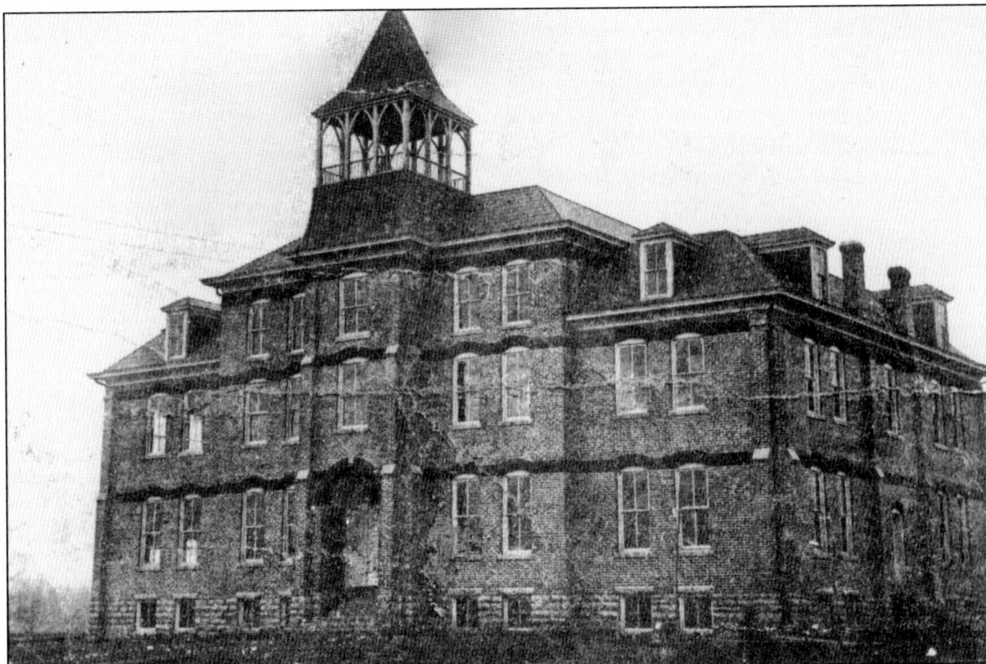

The Russell Creek Academy's original administration building was constructed in 1907. It housed eight classrooms, music and art rooms, a cloakroom, and administrative offices. In 1924, the former Russell Creek Academy became a two-year college known as Campbellsville Junior College. Thirty-five years later the school became a fully accredited four-year school called Campbellsville College. (ABC-CU)

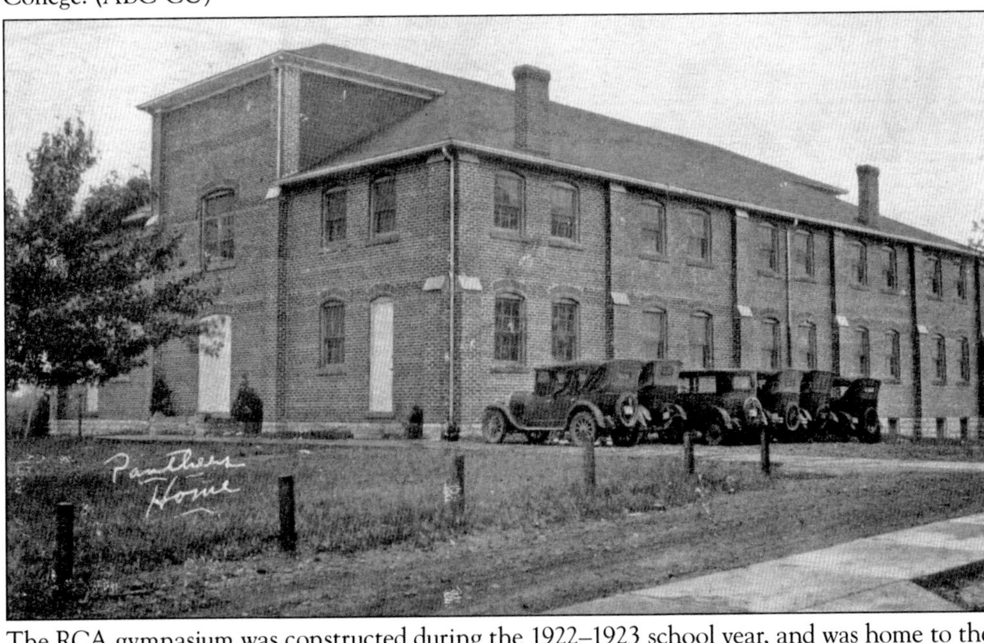

The RCA gymnasium was constructed during the 1922–1923 school year, and was home to the Russell Creek Academy Panthers basketball team. The brick building was renovated in 1991 to become the Student Activity Center for Campbellsville University. It also holds the offices of the Distance Education faculty. (ABC-CU)

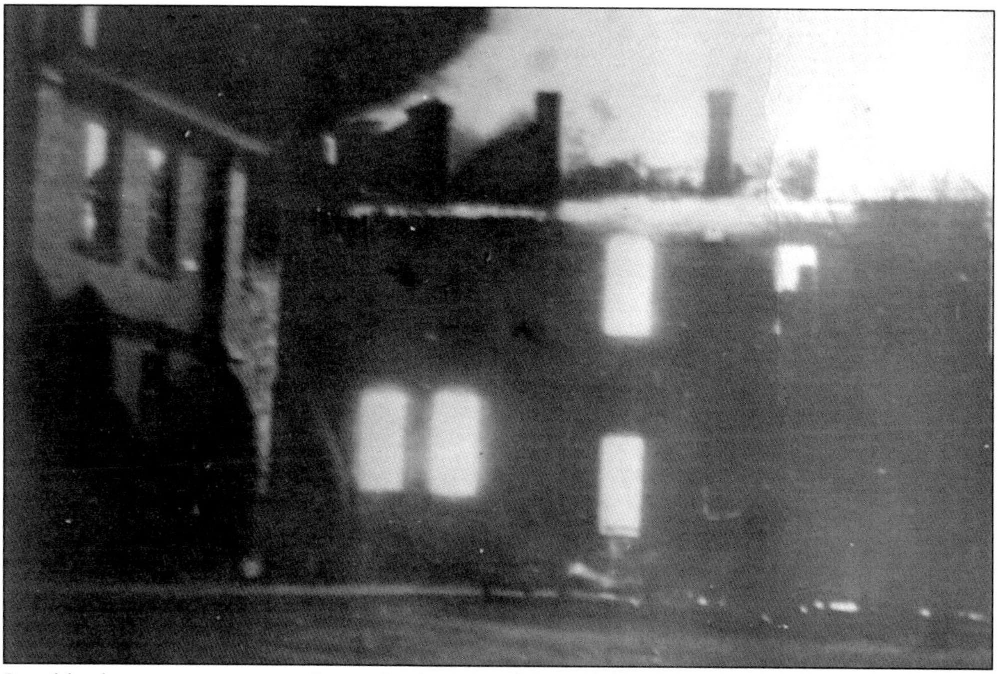

Possibly the greatest catastrophe in the history of Campbellsville University occurred on April 14, 1939, when the original administration building was engulfed by fire. The negative effect of the conflagration to Campbellsville Junior College was obvious to all who watched the flames, because the building housed the administrative offices, classrooms, scientific laboratories, and the library. In the April 1939 meeting, the trustees decided to rebuild the administration building. Completed and opened for classes in January 1940, the building remains in use today. (ABC-CU, above and below.)

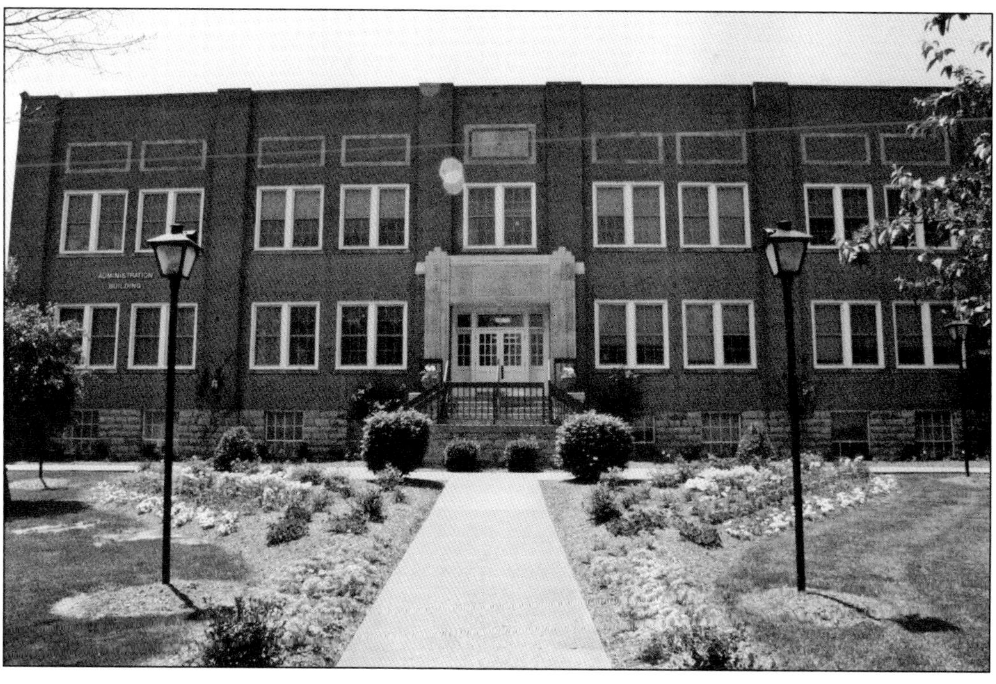

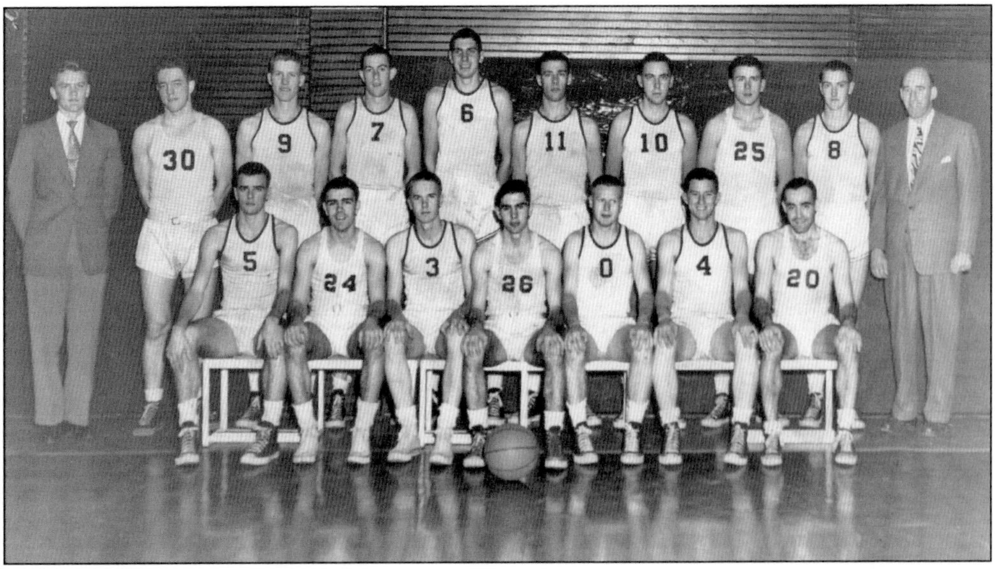

Born in Fayette County, Kentucky, Donald Doyle (standing at right) played basketball for two years under UK Coach Adolph Rupp. Doyle's coaching career included Lewisport High, Mason County High, Campbellsville, and Cumberland Colleges. At Cumberland College, he produced two Southeastern Junior College championships. In 1952, Doyle returned to Campbellsville College where he won the State Conference Championship in 1953 and 1954 and took two teams to runner-up spots in the Junior College Tournament. (DD.)

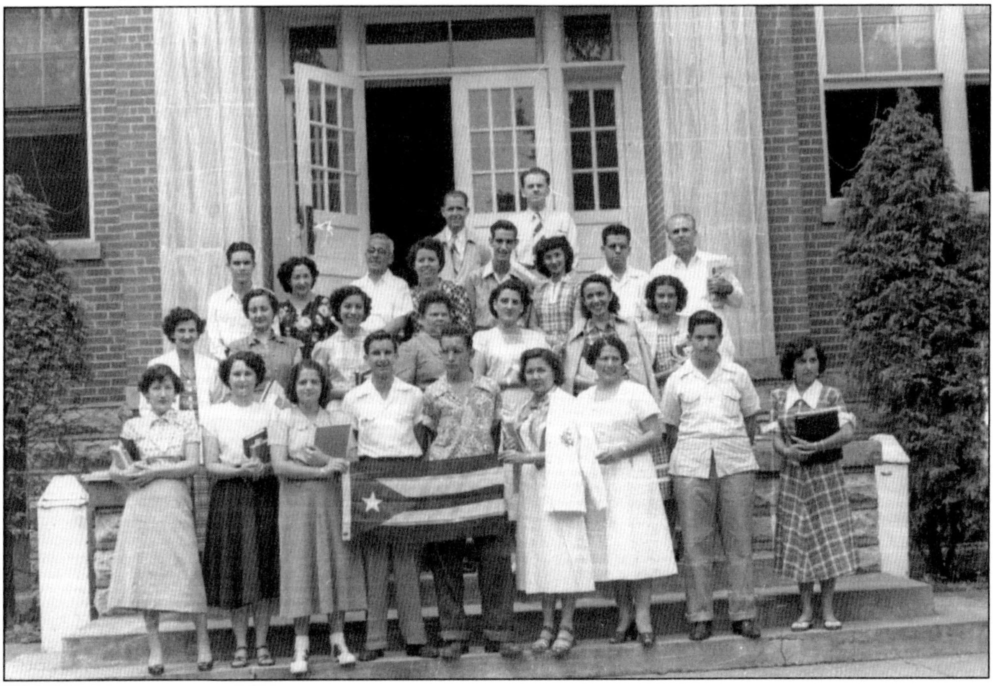

Twenty-five students from Cuba proudly display their country's flag in front of Campbellsville Junior College's Administration Building in 1951. These students represent the beginnings of an increased international student population. Today Campbellsville University has grown to over 3,000 students. Of those students, 229 represent 32 countries around the world. (ABC-CU.)

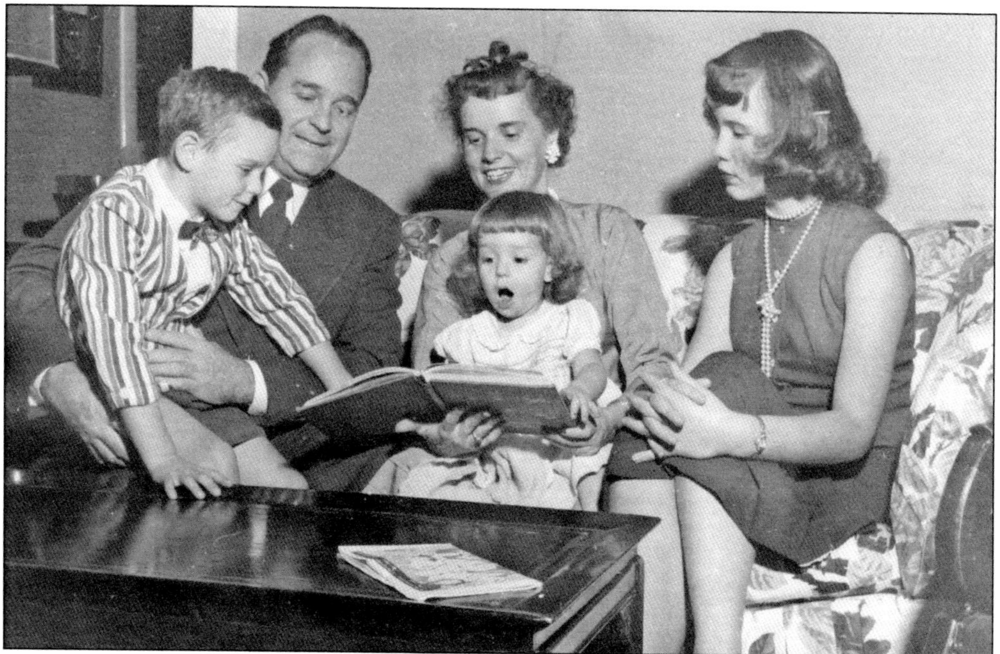

Dr. John M. Carter, president of Campbellsville College from 1948 to 1968, and his wife, June, read a Christmas story to their children in December 1954. The family members are, from left to right, John Mark Carter, sitting on his father's lap; Jill Carter, sitting with her mother; and June Carter. (ABC-CU.)

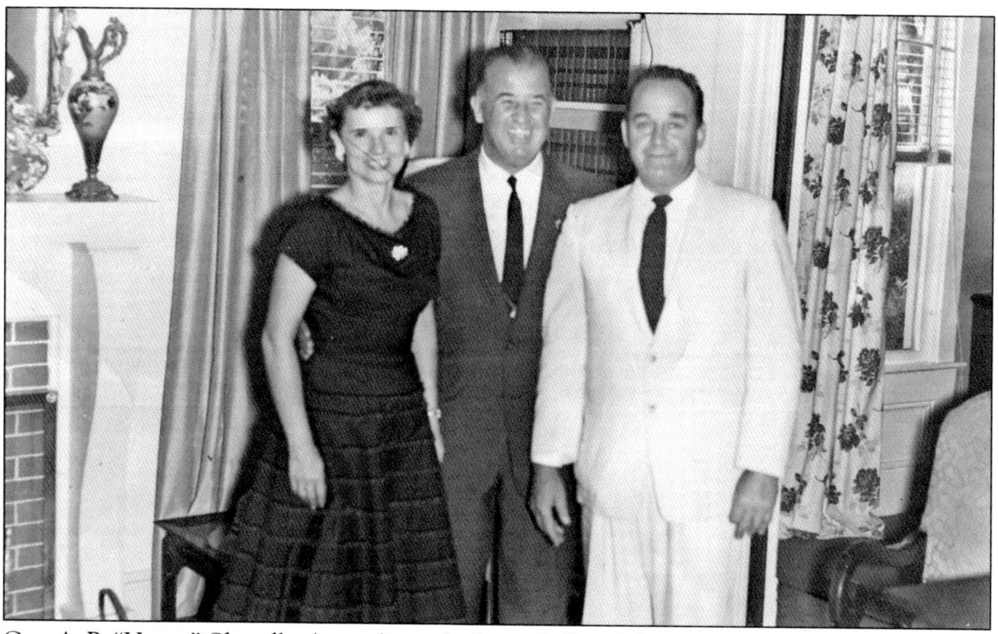

Gov. A. B. "Happy" Chandler (center) stands alongside Pres. John M. Carter and his wife, June, on May 17, 1957, which was designated by the institution as Governor's Day. Governor's Day marked the beginning of Campbellsville Junior College's 50th anniversary celebration. The celebration concluded at commencement on May 26, 1957, when Sen. John Sherman Cooper addressed the graduates. (ABC-CU.)

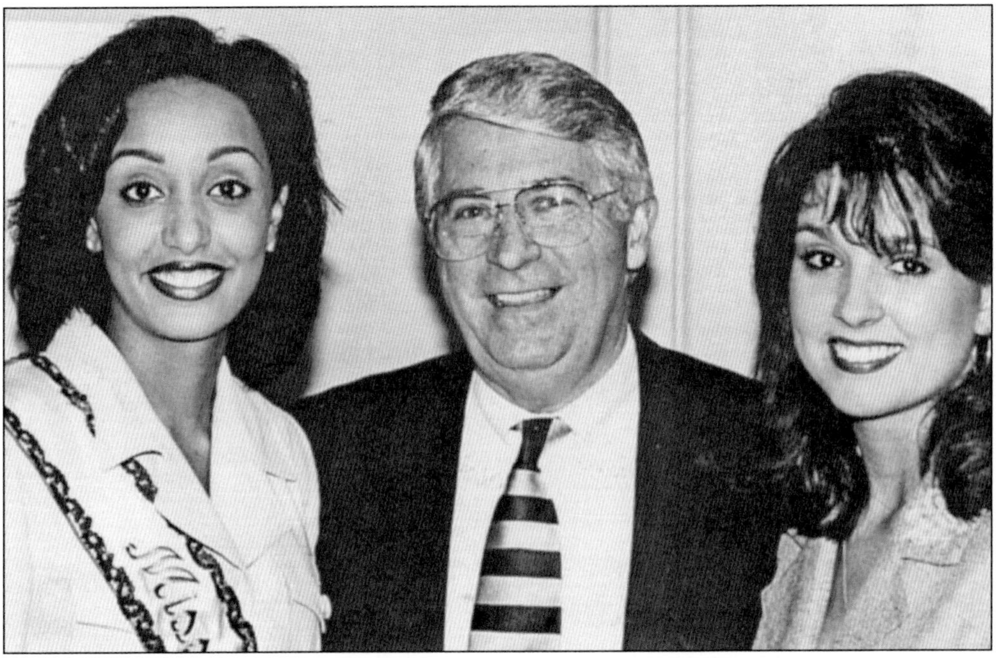

Pres. Kenneth Winters is flanked by two of the four Campbellsville College students who have won the Miss Kentucky title. On the left is Veronica Duka, Miss Kentucky 1996, who finished in the top ten at the Miss America Scholarship Pageant. On the right, Laura Sue Humphress was Miss Kentucky 1994. (ABC-CU.)

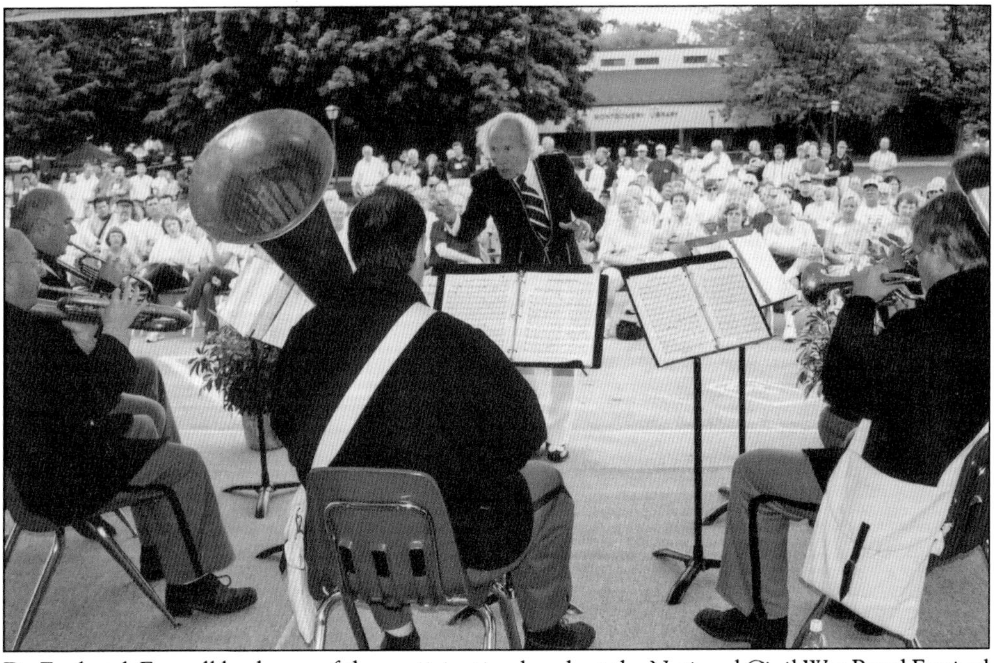

Dr. Frederick Fennell leads one of the participating bands at the National Civil War Band Festival in 2000. Cohosted by the American Civil War Institute and Campbellsville University, the festival featured Civil War bands from 11 states. The events at the second festival in 2003 were among the largest gatherings of Civil War bands since the end of the conflict. (ABC-CU.)

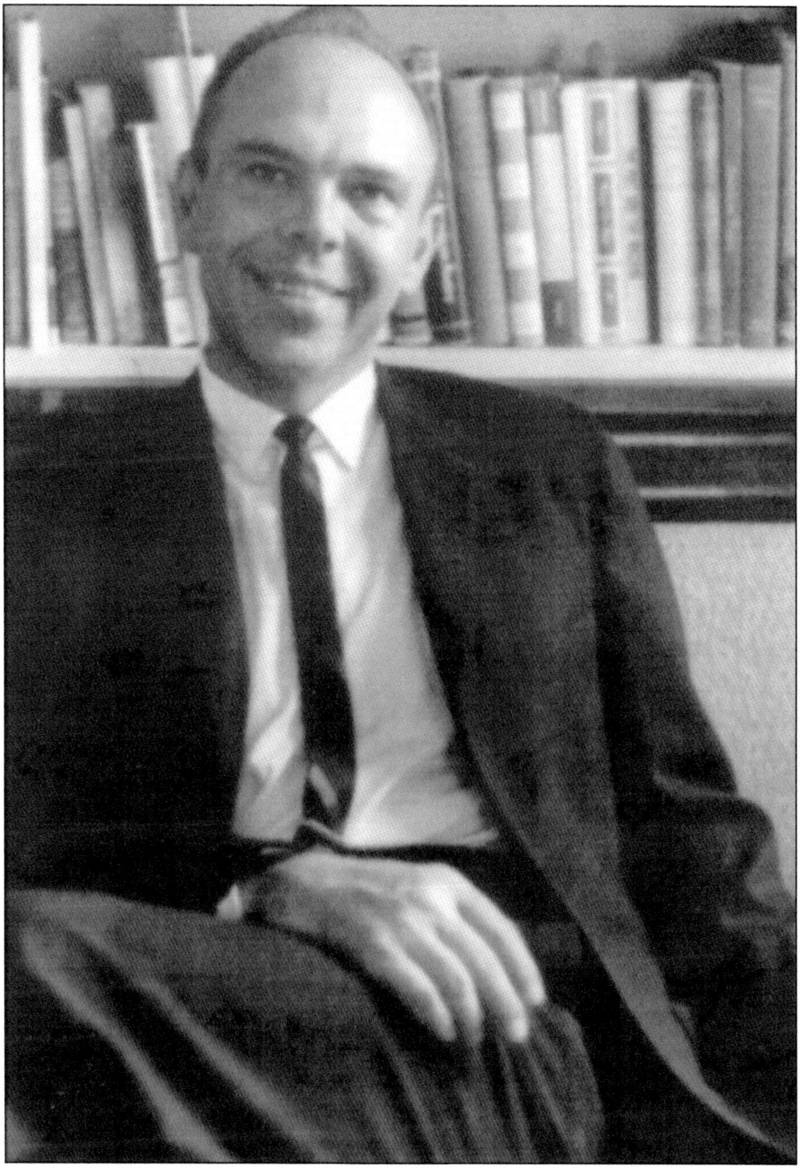

Hollis Spurgeon Summers Jr. spent four years of his early life in Campbellsville, while his father, Rev. Hollis Spurgeon Summers Sr., was pastor at Campbellsville Baptist Church. From this early life, and his time in small Kentucky communities, Summers gained experience that helped inform his 1952 novel *Brighten the Corner*, which was about young boys growing up in a small town where their father pastored. Although he graduated from Georgetown College in 1937, Summers did not follow a family tradition of entering the ministry. He completed a Master of Arts at Middlebury College, and a doctorate at the University of Iowa. His teaching career included seven years in high school at Covington, Kentucky, five years at his alma mater Georgetown, a year at the University of Kentucky, and then twenty-seven years at Ohio University in Athens, Ohio. Summers wrote four novels, numerous poems and short stories, published two collections of his stories, and edited two anthologies. Swallow Press of Ohio University grants the annual Hollis Summers Poetry Prize in his honor. Summers died in 1987. (UK.)

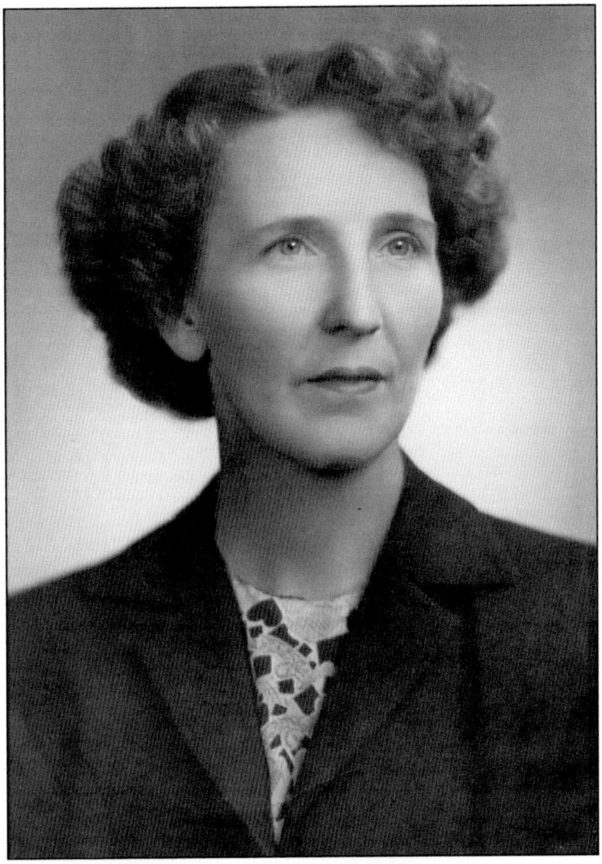

Popular author Janice Holt Giles wrote one of her most successful novels, *The Believers* (1957), while she and her husband Henry Giles lived in a Campbellsville apartment on Central Avenue. The building that housed the apartment no longer exists, having been replaced by an educational wing for the Campbellsville United Methodist Church. Born in 1905 in Altus, Arkansas, Janice, with her husband, lived in Campbellsville from 1955 to 1957, while Henry worked for *The News-Journal*. Janice and Henry are pictured below in the Central Avenue apartment. Janice died in 1979. (TCL, top, ML, below.)

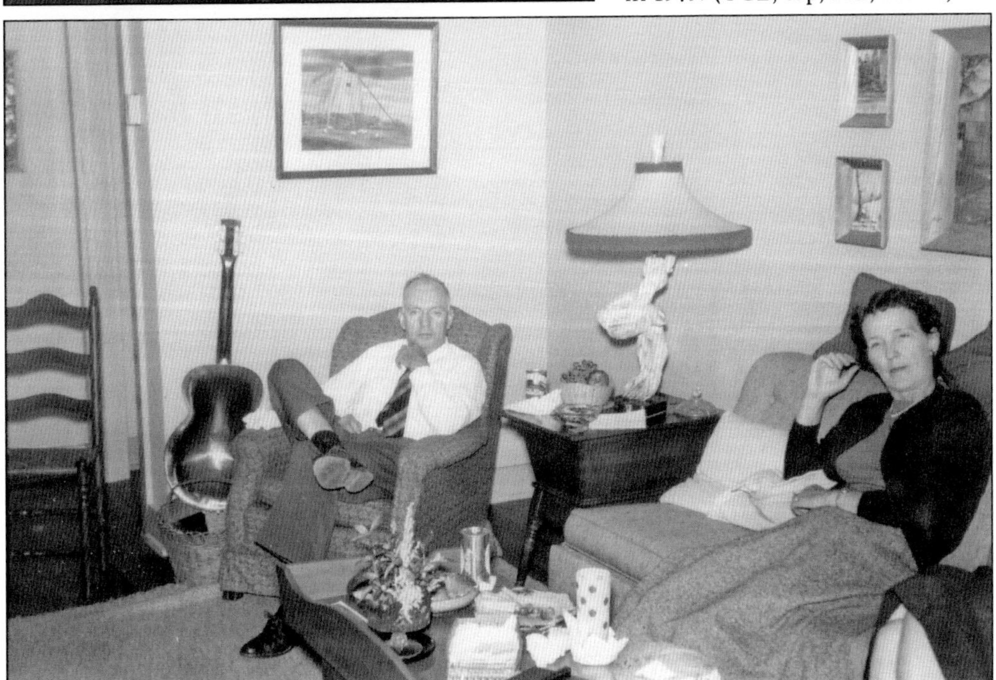

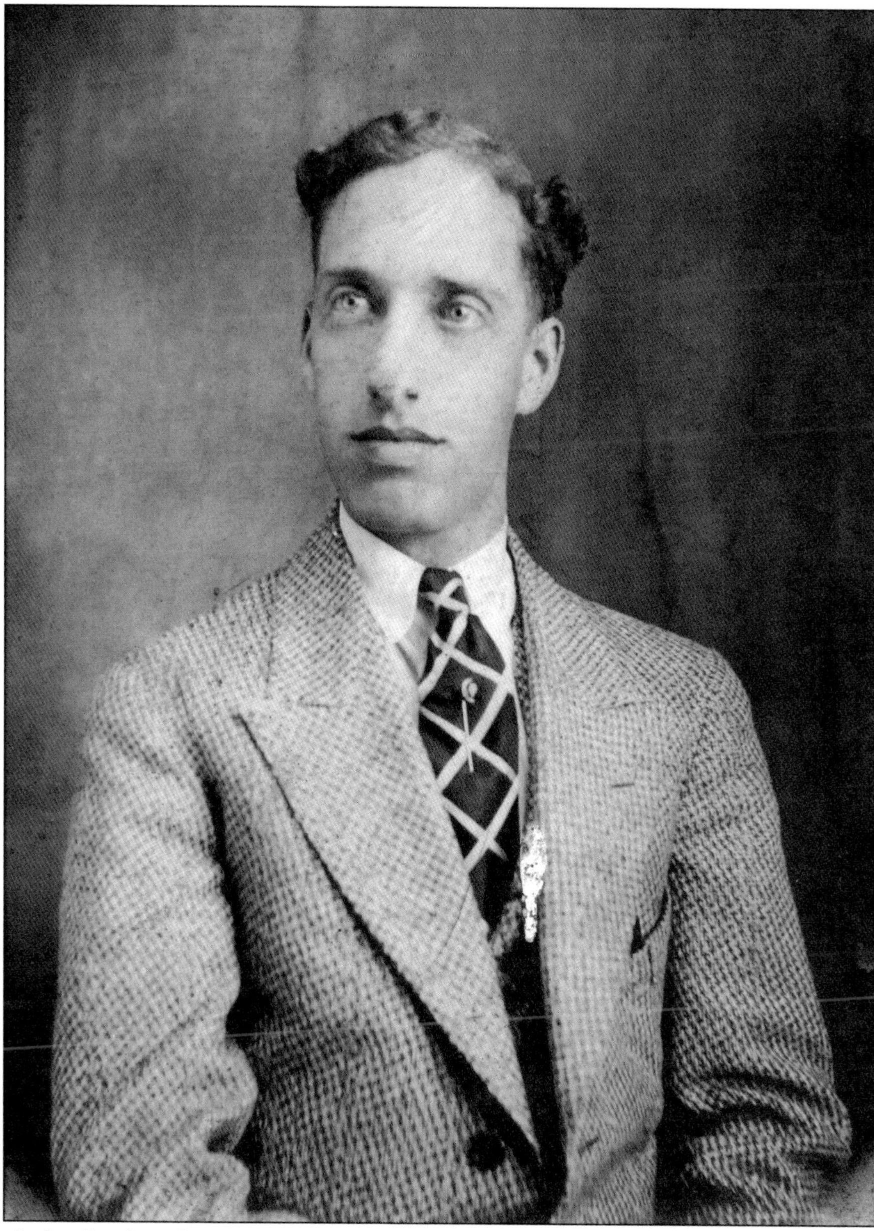

James Luke Creel, a Green County native, graduated from Campbellsville College and the University of Illinois. After winning the Senior Honors in English at Illinois, Northwestern University awarded him a scholarship. He received his Master of Arts degree from Northwestern in 1937 and immediately began teaching at Buena Vista College in Storm Lake, Iowa. Creel spent eight years in Iowa before accepting an English professorship at Gustavus Adolphus College in St. Peter, Minnesota, after considering offers from Eastern New Mexico and Texas A&M. A popular teacher and lecturer, he also served as dean of men, as a member of the Athletic Board of Control, and as chairman of the English Department. After a lengthy, and challenging, research trip to Africa in 1960, he published *Folk Tales of Liberia*, a collection of tales from the Via Tribe of Liberia. He retired from Gustavus Adolphus in 1971 and returned to Campbellsville, where he died in 1985. (MN.)

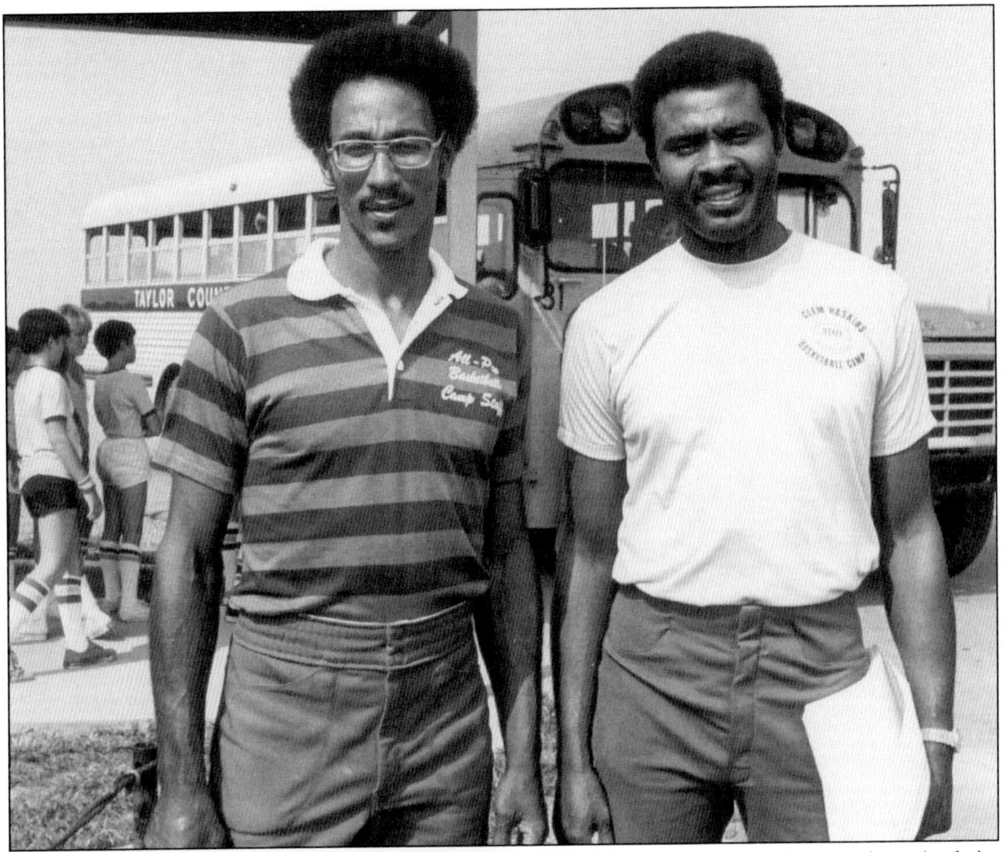

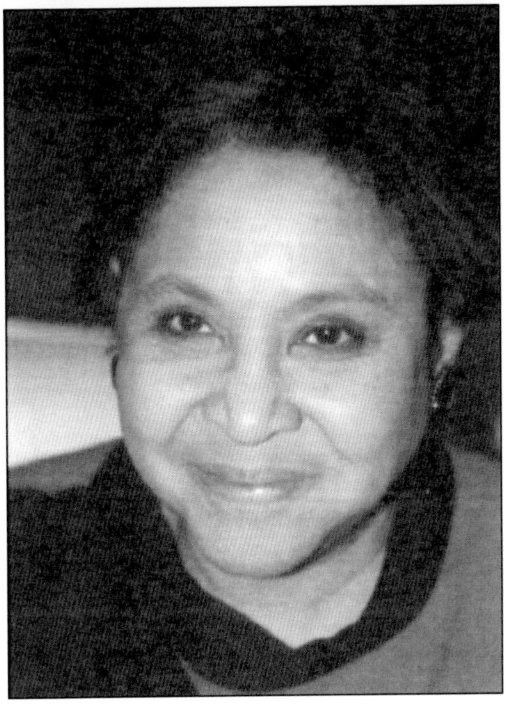

Taylor County native Clem Haskins (right) starred at Western Kentucky University before playing professional basketball for the Chicago Bulls, the Phoenix Suns, and the Washington Bullets. Haskins is pictured with Hall-of-Famer and Washington Bullets teammate Dave Bing, who played college ball at Syracuse. Taken around 1970, this photograph shows Haskins and Bing at Haskins's basketball camp in Campbellsville. (TCHS.)

Born in Campbellsville in 1921, Margaret Buckner received her Bachelor of Arts degree in 1942 from Kentucky State University, where she met her future husband, Whitney M. Young Jr. After earning her Master of Arts degree at the University of Minnesota, she became a professor of educational psychology at Spellman College in Atlanta, where her husband served as the executive director of the National Urban League. Buckner was an educator, author, and civic and corporate leader. (TCHS.)

Three

Life in Taylor County

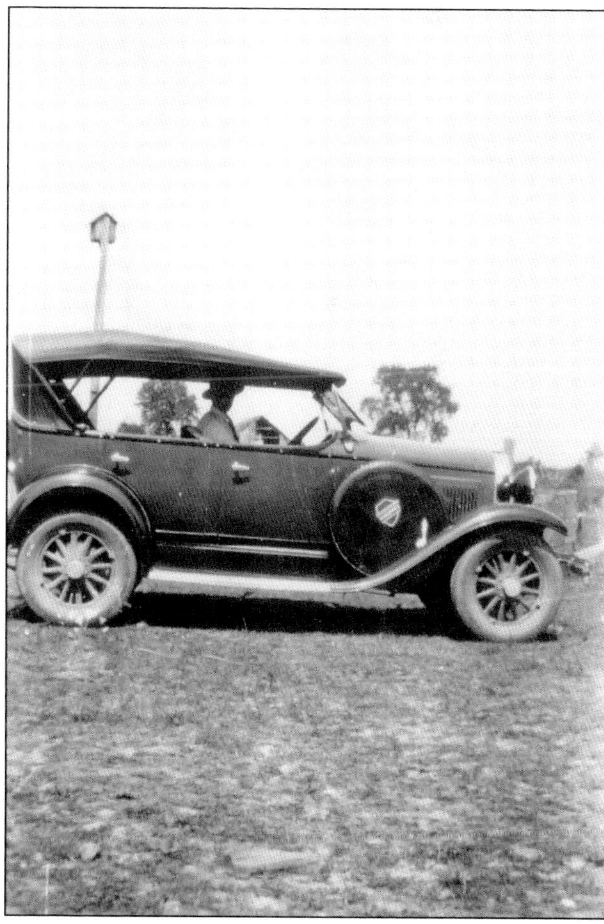

Robert Money bought his first car in 1929—a Whippet. According to Taylor County Court Clerk Oather C. Spurling, Whippets were the third leading car licensed in Taylor County in 1930. Ford led with 925, followed by Chevrolet with 432, Whippet at 71, Star 59, Buick 39, Essex 31, and Chrysler with 30. Twenty five other makes completed the 1,748 cars licensed, including such nearly forgotten names as the Reo and the Hupmobile. (EMC.)

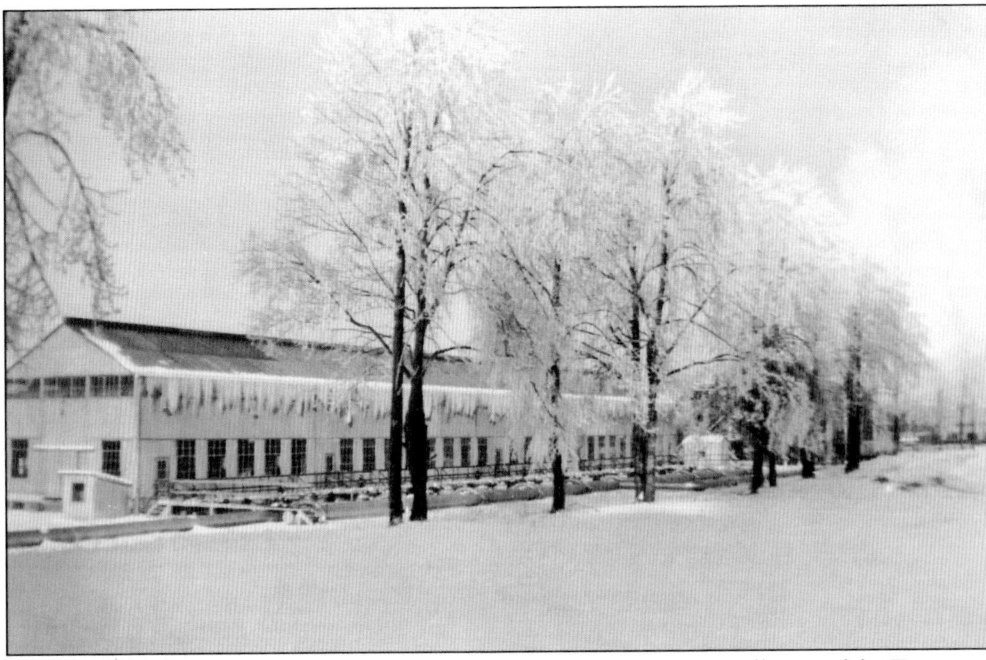

In 1951, nationwide gas distribution reached Taylor County with the installation of the Tennessee Gas and Transmission Company pipeline. The 30-inch pipeline carried gas from the Texas fields to the East Coast. A peak of 300 workers spent time in Taylor County throughout the building process. The company built a compressor station in Saloma (above). In 1952, the compressor's power was increased to a total of 26,000 horsepower. The Saloma station was one of 25 such stations located along the 2,000 mile pipeline. The company built a $10 million liquid hydrocarbon recovery plant in Green County to process most of the gas passing from Texas to the Northeast. (GS, above and below.)

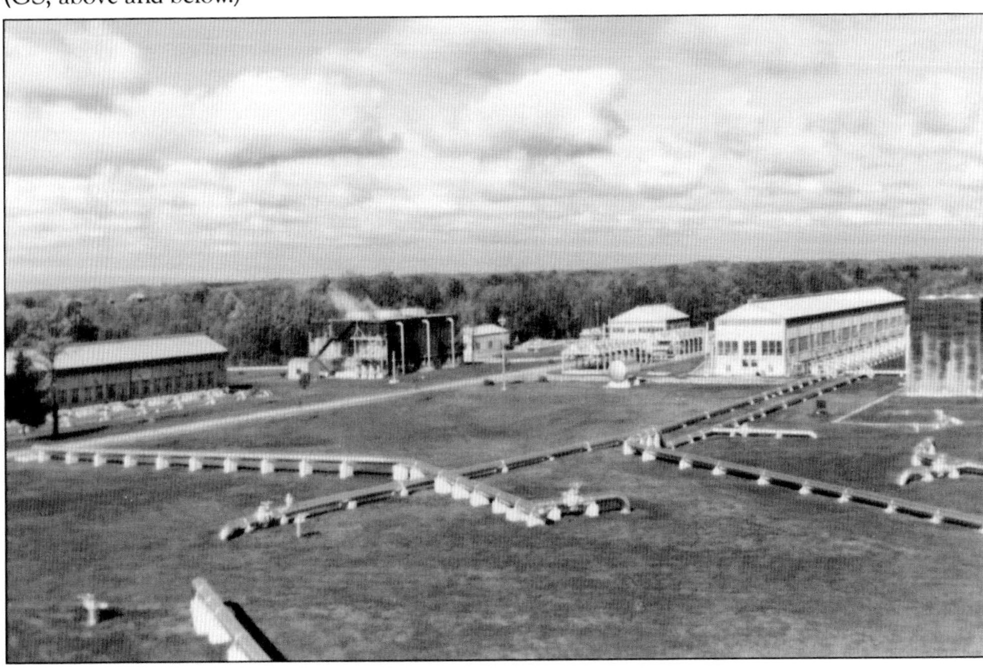

Private investors and small companies drilled for gas and oil in the late 19th century. By the 20th century, a small company provided gas for Campbellsville residents. In 1923, the United Carbon Company purchased the Taylor-Green Gas Company and began service in Campbellsville. United Carbon owned and operated 59 gas wells in Green and Taylor Counties along with 28 miles of pipeline and two compressors to serve their customers. (MJG.)

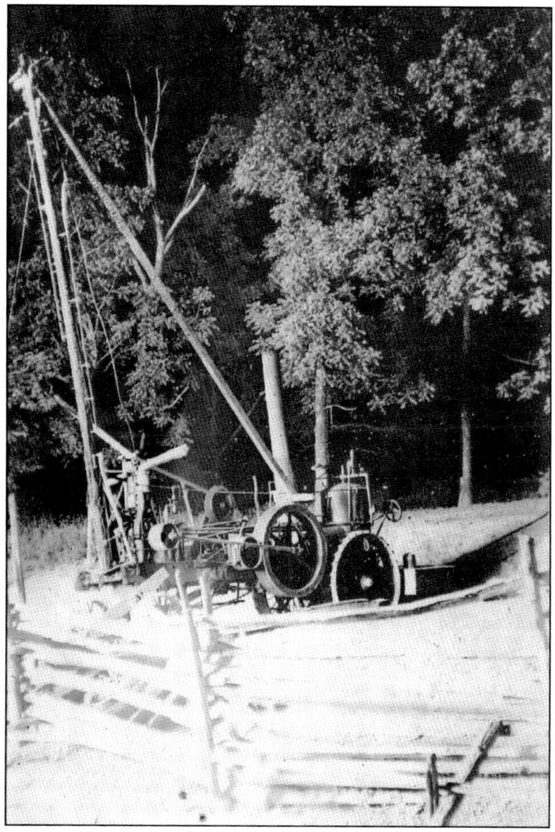

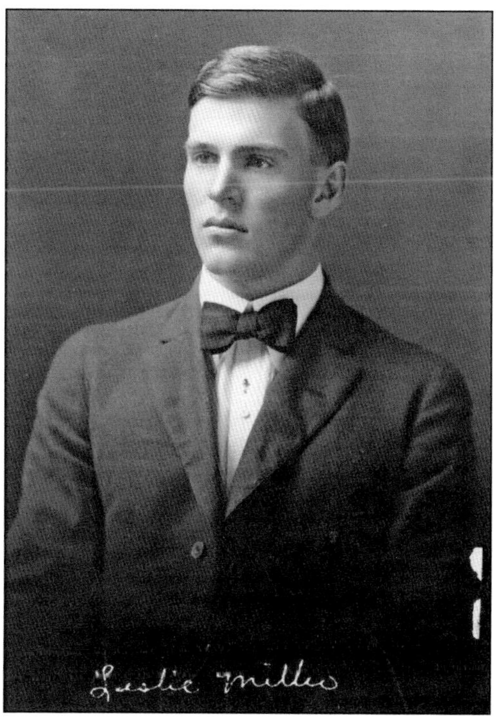

Born in Taylor County on March 5, 1889, Professor Isaiah Leslie Miller graduated from Western State Teachers College and Indiana University. After having taught at Indiana University and Carthage College, Professor Miller became head of the Mathematics Department at South Dakota State College. He wrote two mathematics textbooks that established him as one of the country's mathematics authorities. He died in 1936 at his home in Brookings, South Dakota. (CBG.)

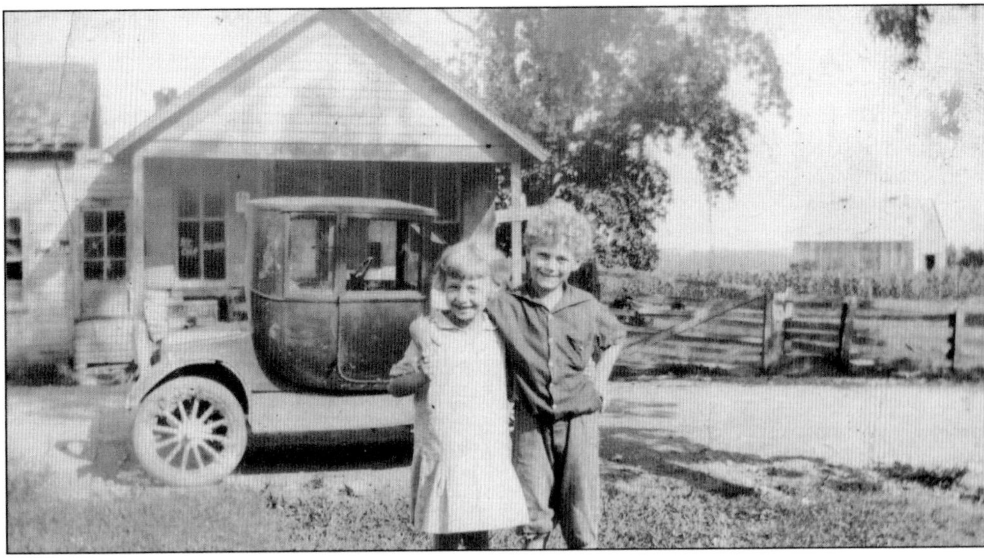

Before good roads and better transportation modes, small country stores provided county residents necessary goods within a reasonable distance. The above photograph shows good friends Adeline Miller and David Hiestand Mitchell standing in front of John Caldwell Buchanan Groceries at Burdick, one of the many small stores that dotted Taylor County in the 20th century. In another part of the county, seen below, Linda Lea Money and Bobby Coakley lounge on the porch of their grandfather Robert Money's store at Black Gnat. The Black Gnat store building remains, but not the store, as most shoppers now choose other options. (CBG, top, EMC, below.)

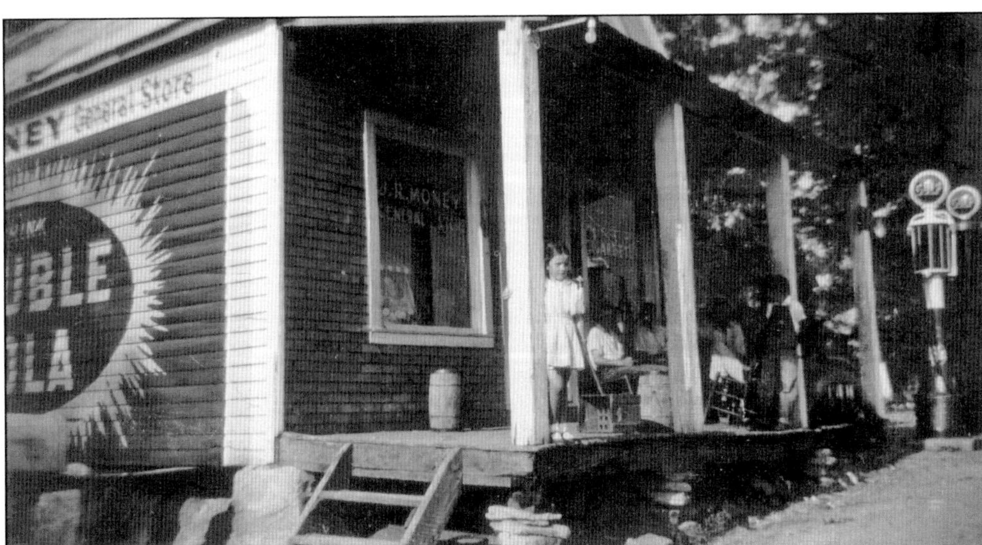

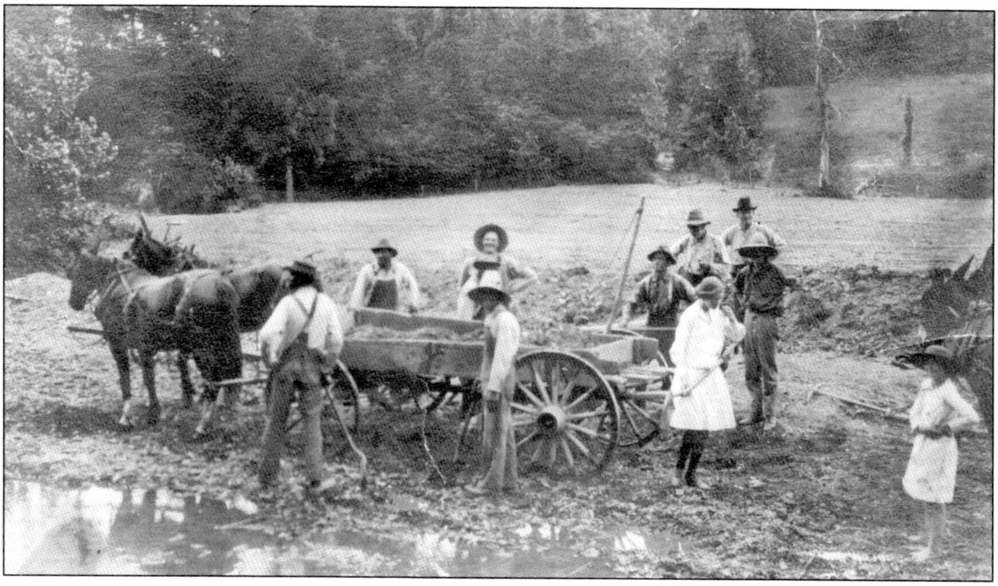

Under a February 1797 Kentucky law, "all male laboring persons of the age of 16 years or more" were required to work on public roads, and counties were allowed to use private equipment for the work. These early-20th-century photographs reflect the requirement applied and the changing ways roads came to be maintained. In the above photograph, workers load creek gravel onto a wagon for use on a county road. Below, workers grade Roberts Road in 1923. When Armour was viewing Campbellsville as a site for locating its cheese plant, the *The News-Journal* editor noted that "it takes good cream to make good cheese, and it takes good roads to get the milk or cream to the cheese factory." His comments reflected a growing awareness of the need for better roads. (FHB, above and below.)

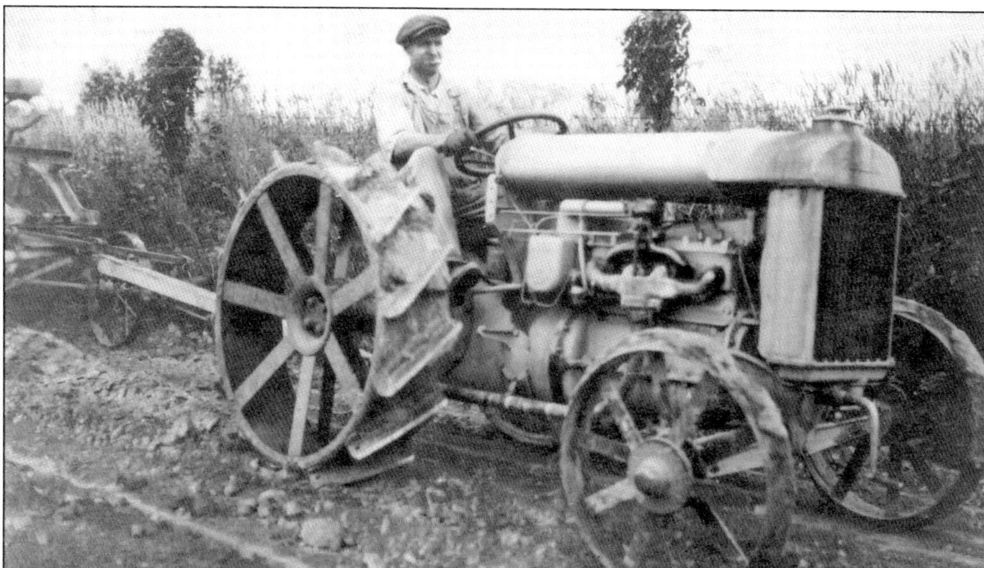

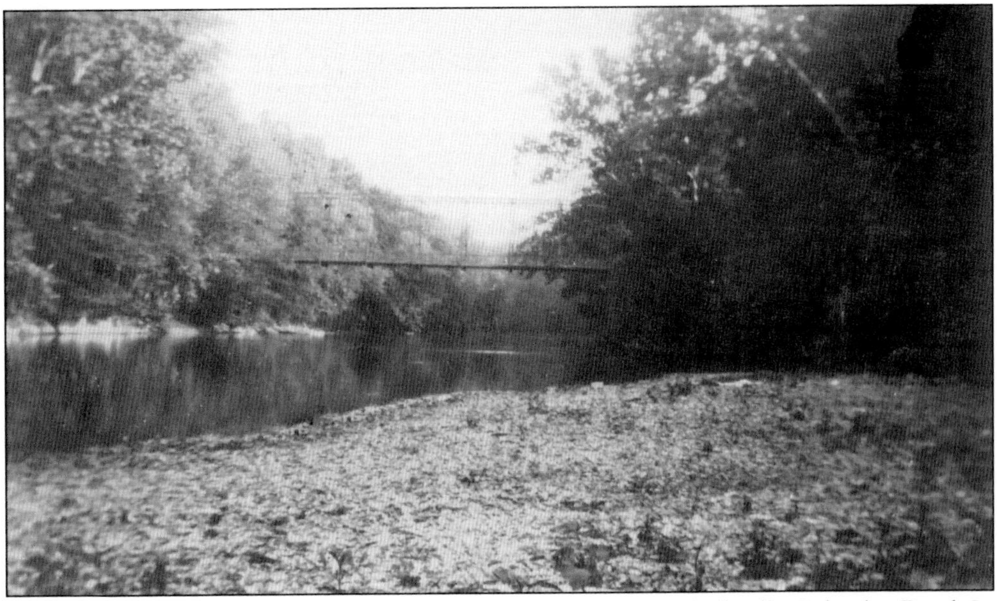

Here is an early photograph of Green River Bridge on the Campbellsville-Columbia Road. In 1933, some unnamed individual investigated placing a hydroelectric power plant near the bridge to supply Campbellsville and Columbia electricity. More significantly, the location achieved recognition during the Civil War, when General John Hunt Morgan unsuccessfully engaged Colonel Orlando Moore in a battle on July 4, 1863. Today excellent markers exist in the area helping visitors understand the engagement. (RR.)

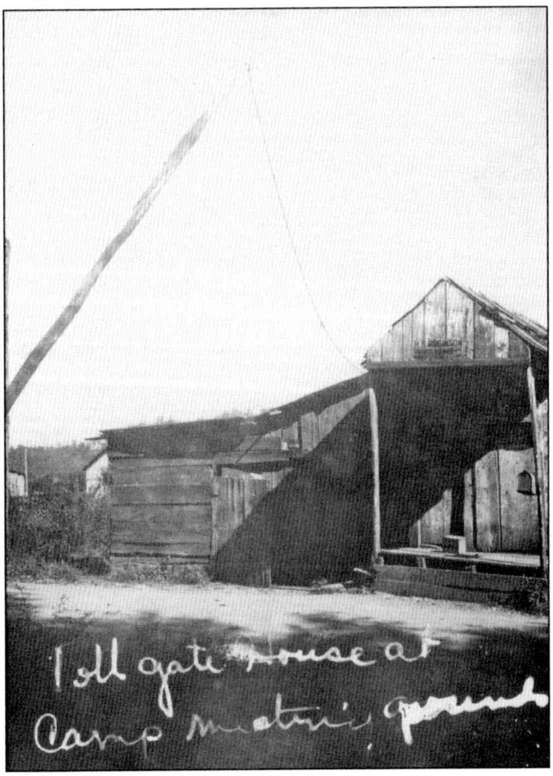

Until the 1920s, private toll roads ran in most directions to and from Campbellsville. The tollhouse in this photograph is thought to have sat on the Columbia pike near Green River. In 1924, night riders expressed a growing opposition when they left the following note at all the toll houses on the Lebanon and Columbia pikes: "Be wise. Don't collect any more toll, or we'll come to see you." (CBG.)

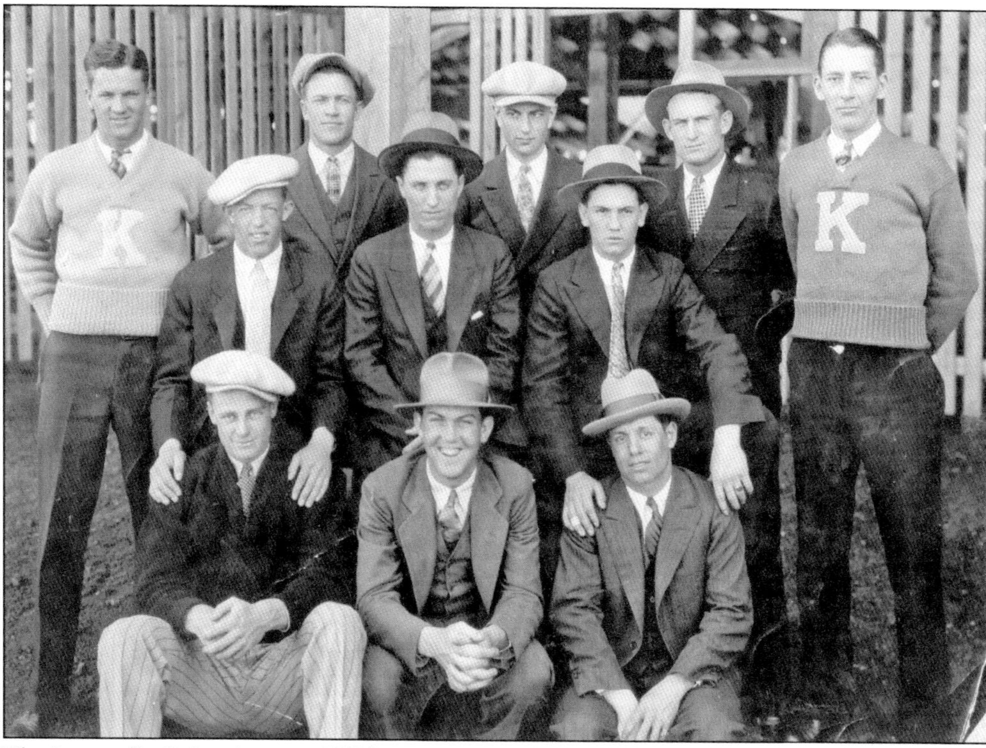

The Louisville Colonels invited Elkhorn native Walter Lee "Zerves" Ramsey to tryouts in March 1927. Despite some early struggles on the mound, the left hander made the cut and joined the team for spring training at Mobile, Alabama. Ramsey, second from left in the third row, eventually hurt his arm, bringing about his release from the Colonels. He continued to play ball for the Mengel Furniture Company team where he worked. (R&WR.)

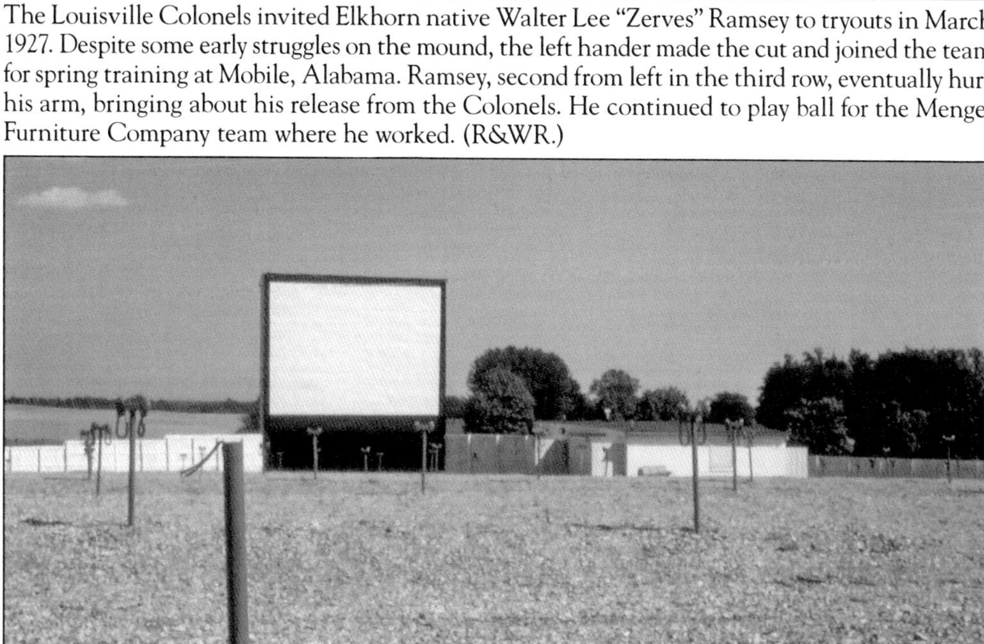

On July 26, 1951, Campbellsville's only drive-in theater opened on the Campbellsville-Columbia Road. A 1950 opening fell through when the initial corporation, Moonbeam Theatre Company, dissolved. The owners, Henry and Conway Whitlock, George A. Kemp, and Richard Lee Smith, reorganized as the Campbellsville Drive-In and constructed a facility with 300 speakers and a concession stand. Adults paid 45¢ admission. J. A. Ball bought the theater in December 1957. (TCHS.)

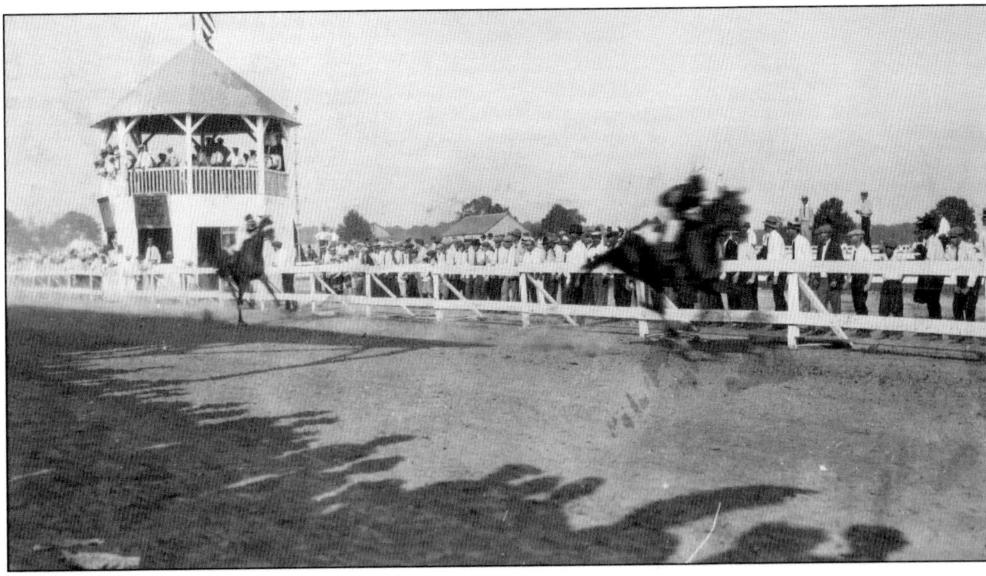

After years of being without a fair, 10 stockholders joined in 1924 to create the Taylor County Fair Association. They held their first fair on land secured from the George R. Holt family. With the coming of World War II, gasoline rationing brought the demise of the fair until 1949, when Claude Huddleston bought the Holt property on February 18 for $12,000, reselling it to the American Legion and allowing them to restart the Taylor County Fair. In absence of a county fair, Campbellsville and Mannsville held community fairs that provided opportunities for parades, displays, and the competitions usually associated with the county fair. Although the men in these photographs are unidentified, I. G. Thomas won $150 by taking first place in the one-mile thoroughbred race. The winner of the free-for-all race trot or pace received $350. (FHB, above and below.)

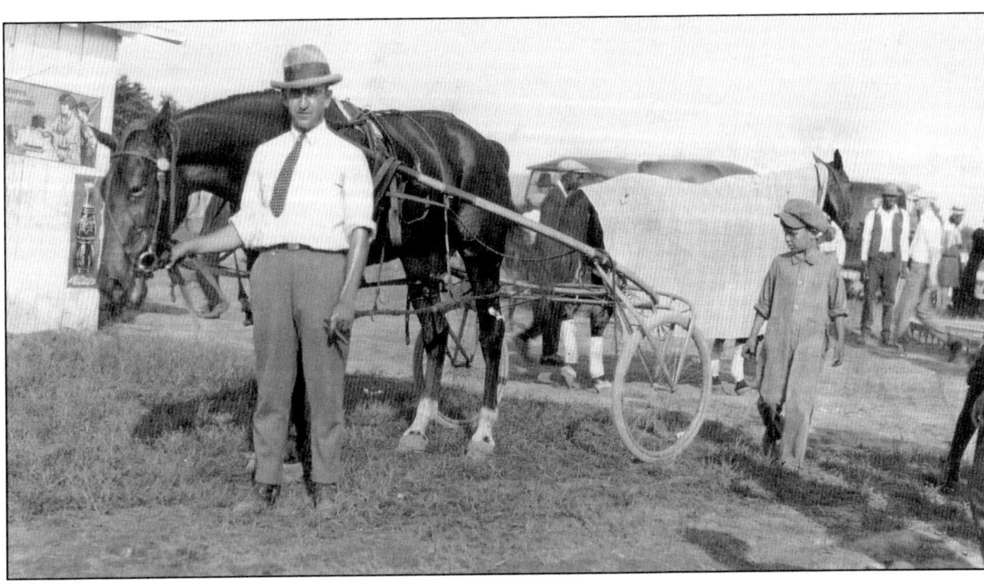

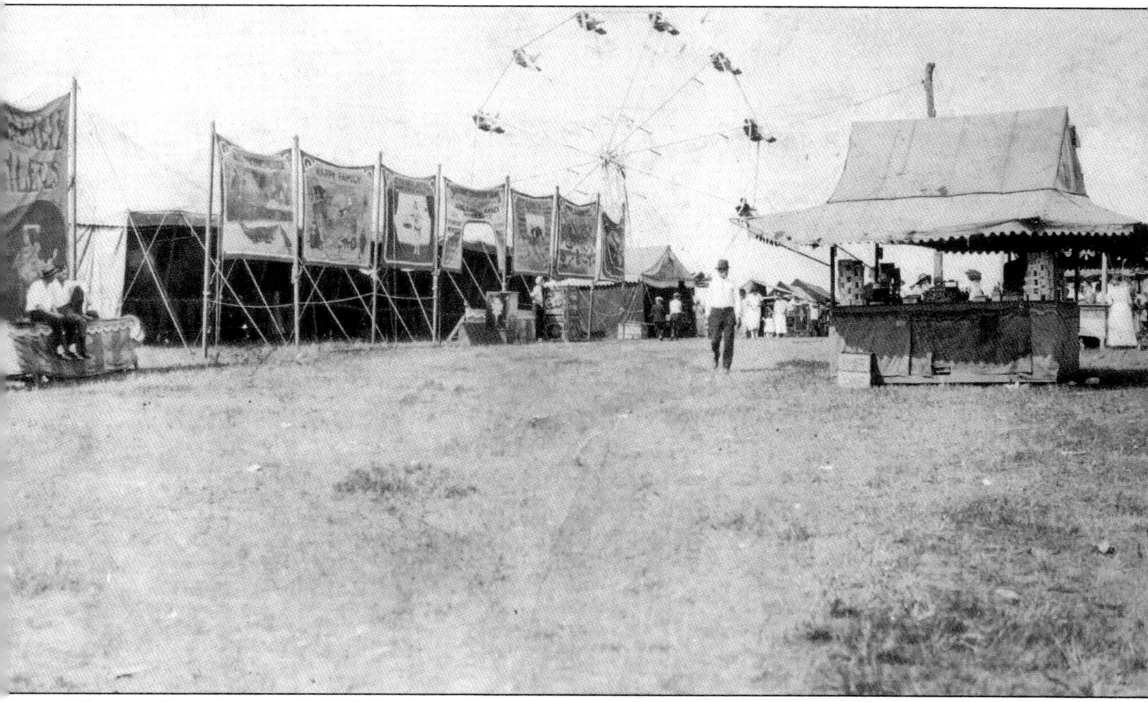

The newly reorganized 1924 fair brought a variety of entertainment. According to the carnival promotional banners, one could see a "Congress of Wonders" that included incomparable athletes, alligators, juggling, and a happy family. Coca-Cola shells stand beside what appears to be a food booth. According to the fair board, they spent $15,000 for new buildings and equipment. (FHB.).

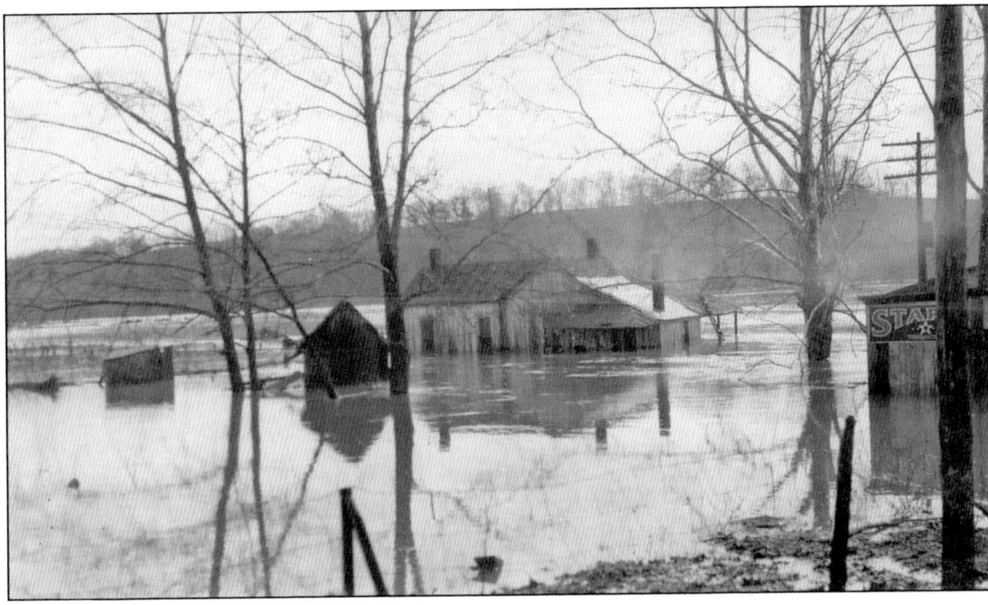

On Friday afternoon, January 18, 1929, a severe storm struck Green, Marion, and Taylor Counties, damaging trees and property. Many Campbellsville residents lost electricity when the Kentucky Utilities poles fell. The Lerman Brothers building on Main Street lost much of its roof. Just east of town, the Taylor County Fair Association's grandstand was moved an estimated 6 to 8 feet off its foundation. Tragically, seven-month-old Nellie Catherine Miller died in her bed when the storm demolished her home and bricks fell from the chimney and struck her. Heavy rains accompanied the storm, causing flooding in the Elkhorn area, as seen here. (FHB, above and below.)

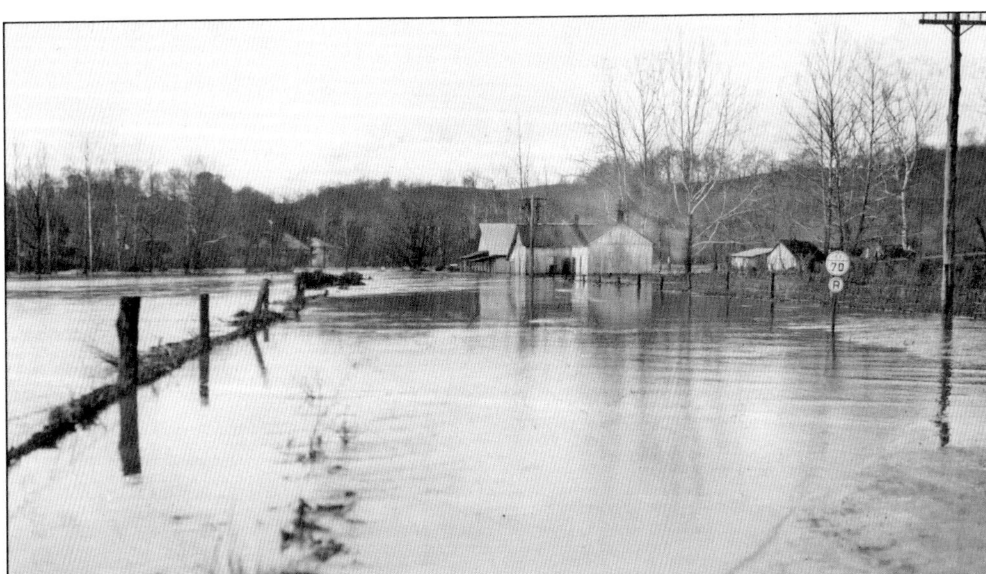

In 1958, the magazine *Progressive Farmer* recognized the Speck Community Center for the recreation and other resources it provided for the community. Members of the Center pictured include Lemmie Cox; William M. McVey, president of the board; Mildred Pike; Mrs. Russell McVey; Curtis McDaniel; Dina McDaniel; and Mrs. Calvin Risen, associate county agent. The group joined in supporting the Speck Community Fair of August 8 and 9, 1958, which included exhibits and prizes for livestock; farm products; food, like best apple and chocolate pies, best jam cake, best peaches, and best apple jelly; and fancy work of quilts, pillow cases, scarves, and dish towels. Consistent with larger county or community fairs that encouraged improved livestock, Speck included a dairy cattle show. (TCL, right and below.)

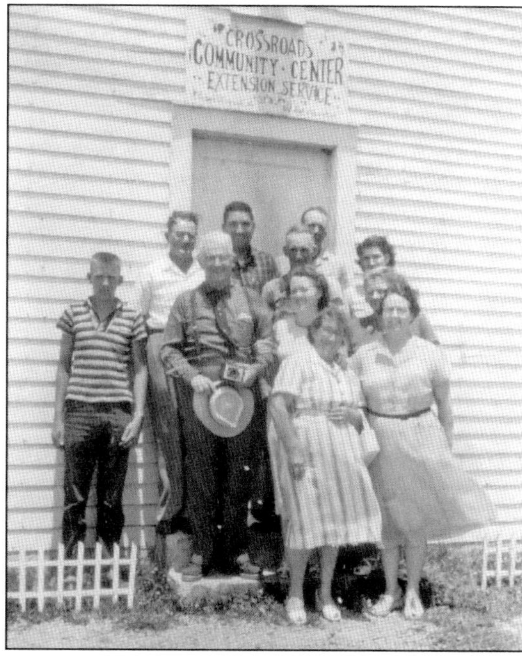

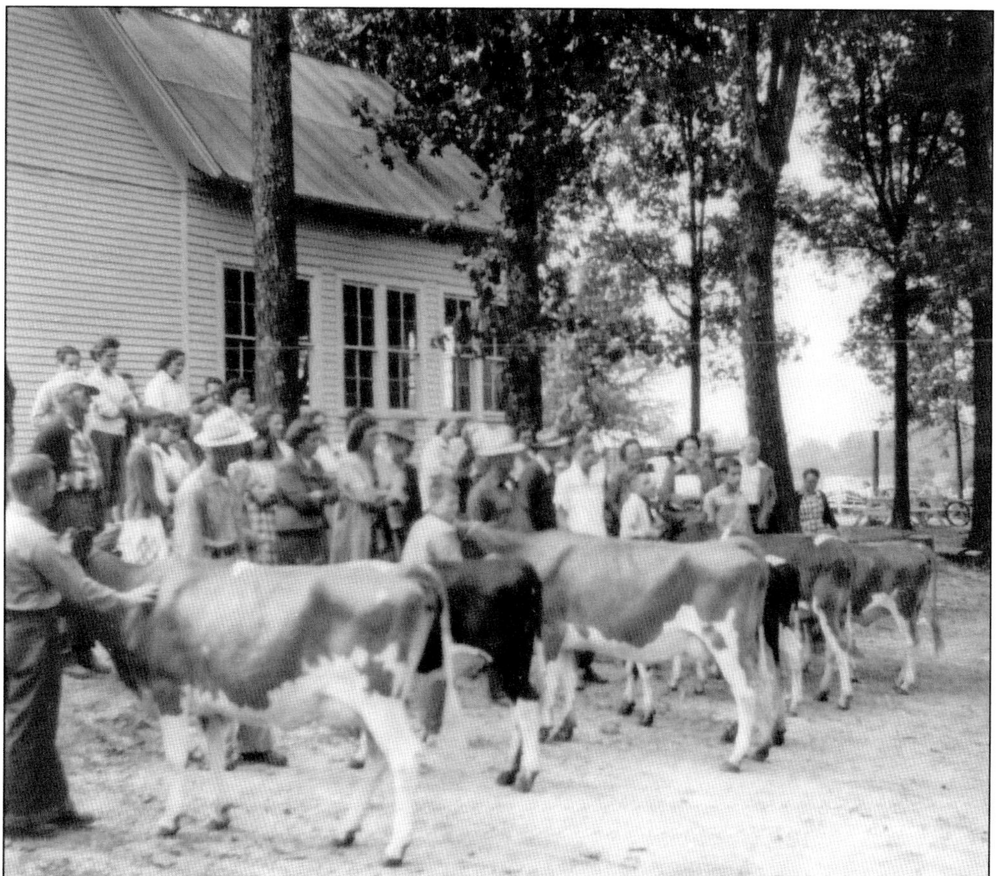

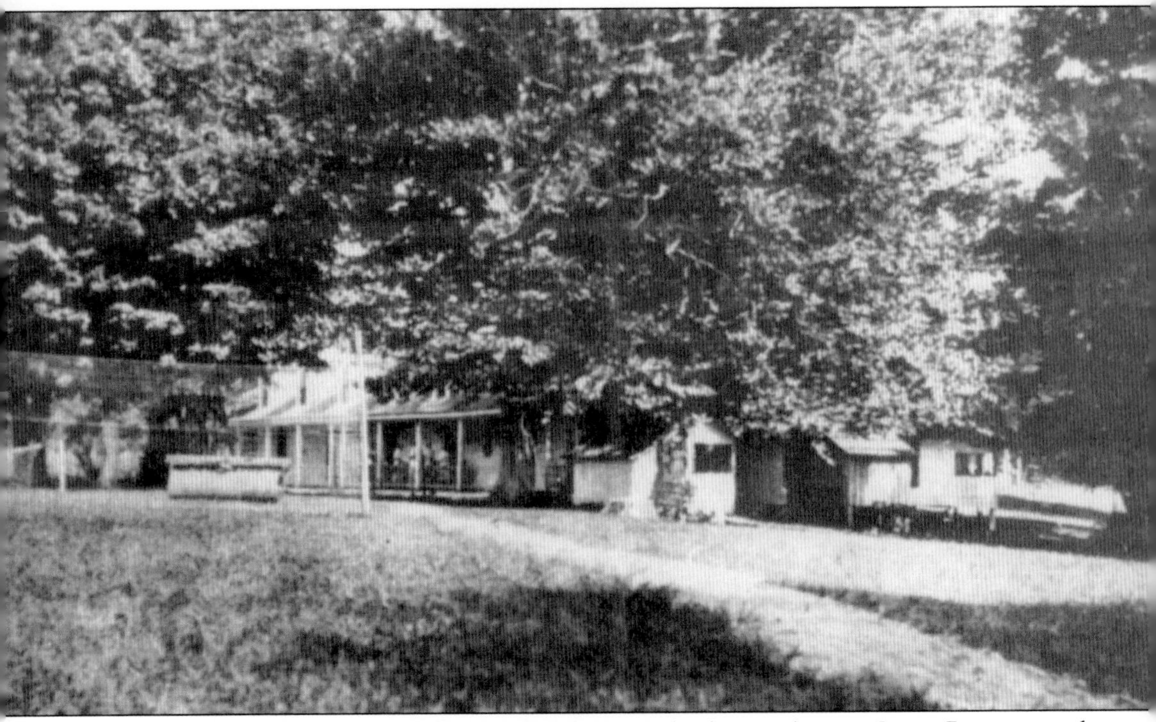

According to tradition, the Griffin family, who were the first settlers on Green River, started Griffin Springs. Known for its sulphur water, visitors came to the resort on Columbia Road, near Romine, for its alleged curative value. Closed during World War I, owner Col. Robert Lee Faulkner reopened the resort in June 1922, offering "fine water, bathing, and excellent board." In 1922, boarders could stay for $12.50 a week or $2.50 a day. Faulkner made other changes, which included adding tennis, croquet, swimming, and dancing. This *c.* 1913 picture shows the tennis court to the left with the roller used to smooth the court. In the left center stands the hotel, with visitors standing on the porch. In the center, the smaller building with a screened porch covers a spring and well. To the right another screened porch reveals the location of the dining room and the area used for registration. The hotel was torn down in 1933. (BW.)

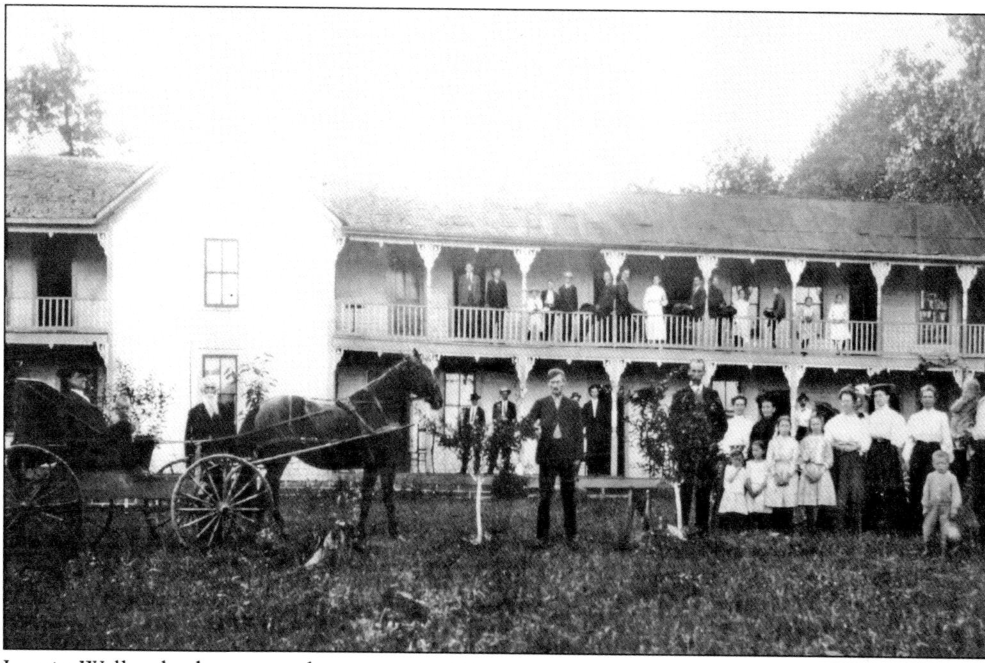

Lorain Wells, also known early as Morrison Well, was located five miles from Campbellsville on the Greensburg pike in the Shiloh area. The Caldwells assumed ownership from G. D. Smith and Jim Morrison. Alfred V. Caldwell is the tall man behind the tree. In 1927, J. L. Bradshaw managed the resort when the owner, Julia Caldwell, sold to L. E. Woodward of Deatsville, Kentucky. The buildings accommodated 42 people in a two-story hotel. Along with residents from Taylor and surrounding counties, visitors from other states vacationed at Lorain Wells and Griffin Springs. Analyzed and promoted for its curative components, water from the wells contained 13 to 18 different minerals with "a very considerable quantity of hydrogen sulphide," according to the local newspaper. The analysis at right was provided to customers. (TC, above and right.)

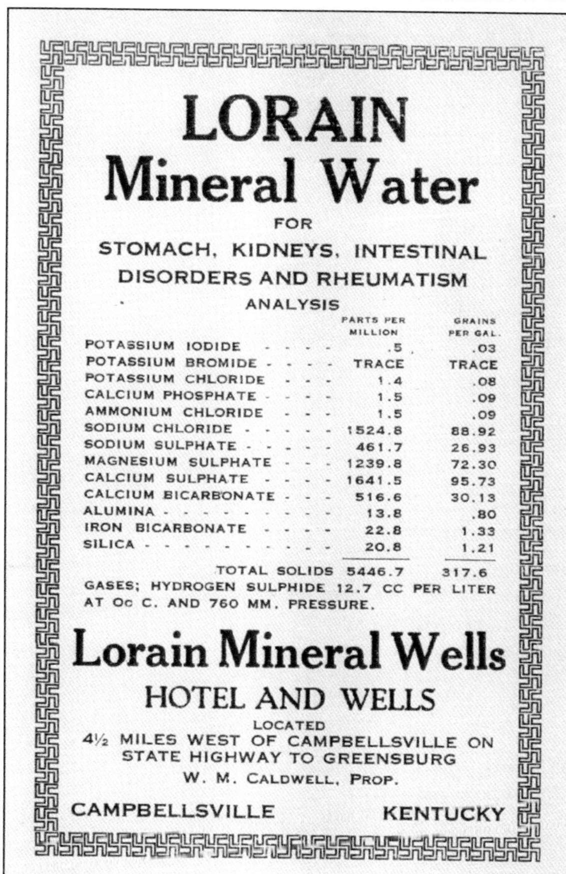

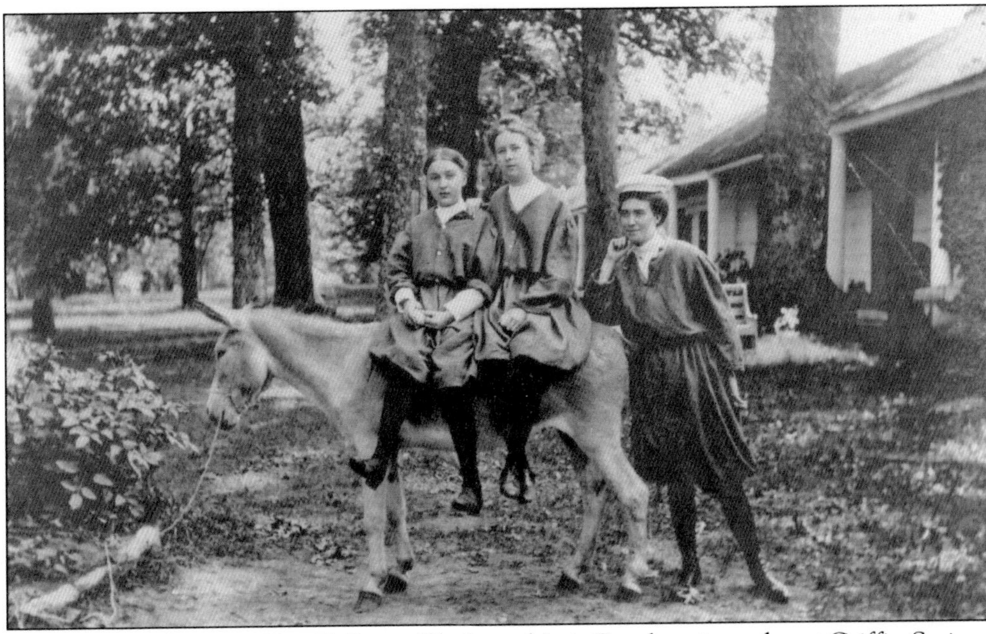

From left to right, Irene Yowell, Emma Black, and Lois Gowdy enjoy a day at Griffin Springs. Irene Yowell graduated from the Cincinnati Conservatory of Music, where she eventually taught. She returned to Campbellsville and continued to teach music until 1962, when she moved to Washington state. Emma Wood also became a music teacher in the Campbellsville schools and taught private students. (TCHS.)

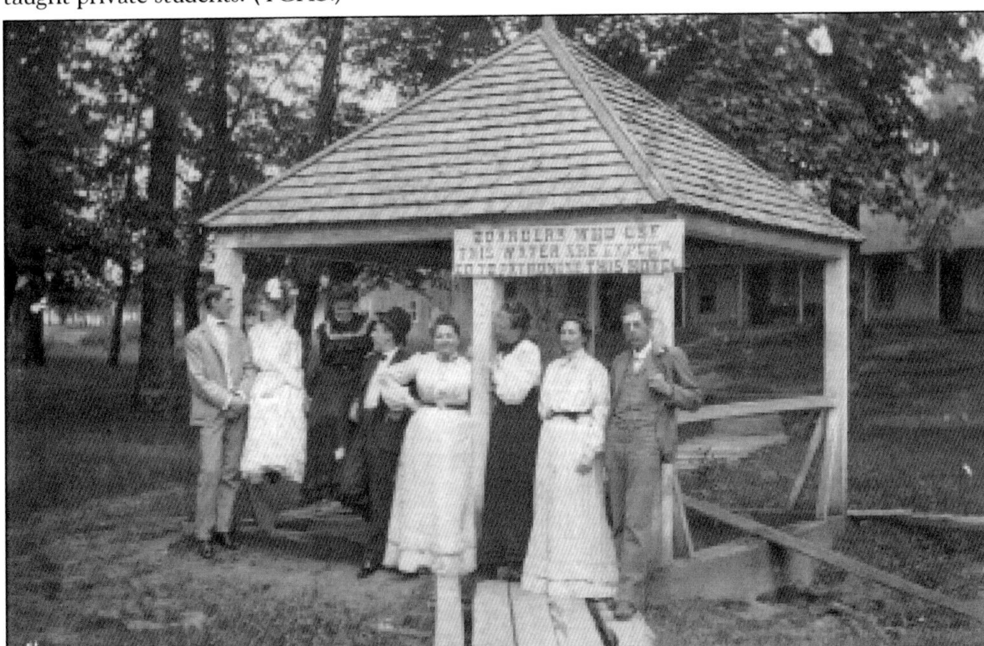

This group gathered at Lorain Wells c. 1910. The sign over the well gives specific instructions to the public about using the curative waters. The only identifiable individual is Olive Walling, daughter of Ulysses P. Walling, who was associated with Campbellsville Lumber Company. Olive is standing third from left in the black dress. (TCHS.)

Simultaneously working from the southern and northern approaches, the Cumberland and Ohio Railroad began the Spurlington Tunnel in March 1872. About 100 to 125 men worked continuously day and night, six days a week, to complete the tunnel. They first saw daylight through the 1,836-foot tunnel on January 29, 1874, after which they reported the tunnel complete and ready to open on March 11, 1874. The first train ran through the tunnel on October 3, 1879. (MJG.)

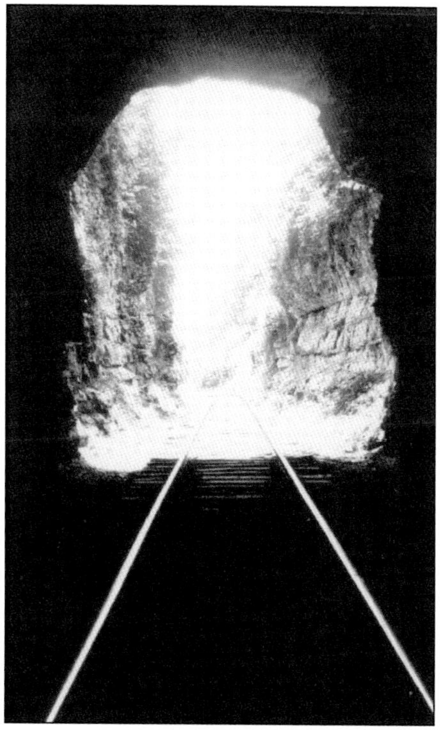

During the Civil War, James Atchley left Tennessee and came to Taylor County, where he operated a general store and mill. Situated at Lemmon's Bend of Green River, the mill produced flour on the upper floor and meal on the lower, using 30-inch French burr wheels. The mill stopped operating in the 1940s. As this c. 1901 picture shows, Atchley's Mill was also a popular picnic location. (TCHS.)

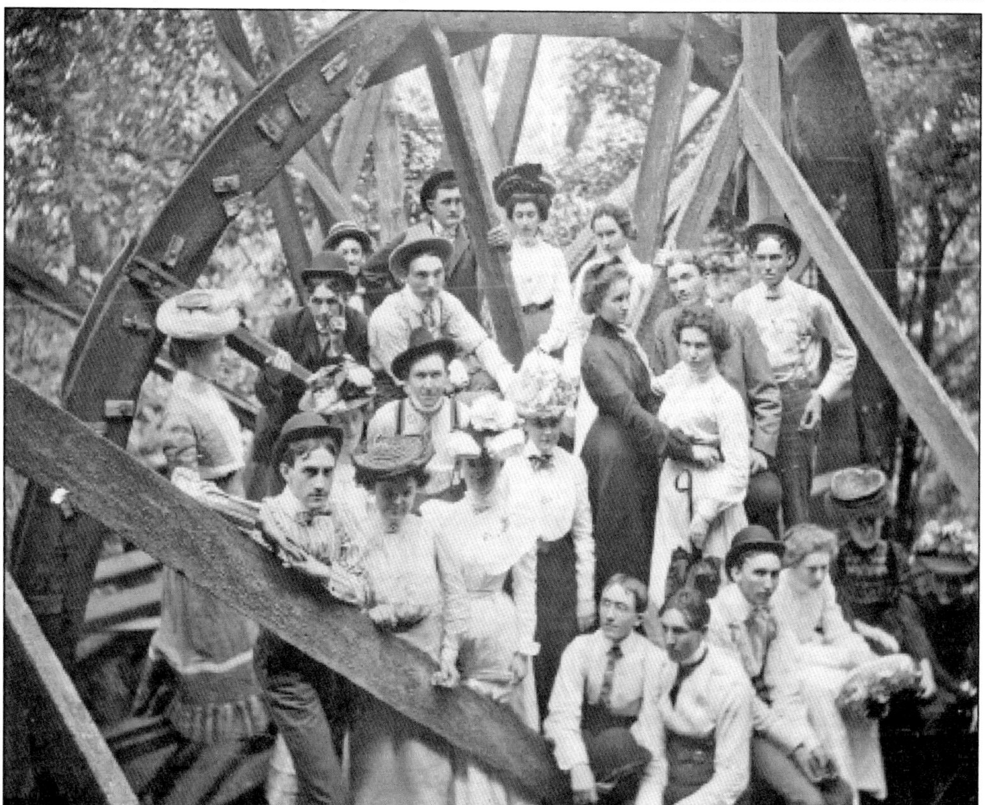

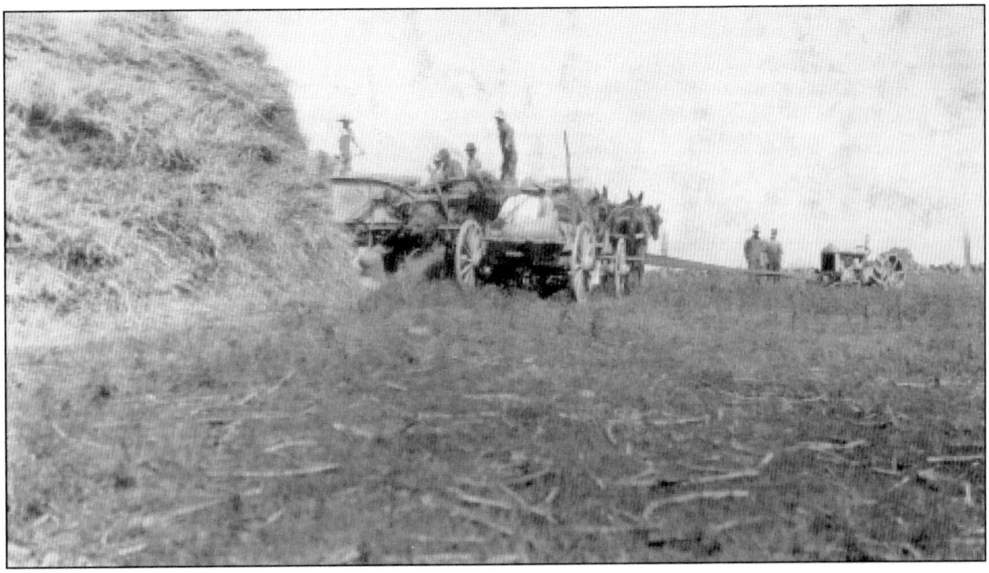

A Campbellsville company, Central Sales sold both Ford automobiles and Fordson tractors. New mechanized farming machinery allowed farmers to increase cultivated acres and reduce manual labor. Work that had previously been done with the help of animals could now be adapted to implements that could be attached to tractors. Such mechanization helped Taylor County rank 28th in soybean production in Kentucky for the year 2007, 31st in all other hay production at 30,100 tons, and 36th in corn for grain production. Here Fordsons are shown driving a threshing machine on Read's farm in 1923 and disking George W. Redman's field in preparation for planting. (FHB, above and below.)

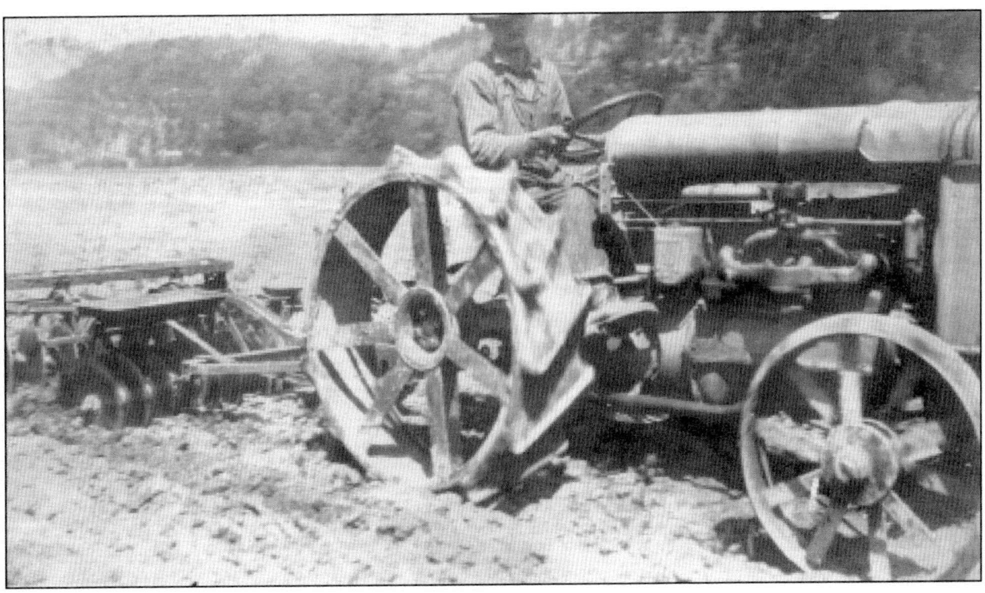

Tobacco has played a major role in the county's economic life. From 1808, when the Kentucky Legislature authorized Diskin Tibb's tobacco inspection on Robertson's Creek, known for Diskin Tibbs on whose land the warehouse sat, to the cigar manufacturers who operated in Campbellsville in the early 1900s, tobacco has provided employment and income to farmers and businessmen alike. Here Paul Johnson Sr. displays an example of a successful crop. (PJ.)

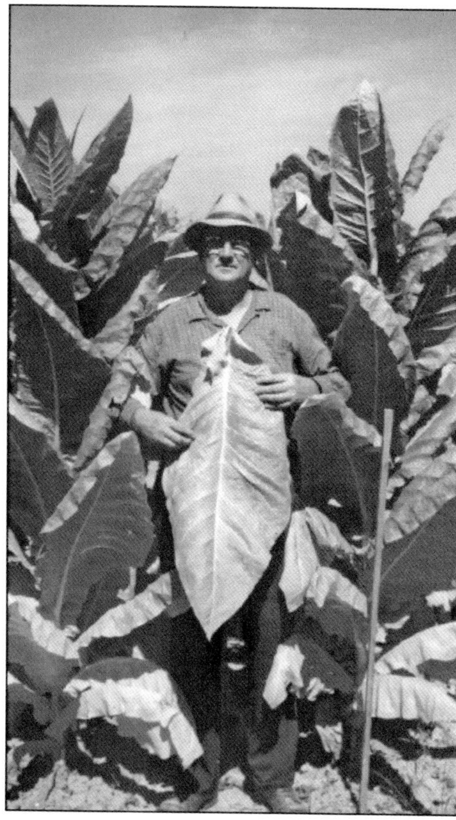

Few photographs capture the value of tobacco and the pride in production for the Taylor County farmers than this photograph of Sanford Minor and his barn full of tobacco. Minor farmed on Dutton branch in the Mansville community. A progressive farmer, Minor adopted suggestions made by his friend, county agent C. V. Bryan. After working with Taylor County farmers for a third of a century, county agent C. V. Bryan reported in 1955 that he had seen tobacco production jump from 535 pounds per acre average to 1,600 pounds. By 2007, Taylor County harvested 1,260 acres of tobacco with an average of 2,030 pounds per acre, bringing total tobacco production for that year to 2,557,800 pounds. (BJGS)

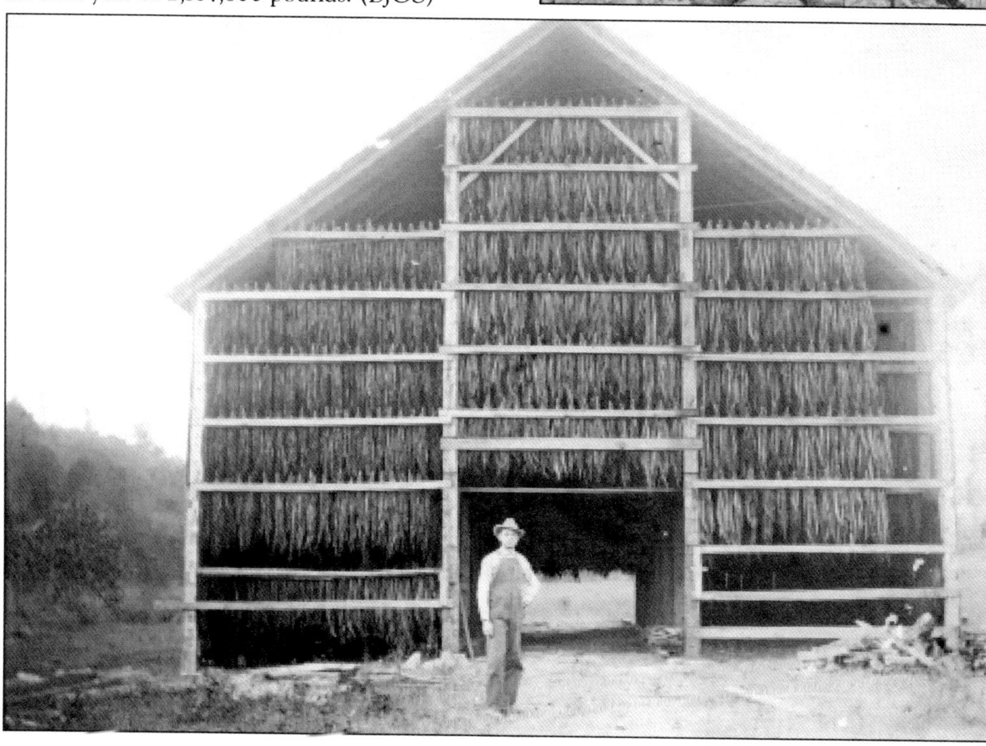

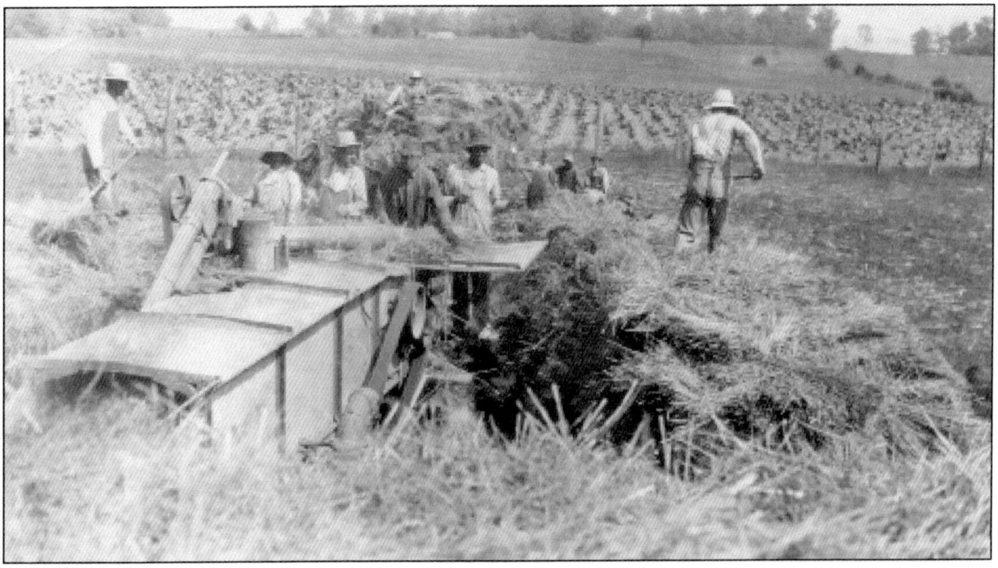

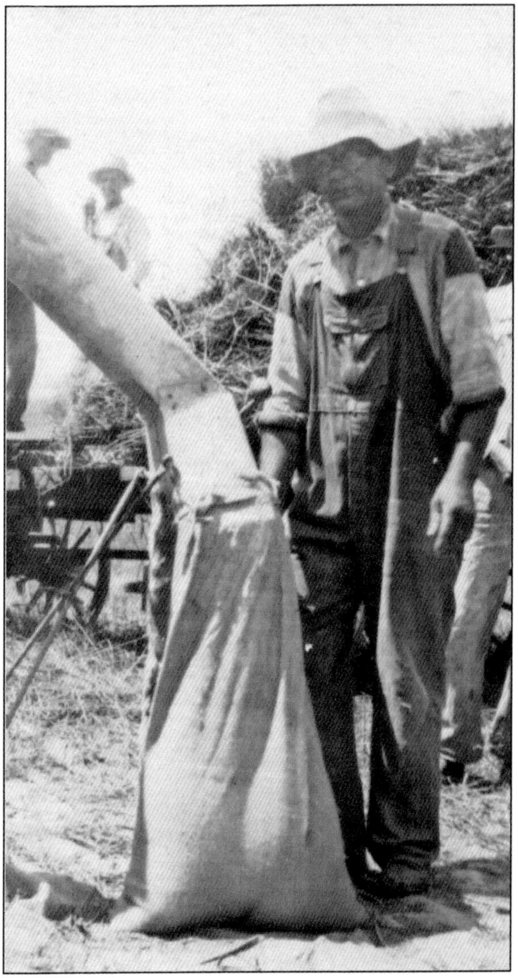

In an effort to introduce new farming practices and cash crops, county agent C. V. Bryan encouraged farmers to grow Korean lespedeza. These photographs demonstrate the wheat threshing of the lespedeza seed on a Shipp farm *c.* 1933. This was the first time lespedeza was grown in Taylor County. A sweep rake gathered the lespedeza, but substantial hand labor was still required to feed a thrashing machine that removed the seed from legume. The seed was then bagged. According to a 1934 report, Taylor County farmers grew 5,000 acres of peas and beans; 35,000 acres of mixed clover, timothy, and red top; and 5,000 acres of lespedeza. (FHB, above, and CBG, left.)

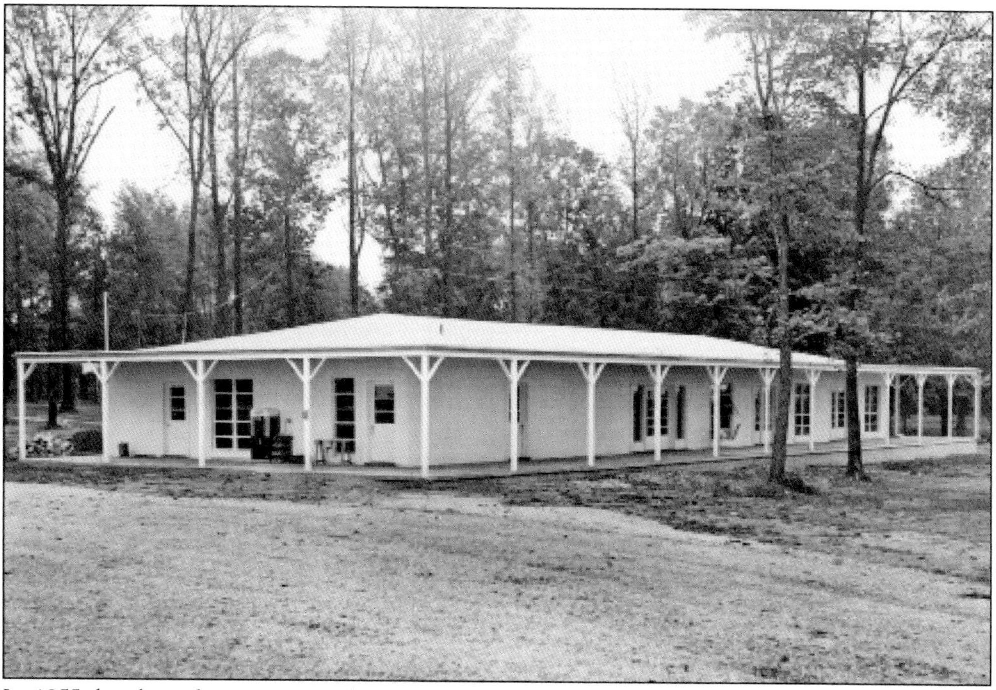

In 1955, local residents interested in promoting golf met to make plans for a country club. By raising private contributions and memberships, the Campbellsville Country Club completed its first golf course club house in 1957. Members subscribed $25,000 to build the clubhouse. Built on the Hodgenville road, the course consisted of nine holes. This golf course followed the first course built by Harry Edwards on West Main Street. (TCL.)

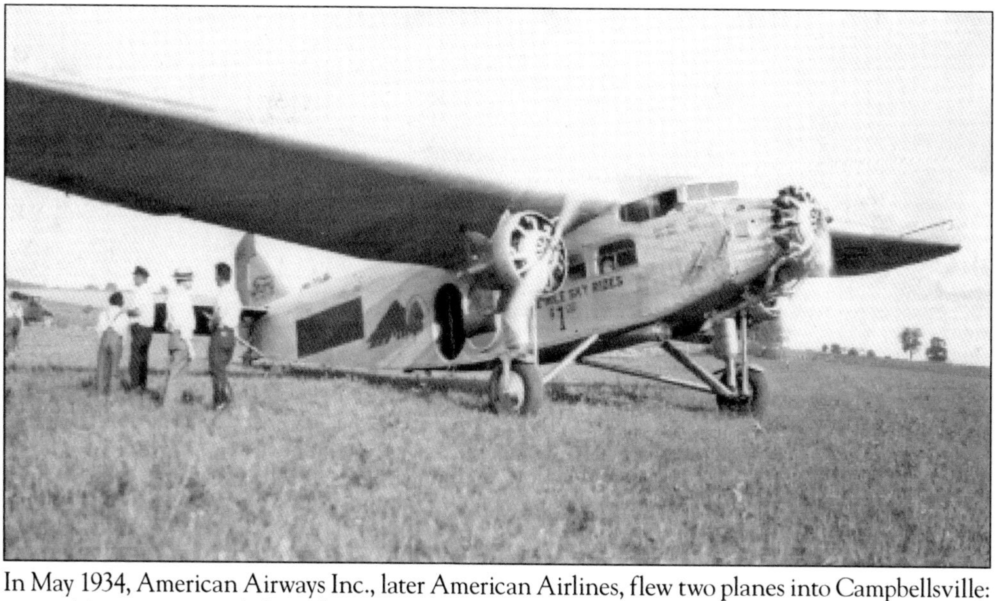

In May 1934, American Airways Inc., later American Airlines, flew two planes into Campbellsville: one a 14-passenger and the other a 4-passenger. This Ford Tri-Motor provided rides to Taylor County residents for $1 per person, which was a significant drop from the $15 per person for 15 minutes that O. W. Pearson and Robert Smith charged in August 1920 when they arrived from Troy, Ohio, in their Curtis. (FHB.)

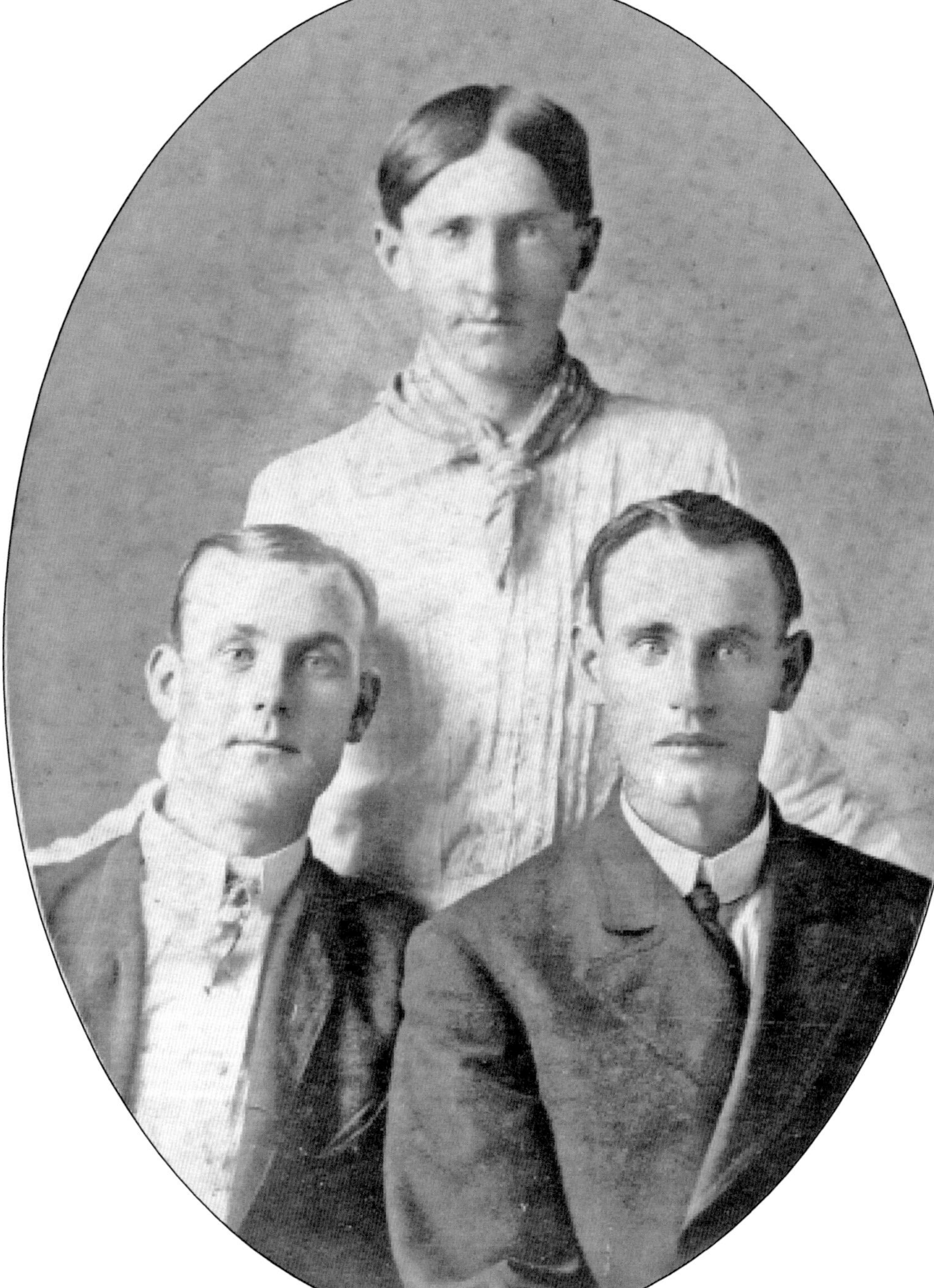

Adair County native Foree Hood moved to Campbellsville in 1926 and leased a warehouse in which to manufacture his paint, "Sal-Lac," a product later patented in cooperation with a company form Norfolk, Virginia. In this picture, made in Elida, New Mexico, are, from left to right, brothers Buster, Foree, and Allie Hood. Family history says that before his paint career, Foree worked on Bat Masterson's ranch while traveling the west. (JF.)

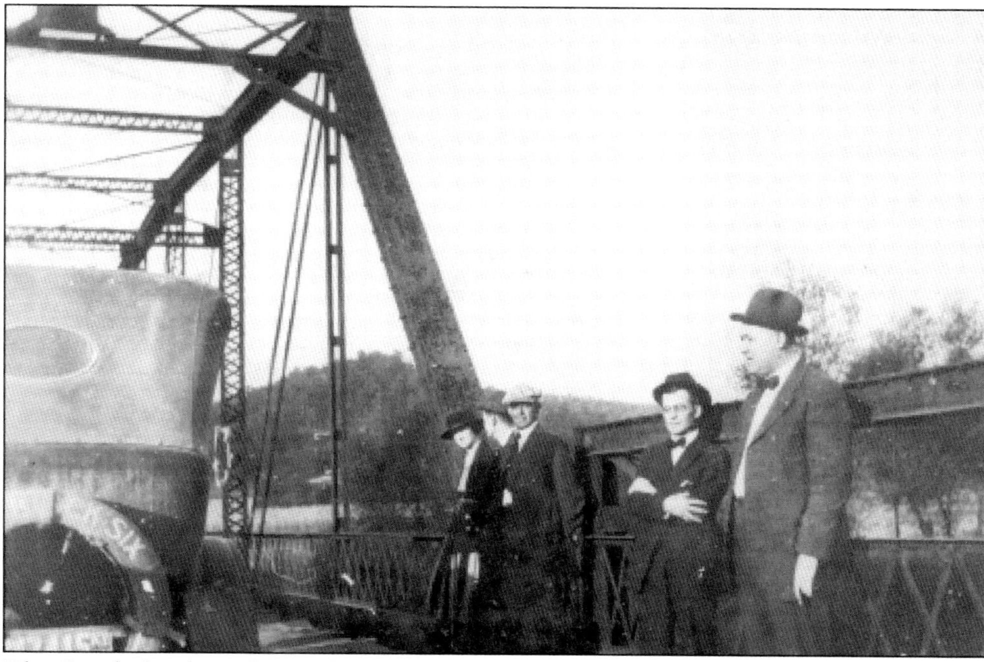

The Gowdy family made significant contributions to Campbellsville and Taylor County life. Reportedly, this picture captures George H. Gowdy (right), one family member whose business and civic contributions were wide. A Princeton University graduate, he founded the Taylor National Bank in 1902. He donated approximately $12,000 to construct the new Christian church, and he owned the turnpike from Columbia to the Marion County line for more than 25 years. (CBG.)

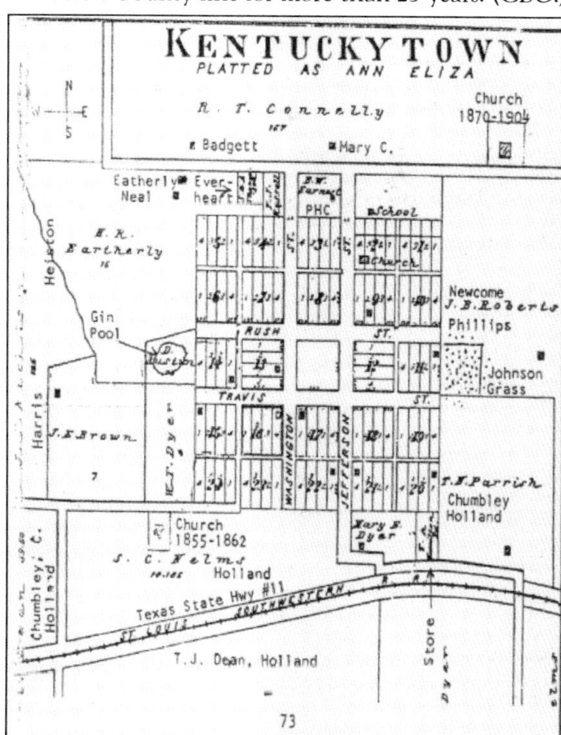

Taylor County resident Dr. Josiah Hiestand and a group of Kentuckians migrated to Texas in 1852 and established a town named after his daughter, Ann Eliza. By 1878, so many Kentuckians lived in the area that the name became "Kentuckytown," and it even had an established post office. Hiestand and other Taylor Countians, like Benoni Hotchkiss who moved to California, helped contribute to settling the West. (BT.)

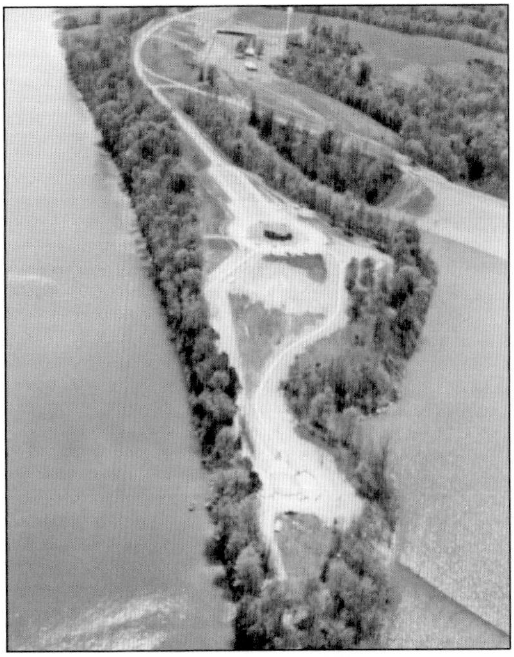

The Green River Lake was a project selected for construction under a Congressional Act of June 1938. As part of a larger effort to determine ways to improve water for municipal, industrial, and agricultural use, the Kentucky Department of Conservation-Division of Flood Control completed a survey of the Green River Basin in June 1951. The survey called for a number of flood control dams to assist in reducing flood problems on the Green, Ohio, and Mississippi Rivers. Construction began on Green River Lake in April 1964, with the lake completed in June 1969. Green River Lake covers 1,300 acres with facilities for boating, swimming, picknicking, and camping. A 141-foot-high, 2,350-foot-long dirt and rock filled dam impounds the lake, which is stocked with rock fish, striped bass, and walleye, in addition to native Green River fish. (TCHS, left and below.)

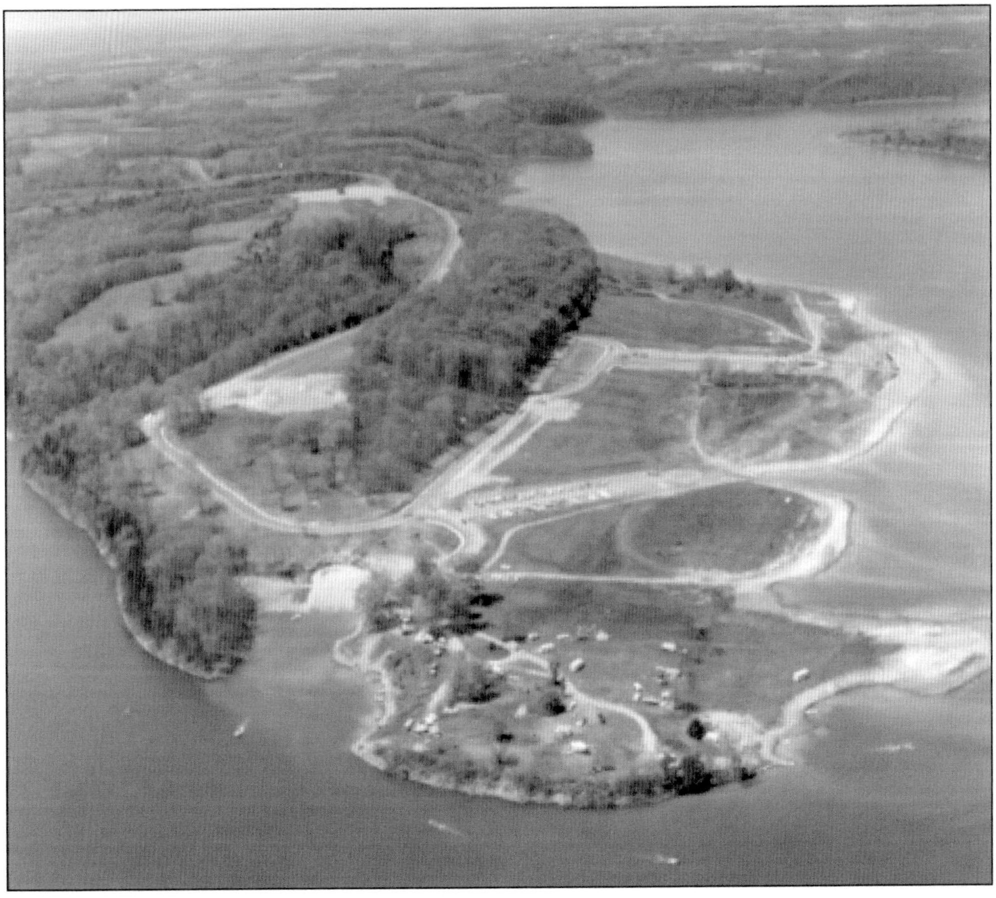

Bibliography

Burch, John R. Jr. and Timothy Q. Hooper. *Campbellsville University*. Charleston, South Carolina: Arcadia Publishing, 2007.

Central Kentucky Researcher. Campbellsville, Kentucky: Taylor County Historical Society.

Chumbley, Joe W. *Kentucky Town and its Baptist Church, or, Ann Eliza and Pleasant Hill*. Houston, Texas: D. Armstrong Company, 1975.

Clark, Lillian; Betty S. Cravens, and Pat C. Webster, eds. *The History We Were Living: Education in Taylor County, Kentucky*. Campbellsville, Kentucky: Taylor County Retired Teachers' Association, 2007.

Dicken, Debbie, compiler. *Obituaries of Taylor County and Surrounding Counties*. n. d.

Gorin, Betty Jane. *"Morgan Is Coming!": Confederate Raiders in the Heartland of Kentucky*. Louisville, Kentucky: Harmony House Books, 2006.

Historic Taylor County Calenders: 1982-Present. Campbellsville, Kentucky: Taylor County Junior Historical Society.

Nesbitt, Col. Robert Lee. *Early Taylor County History*. Reprint. Campbellsville, Kentucky: Creative Press, 1990.

Taylor County Star, Campbellsville, Kentucky.

The News-Journal, Campbellsville, Kentucky.